Where We Call Home

Where We Call Home

Lands, Seas, and Skies of the Pacific Northwest

Josephine Woolington

Where We Call Home: Lands, Seas, and Skies of the Pacific Northwest
© 2022 Josephine Woolington

ISBN13: 978-1-947845-36-7

Ooligan Press
Portland State University
Post Office Box 751, Portland, Oregon 97207
503-725-9748
ooligan@ooliganpress.pdx.edu
http://ooligan.pdx.edu

Library of Congress Cataloging-in-Publication Data
Names: Woolington, Josephine, author.
Title: Where we call home : lands, seas, and skies of the Pacific Northwest / Josephine Woolington.
Description: Portland, Oregon : Ooligan Press, [2022] | Includes
  bibliographical references.
Identifiers: LCCN 2022012684 (print) | LCCN 2022012685 (ebook) | ISBN
  9781947845367 (trade paperback) | ISBN 9781947845374 (ebook)
Subjects: LCSH: Natural histor--Northwest, Pacific. | Wilderness
  area--Northwest, Pacific.
Classification: LCC QH104.5.N6 W66 2022 (print) | LCC QH104.5.N6 (ebook)
  | DDC 508.79--dc23/eng/20220324
LC record available at https://lccn.loc.gov/2022012684
LC ebook record available at https://lccn.loc.gov/2022012685

Cover design by Megan Haverman & Elaine Schumacher
Cover art and interior illustrations by Ramon Shiloh
Interior design by Frances K. Fragela Rivera

References to website URLs were accurate at the time of writing. Neither the author nor Ooligan Press is responsible for URLs that have changed or expired since the manuscript was prepared.

Printed in the United States of America

for the petaled ones
feathered ones
woody ones
fuzzy ones
slimy ones
fruiting ones
furry ones
leafy ones
floating ones
and swimming ones

CONTENTS

Introduction   1

SPRING

Camas, *Ant'ip, Camassia*   5
Sandhill Crane, *Grus canadensis*   23
Yellow-Cedar, *Sgałaan, Callitropsis nootkatensis*   39

SUMMER

Western Bumble Bee, *Bombus occidentalis*   64
Coastal Tailed Frog, *Ascaphus truei*   83
Huckleberry, *Wiwnu, Vaccinium membranaceum*   97
Olympic Marmot, *Marmota olympus*   119

FALL

Moss   141
Clouds   163

WINTER

Gray Whale, *Sih-xwah-wiX, Eschrichtius robustus*   180

Gratitude   215
Bibliography   219

In the nature of things,
all things are natural.
With the advancement of human civilization,
we will never
burn the sun,
drown the sea,
halt the wind,
stop time,
or stay young.
There is nothing left to create.

—*Ramon Shiloh*

Introduction

I'm from the Willamette Valley, where my home was once a lake bottom after a two-thousand-foot-tall ice dam hundreds of miles away collapsed and inconceivable amounts of water flooded the ground I now walk on. I grew up near the confluence of the Columbia and Willamette Rivers, where snowmelt and rainwater from all over the region join to complete their journey back to the ocean. Not far from my childhood home, grizzly bears once indulged in Oregon white oak acorns, condors showed off their wingspans, and long ago, bison roamed.

Until a few years ago, I didn't pay much attention to what kinds of birds visited my backyard or what types of trees lined my neighborhood's streets. I didn't think much about how Portland's Tualatin Mountains had formed from ancient basalt flows that now give the rich the best views in the city. I didn't know how long Wy'east, who we now call Mount Hood, has watched over the valley. I didn't know the names of the many Native tribes and bands, like the Kalapuyans of what we call Willamette Valley, who were forced to give up their land and culture for people like my great-grandparents. I knew next to nothing about their relationships to native plants and animals.

As I got outside more and befriended wildflowers, trees, glaciers, birds, and rocks, I realized how little thought I had given to the processes that create our landscapes. I never wondered where native species came from, how long they've been here, or what makes them unique. I didn't hike until after I graduated college and never owned a pair of KEENs or any earth-toned clothing until a few years later. I've always known, though, from visiting the Oregon Coast and Columbia River Gorge as a kid with my family, that waterfalls and big trees within thirty minutes of my home are the kind of friends who give good hugs and listen deeply. Clouds and salt water remind me of something bigger than our day-to-day. In the last several years, my journalistic curiosity prompted many questions and inspired me to deepen my shallow understanding of home. I wanted to learn about native plants and animals to connect with something real, especially when so much of our digital world distorts concepts of time and place.

I started to notice how trees in logged forests grow at the same height. I recognized invasive plants where native plants should grow. I reflected more on how our way of life and desire for progress, all of which I participate in, require the perpetual destruction of landscapes, even in our supposed liberal, "green" Pacific Northwest.

In an age of distraction, personal brands, and constant market growth, I started to realize that maybe it's somewhat radical to be rooted in a place and entertained by things that can't be commodified.

The idea for this book came to me in 2020 when I couldn't hug my parents for over a year and the world felt close to its end. While hazardous wildfire smoke required an N-95 mask to simply take out the trash, I read natural history books about local geology, birds, mountains, and people. I felt comfort in looking far back, to climate changes of the past, to species' evolution, and it helped me, in some ways, to wrap my mind around our own impermanence. In writing this, I hoped that maybe I could try to better understand our climate crisis, relationships we have with the natural world, and where people have historically fit into ecosystems.

These essays are my attempt to tell natural histories of ten native species in the Northwest, defined mostly as Oregon and Washington. I selected each species based on my own interest, but also their ability to tell broader stories of landscapes and people. In some essays, I detail fascinating animal biology and evolution—like how bumble bees manage to heave their hefty bodies into the air and fly, or why coastal tailed frogs belly flop after they jump. Influenced by the Indigenous perspective of viewing plants and animals as relatives, I refer to these creatures not as "it" but as they/them, she/her, or he/him, because we don't call people "it." Merriam-Webster says "it" typically refers to a "lifeless thing." Just as I wouldn't call my cat "it," moss, marmots, and gray whales deserve a pronoun that acknowledges that they are alive, too.

Many aspects of these stories aren't happy, and I felt that leaving out or glossing over logging, development, fire suppression, commercial hunting, and the removal of Indigenous peoples from their land would be a disservice to these plants, animals, and the people who have taken care of them.

The only perspective I learned about Pacific Northwest history growing up was the white colonial one, where I thought Lewis and Clark marked our region's beginning. For many years after, I assumed historical places were across oceans and borders, a plane ride away. I thought human art, stories, inventions, and technologies developed somewhere else. In four of these essays, I write about Kalapuya, Haida, Yakama, and Makah cultures, histories, treaty rights, and land and ocean management. I am so grateful for those who shared their time, art, expertise, traditions, and pain with me. Micah McCarty, a Makah artist and leader, taught me about his family's whaling traditions. He challenged me to think deeply about people's place in ecosystems and how conservation in a colonized world can be misled. Scholar and Yakama Nation member Emily Washines reminded me that Yakama people hold the world's oldest data set for living with their central Washington plateau and Columbia River landscapes. Their stories are based on real long-term observation, experience, and science.

The essays are ordered seasonally, beginning with spring camas blooms in the Willamette Valley and ending with gray whales migrating past Cape Flattery in winter. I read dozens of new and old, scientific and traditional papers, articles, tribal histories, and natural history books; traveled to most of the places I wrote about; and interviewed more than fifty people, including biologists, ecologists, archeologists, artists, botanists, historians, tribal leaders, atmospheric scientists, bryologists, among others, to tell these stories. Each person volunteered their time. Many of them shared resources, answered my many follow-up questions, read drafts of the essays and provided valuable feedback. Any errors are my responsibility.

Aside from being a journalist, I'm also a life-long musician and have practiced mindfulness for more than fifteen years, both of which heavily inform the way I see the world, and how I choose to pay attention. During the narrative, I insert my own thoughts or experiences at times, but I feel most comfortable as an observer, so I share knowledge from the experts I spoke with and information drawn from research about each species.

I hope after reading that maybe you'll notice huckleberries on a trail and think of their longevity and all the lives they've nourished. When you pass camas blooms off the side of the road, maybe you'll reflect on who took care of the flowers before the prairies were plowed. If you see yellow-cedar, perhaps you'll think of all the baskets, hats, and canoe paddles that sustained generations. When you look up at the clouds, maybe you'll admire their changing form for a few minutes. Writing this humbled me and changed me. Whatever city, town, or landscape I visit, I now think of its deep roots that have supported a myriad of diverse lives—human and non-human—at one point in time, and we're here now too, briefly. The Pacific Northwest is much more than hipsters, breweries, coffee shops, and rain. Whether you're new here or a lifelong resident, I hope you'll become a bit more attentive, and that you'll be rooted, mindfully, wherever you call home.

Camas,

Ant'ip, Camassia

New growth suddenly emerges from onion-like bulbs spread out and nestled underground. Journeying up through a few inches of sodden Willamette Valley soil, tiny plants greet the February sun.

They're more like thin blades of grass at first. Slowly, their leaves thicken. They prepare themselves as days grow longer to make room for a single flowering stock that will shoot skyward. Weeks later, indigo star-shaped blooms float among open meadows of chartreuse bunchgrasses as warmer days arrive in the western Oregon valley.

Camas, *Camassia*, welcomes spring.

From six slender, deep-purple petals, which resemble a cat's constricted pupil, are six golden anthers. Their pollen provides native bees, beetles, and flies with nutrients in their long and arduous quest for food in early spring. The petals surround the seed pod, a lime-green oblong pearl that's so bright I wonder whether it would glow in the dark.

The petals are sometimes a soft lavender, other times a deep violet. If you look closely enough, you can see that they often have faint stripes of blue down their center, giving them more definition and intrigue.

The plants take their time to bloom from seed. They stay grass-like for a few years. After five springs, or so, they'll bring color to open fields. Once matured, they're reminiscent of their agave family relatives, as their flower stalk stands tall over cascading bunches of leaves. Some types of camas rise to three feet, or taller. Each leafless stem contains up to a dozen blooming flowers that spiral around the slender stalk in an orderly fashion. They blossom from the bottom up, and flowers toward the tip of the plant often stay closed, creating an asparagus-like blue top. The flowers know exactly the right amount of space to give each other so they can stretch out among the group.

Camas blooms in late April cover an abandoned field, sandwiched between apartments and a busy road, near downtown Salem. It's the only place where the plants fit in our urban lives: on random plots of land that will soon be sold and developed.

Their blooms once brightened fields of open grasslands that stretched hundreds of miles from the Umpqua Valley in southern Oregon to the Willamette Valley and north to the Puget Sound and British Columbia. They gently swayed in a warm spring breeze along streams and rivers, lined with cottonwood and ash trees, or in meadows under the shade of oaks. They were as awestriking as the balsamroot blooms that create yellow hillsides in the Columbia River Gorge, but they had even more open space to show off. They took root in the prairies soon after giant floods brought in nutritious soils, when grizzly bears and gray wolves lived in the Willamette Valley, too. They grew among more than a million acres of rolling hills speckled with white oaks, golden paintbrush, Kincaid's lupine, and more birds and butterflies than we can imagine.

Camas can grow all over the West. It's found from Vancouver Island to as far east as Montana and Wyoming, and south to California. Four species live in Oregon, though the most abundant, *Camassia quamash*, grows from the San Juan Islands and Olympic Peninsula, east to the Palouse and Zumwalt prairies, and to Table Rocks in southern Oregon. The flower has fed the region's first people with its starchy, sweet bulbs for as long as anyone can remember.

In the way that some Northwest tribes are salmon people, Kalapuyans of the Willamette Valley are camas people. With only one spring run of salmon, but boundless fields of edible plants, Kalapuya people ate plentiful amounts of wapato, yampa, acorns, tarweed, and camas. "Our identities are tied together," says David Harrelson, who is Kalapuyan and is the cultural resources manager for the Confederated Tribes of Grand Ronde. "To know yourself and to know a place, it becomes necessary to know both."

CAMAS HARVEST

Although they look delicate, camas likes disturbance.

Kalapuyans harvest the bulbs twice—once in early spring after having few fresh nutrients all winter, then again in early summer when the blooms dry up. They use shovels or sharp wooden digging sticks, called cupins, which are two to three feet tall with an antler handle, to dig up the bulbs. When they harvest, they take only large bulbs and leave smaller ones scattered close to the surface. This method aerates the soil, and gives the plants that can live for several decades more room to grow, Harrelson tells me. With more room comes more camas, which is called *ant'ip* in the central Kalapuya language.

Families traditionally tend to the same camas patches each year, observing the plants' health for generations, and forming deep connections with the fields. In some tribes, families owned specific camas fields, while in others, fields were shared between extended families.

Common camas, *Camassia quamash*, and tall camas, *Camassia leichtlinii*, are the only types in the Willamette Valley. Sometimes, the two species grow together, while in other places, only one type will grow. On common camas, five petals group together in a semi-circle with one lone petal hanging down like a tail. Tall camas petals are typically more symmetrical, and the plant, as the name suggests, is bigger. Scientists recently realized through DNA analysis that all types of camas are most closely related to agaves. Camas actually belongs in the asparagus family, which includes agaves, and not in the lily family as researchers had long assumed.

Young camas plants can be bullied by stronger, faster-growing grasses, especially thick, invasive grasses that cover the entire ground, like the kind we fuss over and fertilize in our backyards. Native bunchgrasses that covered the valley, like Roemer's fescue, grow in tufts or bunches, leaving room for flowers like camas, the

Willamette daisy, and, later in summer, Nelson's checkermallow to stretch out and grow.

To maintain a camas patch, Kalapuyans regularly set fires during late summer or early fall. All the valley's vegetation burned, except for the oak trees. Ash enriches the soil and increases seed growth, while heat controls pests, clears space for people to travel and animals to forage, and keeps conifer trees from suffocating oaks and other plants. During spring seasons after the burns, camas thrives. Many other native plants also rely on fire. "Camas and humans have this reciprocal relationship," Harrelson says. "A camas patch becomes more abundant over time when you interact with it the right way.

"Agriculture today is very extractive," he says. "In a tribal world with camas, there's only obligation and reciprocity. If you're getting something from the camas, you owe them something.

"If everything you take requires reciprocity and exchange, it would affect the way you act."

PRAIRIES

As Coast Range slopes subdue, giant Douglas-firs give way to oaks in a somewhat flat land, which at its widest point spans up to forty miles before the earth swells again into the Cascade Range. I've lived here, in the Willamette Valley, all my life. But I'd never given much thought to the types of landscapes that exist in-between mountain ranges other than freeways, farms, cities, suburbs, and shopping centers. I didn't know we had vast prairies west of the Cascades and didn't know that camas was a wildflower and not just a sulfurous smelling city in Washington. Landscapes that many of us love are outside of the valley, within or beyond the mountains—the old-growth trees, pristine lakes, sea stacks, and salt water. We enjoy the same open, mountainous views the Willamette Valley has offered since the first people arrived, but we admire them from vineyards or tulip farms, in a valley that has been transformed, with different plants that cover the grasslands and camas fields.

The oldest memory Kalapuya people have of living in the Willamette Valley is the great floods that they call *atswin*, or the Missoula floods. A 2,000-foot-tall ice dam broke around 15,000 to 18,500 years ago during the last Ice Age, releasing a Lake Ontario-sized body of water in western Montana, called glacial Lake Missoula. So much water burst through the Northwest that the rush is thought to have been ten times stronger than the combined flows of all of Earth's rivers today. Water tore through eastern Washington and the Columbia River Gorge at sixty-one miles per hour, bringing with it massive boulders, ripping off cliff faces, and shaping the region we know today.

Harrelson's ancestors tell stories from when more than four hundred feet of water nearly filled the entire 120-mile-long Willamette Valley, which spans from Sauvie Island, north of my home in Portland, to just south of Cottage Grove. Mountains that we're familiar with today became islands. Kalapuyans took refuge from the floods on Chantimanwi, known today as Marys Peak, the tallest point in the Coast Range.

One story tells of all the valley's people rushing to "the big mountain" as flood waters quickly rose higher and higher, nearing the 4,097-foot-tall summit of Marys Peak. The story details the birth of panther and deer and the death of coyote before the floods, symbolizing monumental changes to the land, according to anthropologist and Grand Ronde tribal member David G. Lewis.

The ice dam on Lake Missoula continued to form and break, over and over, sending unimaginable amounts of water into the valley every thirty to seventy years. Similar to a pressure washer wiping a dirty surface clean, floods stripped western Montana, Idaho, and eastern Washington's nutrient-rich, diverse soils and brought them to the Willamette Valley. The mixture later nourished prairie plants, like camas.

Prairies may have formed shortly after these Ice Age floods when the region became warmer and drier. Camas soon sprouted. Once established, the plants are thought to have made their way north across the prairies as the ice sheets retreated in northern Washington and Canada. Some patches, however, may have avoided glaciers in small, ice-free pockets. The open landscapes would have been converted to ash or Douglas-fir forests had Kalapuya people not regularly conducted prescribed burns, some of which engulfed large parts of the Willamette Valley. Prairies flourished because of people's care.

People have always been in the Willamette Valley, in human memory. They lived in the Mohawk Valley, Cottage Grove, Blue River, and Fern Ridge areas, maybe hunting bison or woolly mammoths. Projectile points estimated to be twelve thousand years old survived the valley's frequent flooding. Many artifacts are buried deep in flood sediment and colonists didn't save any before plowing fields for agriculture. Tribal elders and scholars also say archeologists haven't dug deep enough in the valley beyond flood sediment to find artifacts that predate the floods.

Near Fern Ridge, archeologists found 350 charred camas bulbs thought to be 7,650 to 8,500 years old, showing how long the plants provided critical carbohydrates and protein to people throughout the seasons. Ancient homes, charred bulbs, and camas ovens—with one measuring two feet deep and five feet across—have been found throughout an area west of Eugene, where fairies and ecstatic dancers now gather each July for the Oregon Country Fair.

When European Americans first saw the valley in the early 1800s, they called it one of the most beautiful landscapes they'd ever seen, with idyllic, rounded hills covered in grasses similar to wheat fields. They described scattered oaks that looked more like orchards of fruit trees planted by people. The circumferences of the trees measured twenty-four feet—larger than the biggest oak that remains in the valley in Silverton. Tree-lined streams gently meandered for as far as they could see. They wrote about it as Eden-like, a promised land, one filled with fertile soils and money-making opportunities. They urged others to join them.

BEFORE

Camas' striking color fades by June, and the plants take a seasonal nap as their favored wet, clay soil dries out. Petals wither and twist, hanging like damp hair from the neon seed pods that stay upright.

The pods eventually brown and split open, revealing black sesame-like seeds that disperse in the warm summer breeze or when brushed off by an animal.

"If you were walking around here in July," says botanist Edward Alverson, while showing me a camas patch at Howard Buford Recreation Area, just southeast of Eugene, "you'd hear a sound sort of like a rattlesnake. That's the seeds of the camas rattling in the seed pods."

Alverson can give a complete natural history on nearly every plant we pass, and his name is on many studies about Willamette Valley prairies. He's worked with the environmental nonprofit The Nature Conservancy and now works for Lane County parks. He looks after one of the largest publicly owned prairie remnants, which spreads across one thousand acres in Howard Buford Park and Mount Pisgah where camas patches give me a quiet sense of what this area used to be.

Some blooms are in the park's 265-acre Meadowlark Prairie, but few meadowlarks and other prairie birds are around to enjoy it. The western meadowlark, a chunky, robin-sized bird with a bright-yellow breast and belly and even brighter song, is the Oregon state bird and is at risk of becoming endangered in the valley. The birds have called this landscape home for thousands of years but don't have enough space now to live, Alverson tells me. A single nesting territory requires about twenty acres, and the birds need multiple territories for a viable population. "Even though we have lots of grass seed fields, they won't really use them," he says. "They'll use pastures, but pastures aren't that big either."

Other small prairie remnants are scattered haphazardly throughout the valley, and many are found on rocky slopes that survived only because they weren't viable for farming.

From the top of Mount Pisgah—named by settlers after the biblical mountain where Moses saw the promised land—a mosaic of dark-green fields, orderly rows of light-green fruit trees, housing, and highways cover the land where it flattens below the mountains. People now grow imported food crops among what was once a plentiful supply of native food, Alverson points out.

Grizzly bears once dined on Oregon white oak acorns in the open grasslands where trees had endless space to grow massive branches to nurture two hundred different species. The bears are gone now, and the oaks are squeezed to smaller versions of themselves as they grow too close together. They're crammed into smaller plots surrounded by vineyards or encroaching Doug-firs. "We have way more trees than we had in this landscape 170 years ago," Alverson says. "And that's one of the primary threats to prairies. It's not really a problem of not having enough oaks, or not having enough trees," he says. "We have too many."

Wolves used to hunt in the bunchgrasses, but they're gone now. Columbian white-tailed deer used to gracefully graze in the valley, but they're gone now, too.

Burrowing owls once nested in the southern Willamette Valley, but when construction workers in the 1950s destroyed a nest to make room for Interstate 5, the owls haven't been seen much since.

Birds still travel south through the valley to their warmer winter homes. The prairies are so fragmented now, though, that birds who used to nest here in summer have been pushed out. Two birds found only in Northwest prairies, the Oregon vesper sparrow and the streaked horned lark, used to commonly breed in the valley but don't really anymore.

Western bumble bees probably feasted on camas' early blooms, but they're not here either. The valley silverspot butterfly, related to the threatened Oregon silverspot, is also gone.

Rivers like the Willamette, McKenzie, and Santiam flowed freely with braided channels that provided nutrients to soils and created unique habitats for unique creatures. Floodplains used to cover large areas near Sauvie Island and along the Columbia River, not far from what's now Portland International Airport, but agriculture, levees, and dense stands of invasive reed canary grass have replaced them.

This bountiful landscape of the West, which sustained birds, bees, butterflies, and people for thousands of years, has nearly disappeared over the past two hundred years.

It's hard to get people to care about grasses, small flowers, and even smaller insects. Funding for prairie restoration and research is dwarfed in comparison to money given to old-growth forests, whose mammoth, moss-covered trees and northern spotted owls, although equally important, are easier to sell to the public than bunchgrass. "When you go out to one of these sites in late summer or fall, there's not much to see," Alverson says. "It doesn't look any different from a pasture. Their uniqueness doesn't really show itself."

The valley is now 96 to 97 percent privately owned. The ability to restore native landscapes depends on how much land tribal leaders and conservationists can come by, and how much landowners care to keep their backyard oak trees, or nurture native grasses and camas. "It could include planting of seeds, doing a certain type of mowing to benefit native species, or removing non-natives," Alverson says.

Trees and plants in my Northeast Portland neighborhood come from all over the world: the Deodar cedars from the Himalayas, the tulips of central Asia, and the fresh, green grass we idolize from Europe and Asia. Plants from here who made this valley special aren't as common.

We move around a lot as a culture, Alverson says, and we can live wherever we want without needing to know native plants and animals who also live in the same places. Anything we need is a drive, or walk, away. "If you were to do random surveys on the street and ask people where you can find camas in bloom, some people would know, but most wouldn't," Alverson says. "That's an indication of our culture and separation of nature, and to some extent, lacking a sense of place and knowing a place.

"People don't really think about being rooted in a place in the same way that Native cultures did," he says. "We don't need that knowledge for survival."

COOKING CAMAS

Camas is the original sweetener. The bulbs caramelize to a nutty brown, becoming candylike. They taste like roasted chestnuts, sweet potatoes, or baked pears with a texture like roasted onions.

Once harvested, the small potato-sized cream bulbs are placed over layers of maple leaves and ferns stacked on top of hot stones within an oven dug into the earth. Kalapuyans arrange more leaves on the bulbs before covering the oven with dirt. They lever the bulbs above the stones, which they replace every eight hours or so, reheating them with fresh fire. The bulbs cook for several days until their starches become both digestible and delectable.

Similar to a potato, camas can be prepared in many ways—dried and stored for winter, smashed into biscuit-sized "camas cakes," condensed into a sweet paste, or paired with acorn mush and tar-weed seeds. Different tribes have different ways to cook camas, and some archeological sites have revealed ovens akin to a brick pizza oven. Some Kalapuyans may have used the same oven repeatedly, heating it first with fire, then packing it with camas, and baking the bulbs for two to four days.

When non-Native cultures think of natural landscapes now, we tend to imagine "wild" places, where we think land is untouched or unmanaged by people. Areas in national parks, forests, or lands now designated as wilderness are often historic food-gathering sites, places where people have lived, traveled, camped, and set prescribed burns for thousands of years, like the high country in Olympic National Park, or huckleberry fields that once covered Indian Heaven Wilderness. Kalapuyans maintained an active collaboration with native plants in the Willamette Valley for more than five hundred generations. Their annual harvests gave camas a needed rejuvenation, and their fire management sustained the prairies. Efforts to save these plants and landscapes often miss this point, Harrelson tells me. "While people are focused on restoration, they don't get at the values that created the landscape," he says.

Kalapuya people lived within the entire valley, from Tualatin and Yamhill areas, southeast to Santiam, and further south to Yoncalla in the northern Umpqua basin. They represent a diverse linguistic group, with three languages and thirteen dialects. When settlers arrived in the valley, tribes initially didn't think they'd lose all their land. They were open to learning about and trading for metal knives and other items that the new people had, but disease devastated communities. It's estimated that twenty thousand Kalapuyans lived in the valley in the late 1700s, and by the mid-1800s, fewer than six hundred had survived smallpox, malaria, flu, and measles that settlers brought with them.

White newcomers wanted Native tribes and bands out of the coveted valley, and initially tried to remove them to eastern Oregon. The US government drafted treaties to acquire Native land, but many of the early treaties were tabled once they reached Congress and were never ratified as militias waged war and genocide against Native people.

Camas fields became huge wheat, corn, oat, and, later in the 20th century, hop fields, where Kalapuyans worked within the changed valley, from Brownsville to Tualatin, providing food for other people. Oak trees were fenced off on land for new homesteads. Some were cut and became barns. By 1851, white settlers had claimed all land within the Willamette Valley, leaving no room for tribal villages, culture, or camas.

The tribe eventually ceded millions of acres of land—most of western Oregon—and owned just sixty-one thousand acres after signing seven new treaties ratified by Congress. Between 1853 and 1855, the US government forcibly removed hundreds of people from their western Oregon homelands to temporary reservations, first at Umpqua and shortly afterward, to Table Rock in southern Oregon. People at other temporary reservations in Cow Creek and Kalapuyan encampments throughout the Willamette Valley and coastal towns were removed within months. In 1856, tribal people were then forced to travel 265 miles in harsh winter conditions to a newly established permanent, remote site at Grand Ronde. Native people from southwestern Washington to Northern California now live at the headwaters of the South Yamhill River in the Coast Range. They became the Confederated Tribes of the Grand Ronde Community of Oregon, which represents people from thirty-two tribes and bands, including Kalapuya, Umpqua, Rogue River, Molalla, Klickitat, Klamath, Clatsop, Chasta, Clackamas, Cascades, Multnomah, and Tillamook peoples.

A few decades after the treaties, Congress passed the Dawes Act of 1887, the cornerstone of federal assimilation policies, forcing Native people into the new, white, Christian culture through individual land allotments. The US government wanted Native people to become farmers and believe in American individualism as an attempt to destroy tribal communities, traditions, and sovereignty.

When Native people accepted their allotments, the government declared the remaining tribal lands as surplus, breaking up reservations and selling plots to non-Natives. The Dawes Act cut the Grand Ronde's treaty-given sixty-thousand-acre reservation to thirty-three thousand acres by 1901. Only those who accepted land allotments could become US citizens, a right not guaranteed to Native people until 1924.

Among other assimilation efforts, many Grand Ronde children were forced to attend two on-reservation boarding schools, run by Methodist and Catholic churches, in unsafe conditions, devastating families and their cultures.

In 1954, about one hundred years after the original treaties were signed, the federal government closed the reservation, stripped the Grand Ronde of most of their land, and took away the tribe's federal status, in an era known as termination. All they had left was the tribal cemetery. For several decades, Grand Ronde people had no land. Many moved away.

When David G. Lewis was growing up in Salem, there was no Grand Ronde tribe. They were still terminated. The anthropologist and Oregon State University assistant professor didn't know much about his family's story. "I had been taught by my dad and grandparents about some little things about the tribe," Lewis says. "I don't think they knew much. They knew some of the reservation history. They'd tell me I was Chinook.

"My dad would take me to the forest and would sometimes drive through reservations, and we'd talk a little bit about it," Lewis says, but as a young kid, he didn't care that much. In college, though, he started taking anthropology, Native studies, humanities, and history classes. He wanted to learn more about his identity.

Tribal members in western Oregon, and nationally, worked in the 1970s to restore what was taken from them. A tool shed on the remaining two and a half acres of the tribal cemetery became the Grand Ronde's headquarters, where they started issuing regular newsletters to members. After years of relentless work, the tribe in 1983 regained federal recognition: a renewed acknowledgment to treaty-protected rights of sovereignty, land, education, housing, and health care.

Lewis initially studied in California, but after Grand Ronde began rebuilding, he wanted to do something with the tribe. "My dad had been telling me that the tribe needs a history," he says, "so I came back.

"I was trying to understand what Native people were because I didn't really know," he says. "Even today, there's very little teaching about Native people in schools at all. The tribe wasn't able to reach out yet and teach us who we were."

He enrolled at the University of Oregon and became a member of the tribe. He's a descendent of the Santiam, Takelma, and Chinook tribes, and he led Grand Ronde's cultural department for eight years in the mid-2000s. He helped write the tribe's own history and develop their plank house, and museum. "We're kind of still in this process of recovery of tribal identity based on the histories that were essentially taken from us for a while."

He's worked to piece together the story of the Grande Ronde, which became his dissertation and life's work. He's collected Kalapuyan stories of the Missoula floods and continually publishes on his blog, *Quartux: Journal of Critical Indigenous Anthropology*, new histories of Native people and how they lived in the valley.

The Grand Ronde now owns 16,100 acres throughout the valley, but displacement deeply damaged the community. Many elders didn't want to talk about their culture or traditional foods, like camas. The iconic plant represented what Harrelson describes as "poverty food."

"It wasn't something to be celebrated, and a lot of people had shame," he says of eating camas. "The kids were conscious of what poverty food was, and they felt bad about it around their friends. That was the reality of it. It was weird poverty food—what Indian food was considered to be. That made conversations [with my grandparents] different."

Other families, he says, had great resilience and kept traditions alive.

Once the tribe was restored, people focused on developing infrastructure before recovering culture. "Part of the problem was that nobody really knew how they got there and what happened to put people on the reservation," Lewis says. "What were our people like before we got to the reservation? We've been working for thirty or forty years to answer that question. And people began realizing the importance of some of these plants.

"It's almost become synonymous with Kalapuyans as kind of an identity plant, in a way," Lewis says, "an identity symbol of the Kalapuyans because there was so much camas in this valley."

Soon, they started replanting camas.

TODAY

Prairies and oak lands once covered most of the valley—more than 1.5 million acres. They were especially plentiful around and south of Salem. The fertile soil and the area's wet winters created a biologically rich landscape, a kitchen full of food maintained by Kalapuyans.

Their descendants, though, have few places to harvest camas safely. Many patches are contaminated with chemicals and some soil shows signs of DDT fifty years after the government banned it.

The tribe can harvest camas from a two-acre site at Champoeg State Heritage Area south of Wilsonville, but the soil has traces of chemicals in it. Though the amount falls within what the government says is safe, it's still not what tribal people want, says Lindsay McClary, the tribe's restoration ecologist. The park, whose name is a Kalapuyan word that means "the place to dig yampa root," is treated with herbicides to manage the prairie surrounding the camas patch.

It's hard to find a place in the valley where the soil hasn't been contaminated. Tribal members might notice decent camas plants on private land but can't come and go as they would like to since it's someone else's property. "I want to make sure I can continue digging in the patch for the next thirty years," Harrelson says. "It falls short of the mark."

The tribe has two thousand acres—and will soon receive another one thousand—that they hope to turn into something like a native prairie, or oak savanna, which is a similar grassland landscape but with more trees. Some of the land the tribe acquired used to be a farm, and some is so overgrown with aggressive and persistent Himalayan blackberry, Scotch broom, tall oat grass, and tall fescue that it'll take at least ten years to remove.

"Once you remove it, there's a large native component," McClary says. "They just need a little breathing room. The seed sources are there, the root sources are there, they just need a bit of sunlight to reemerge from these suppressed landscapes."

A large portion of the country's grass seed is grown on Willamette Valley farms, especially in Linn County, whose sign welcomes you to the "grass seed capital of the world" as you pass by on Interstate 5. The valley's farmers produce more than six hundred million pounds of invasive grass seed for the million-dollar global industry.

Native seeds, meanwhile, are sometimes difficult to come by. Seeds are expensive, and to do a good restoration, conservationists would need many different species, Alverson explains to me. "There are seeds out there," he says, "but you couldn't just go and order enough seed to plant fifty species over one hundred acres. And even if you could, it would cost a huge amount of money."

Organizations, like the Willamette Valley Native Plant Partnership, are trying to make seeds more accessible. "People are working on it," he says.

FUTURE

Prairies are healthiest when they are big, and they are now critically small. Less than 1 percent of native Willamette Valley prairies remain. Other nearby prairies, like those in the Puget Sound area, face a similarly grim reality, making the landscapes some of the most endangered in the county.

It's complicated to try to regrow what used to be in this valley where most Oregonians live, and where more and more people are coming to live. Tribal members and conservationists are trying to sew together a patchwork of prairies, fragments stitched in among farms and homes. The lives of tiny flowers, birds, butterflies, and bees depend on who owns the land. The relationship between people and plants that developed in this valley before memory continues to face challenges.

"Our history isn't written in books," Harrelson says. "It's written on the landscape. They remind you of all these lessons and all these things that give you a fuller way to live your life."

A small camas patch grows on a rocky outcropping next to a West Linn High School parking lot, not far from the Camassia Natural Area, where camas and other prairie plants are preserved. Empty bags of chips and soda cans are left scattered among the blooms. Rocks, soils, and debris brought here by the Missoula floods overlook Interstate 205 and Willamette Falls, where the Charcowah village of the Clowewalla people and the Kosh-huk-shix village of Clackamas people used to be. At the falls, people once traded camas with nearby tribes for dried salmon, obsidian, buffalo hides, whale products, and shells.

Prairies clean the air, minimize flooding, and provide food for bees who give life to our food, says Tom Kaye, a local ecologist who studies and restores prairies at the Institute for Applied Ecology. These ecosystems also hold carbon in their soils that can help take it out of our atmosphere.

Living near a healthy ecosystem makes humans healthier by way of microscopic organisms that blow off the plants and soil, find their way through our windows, and onto our skin. "Literally, a healthy environment can make you well, or a sick environment can make you sick," he says.

People also love what prairies provide—an open landscape. One where we can see for miles while shaded underneath an oak tree whose lichen-draped branches blow in the wind like linens hanging to dry on a warm day. Prairie parcels on the outskirts of towns often become vineyards, farms, or apartment complexes, unless they're scooped up by tribes or conservationists first.

Tribal leaders and conservationists are trying, camas patch by camas patch, to create a collage of native prairie. They might get lucky and buy land from developers or acquire it through land trusts, but they still face the years-long task of removing and keeping invasive plants out.

Some plants, though, like the fluorescent-yellow golden paintbrush, have been reborn.

The wildflower went extinct in Oregon during the late 1930s when housing and farming took over the prairies. Recently, one hundred to two hundred thousand plants were reintroduced to more than twenty different sites in the valley, including one on Sauvie Island, Kaye tells me. The plant connects to roots of other plants for nutrients and was difficult for ecologists to understand how they grow. They'll require care and monitoring, but their comeback is hopeful.

The sun illuminates their neon blooms on a warm May afternoon on the island, where they now grow next to bigleaf lupine and camas. "You can go see this plant today in Oregon," Kaye says. "A few years ago, it was gone."

Another native plant, Bradshaw's lomatium, was taken off the federal endangered species list, though it remains on the state list. The herb boasts bursts of small, creamy yellow flowers and was thought to be extinct but was rediscovered in the late 1970s near Fern Ridge, west of Eugene. Several other populations were soon found in other areas like Willow Creek Preserve and Mount Pisgah in the late 1980s, where they still grow.

Not far away from the lomatium at Mount Pisgah, one-hundred-year-old oak trees can breathe a little easier after a stand of Doug-firs was recently thinned in a Lane County project.

Conservationists and tribal leaders are working to revive traditional burning practices. Patches of Buford Park, which now has ten times more trees than it did two hundred years ago, were first burned in 1999 and have since been burned half a dozen times.

Scientists are also studying how a warming climate could threaten some prairie plants, like the Southern Oregon buttercup, who may not survive higher temperatures. Since the prairies are so fragmented and plants can't naturally migrate to cooler temperatures, some scientists toy with the idea of moving plants themselves, but it's expensive and ethically touchy.

People travel hours away to see late-summer explosions of lupine and paintbrush in Mount Rainier's alpine meadows. Hundreds flock to tulip fields where native flowers used to similarly bloom in the Willamette Valley. Caring for a landscape, from a tribal perspective, requires generations-worth of respect and exchange. "It can be as simple as returning the fish bones to the system that it was harvested from, and in a way, giving back to that river system," Grand Ronde's McClary says. Or, it could be leaving the small camas bulbs, spreading them out, and then burning the land.

Native people look seven generations into the future, making sure to use what the land provides them with today, but leaving enough for others decades from now.

Grand Ronde people want to restore burning to a newly acquired site, one that, like the rest of the Willamette Valley, belonged to them. The burns will hopefully clear ninety acres of blackberry and oat grass and welcome back bunchgrasses and oak trees.

And, in time, welcome again, camas.

Sandhill Crane,
Grus canadensis

We see her on Mother's Day off the side of the road. The sun peeks through mid-afternoon clouds that stretch forever across the basin. Her slender, long pastel-gray neck drapes elegantly across her cattail and tule nest while she rests. Her orange eyes, barely distinguishable against her burgundy forehead, keep watch.

We see another mother, or maybe a father, close by on the same road in Harney County, neck upright though slightly tucked inward and curved toward her body. The large, mound-like nest is her throne in the open, marshy field. Like royalty, she sits high among the black coots and Canada geese while keeping her young ones warm.

Here, sandhill cranes bring new life into the world. They return here, year after year, to marshes, ponds, barbed-wire fencing, and the rumbling of occasional speeding trucks in this open southeastern Oregon landscape, where birds and cows outnumber humans.

As my partner and I drive through the Silvies Floodplain, just north of Burns, we immediately notice their massive builds and catch a glimpse of their crimson foreheads moving up and down as they pick and prod at the marshy land. Before, we had only heard their unmistakable bugles—almost dolphin-like, resonant staccato calls—echo through a Sauvie Island pumpkin patch.

Sandhill cranes, *Grus canadensis*, mesmerize us with their grace. We've honored their elaborate dances and powerful trumpet-like voices for thousands of years through song, paintings, and literature. They perfected themselves long before modern humans shared the earth with them, at least 2.5 million years of life experience that they seem to carry with each step and flap of their wings.

Sandhill cranes stand as tall as a third or fourth grader—some even the same height as a petite woman—with a wingspan more like Michael Jordan's. They weigh as much as a house cat and can live to be middle-aged.

They're monogamous and tender and sing with their partners during their synchronized songs with the resonance and range of Maria Callas. They share chick-rearing duties and do yoga-like stretches in the morning. They're wary of humans, but if a coyote comes near one of their chicks, it's over with a mighty jump and quick kick of their pitchfork feet.

Their bodies are a brownish, delicate gray, which reminds me of hues I've seen just above the horizon during a soft sunset in May, or somewhere within a towering *Cumulus* cloud's violet and silver ombré. Their wings are a combination of gentle pastels that appear golden taupe on the tips, depending on the light. In contrast to their dreamscape feathers, their legs, feet, and bills are jet-black, obsidian. Their elongated tail feathers protrude far past their rumps, creating what's called a "bustle," like they're wearing short tulle skirts, the perfect outfit for their sophisticated dances. Similar to most other species of cranes, sandhill cranes have a bare patch of scarlet skin on their heads that extends from their long, sharp charcoal bills to their striking tangerine eyes. Below the red patch, the cranes have triangular, powdery-white cheekbones that fade to a subtle gray down their slim necks. I wonder how they evolved this enviable color combination as I admire them, with slightly sunburned flesh, through binoculars just outside of Malheur National Wildlife Refuge in the Oregon high desert.

Just two types of cranes—sandhill and whooping—live in North America, and the former views our Oregon and Washington landscapes worthy of bringing up young in spring. Some types of sandhills even stay for winter just north of Portland along the Columbia River, eating in their preferred grain fields on Sauvie Island, Ridgefield National Wildlife Refuge, and Frenchman's Bar

Regional Park. Hundreds flew over me one sunset in November at Ridgefield, calling in their thundering voices as they prepared to roost for the night. Some of them danced.

On New Year's Day, we visited them at Frenchman's Bar as they ate, danced, and talked loudly to each other next to thousands of snow geese in an open grain field under the winter sun. Nearby smokestacks emitted thick, gray clouds into the air and massive barges slowly passed by, yet just downstream, several thousand cranes and geese journeyed here to survive winter. We watched the clear sky turn pastel pink as the low sun cast a warm glow on Mount Hood in the distance. Our breath was visible in the thirty-degree air. Suddenly, the cranes and snow geese flew off. All at once, in a thunderous sweep, thousands of wings flapped, thousands of voices chattered, thousands of bodies swarmed and darted in different directions. The exhilarating rush of witnessing it felt like I splashed cold water on my face. The birds gave us the hope and rejuvenation that we needed after a long two years living in a global pandemic. We went back every weekend in January for that sound, feeling, and optimism from so much life so close to home.

Cranes, and millions of other migratory birds, choose whatever marshy or grain-covered open land they want to feed, rest, or nest on, regardless of our arbitrary borders and private properties. Once cranes who winter in northern California arrive in southern Oregon's Harney County in February and March, they build impressive nests if the water level is to their liking, whether the site is within the Malheur refuge or on private land.

Cranes have welcomed spring in the high desert for as long as water has been here to greet them. They've seen colonists wage war on the land's original Wadatika people and remove survivors from the vast basin. They've seen egrets killed for feather hats. They've seen their own killed off, nearly for good, just to be served on a dinner plate. Wetlands here used to be better, with more grasses, water, and fewer farms, but they make do. They nest in areas we may deem as drab, flooded meadows, but for them, the marshes are life-giving.

VOCALIZATIONS

I hear them before I see them. Their voices carry powerfully over the flat landscape, speckled with sagebrush. Their calls manage to penetrate the endless cackling choir of yellow-headed and red-winged blackbirds, who seem like they can make any sound. The quiet of the high desert is often interrupted by the blackbirds' robot-like buzzing, *splat, splat,* hacking as if they have thick phlegm lodged in their throat. My favorite sound is their sweet and unexpected descending two-note phrase, like a cuckoo clock striking the hour.

If one bird can project through the rambunctious blackbirds, it's the sandhill crane. The dozen or so of them I see in V formation reflect early morning sun while they travel over the community of Crane, just northeast of Malheur Lake. My partner and I admire them from a hot spring.

"You hear that?" one man nearby says to his partner, as the cranes come closer. "I just love that sound."

Cranes are the envy of any singer. Their voices can be heard from several miles away, the effortless high notes bouncing off juniper and pine trees like a soprano's voice in a church. They're often heard before they're seen, especially when they're in flight.

Unlike human singers and songbirds who have to practice their tone and resonance, cranes make their musical sounds naturally. They start vocalizing soon after hatching, beginning with high-pitched peeps that develop into powerful guttural calls. Cranes don't sing elaborate songs like a western meadowlark perched on a juniper fence post, showing off his yellow belly and clear tone. Rather, they let out calls, short and simple sounds, a rattling *kar-r-r-o-o-o*. These calls are innate, like our screams or laughter. Cranes are flexible in their vocal agility and can purr, growl, snort, and perform complicated duets with their partners.

A complex acoustic system embedded within their chest gives cranes their thundering voice. The birds have extremely long tracheas. Greater sandhill cranes, who breed at and around the Malheur refuge, can have a tracheal length of more than two feet— nearly six times the length of our windpipe.

To fit inside the crane's chest, the windpipe loops and spirals, creating an *s* shape similar to the curving of a trumpet or bugle. Tracheal coiling, as one 2014 study notes, is a bizarre morphology. It's relatively rare in birds, especially migratory birds like cranes whose bodies need to be as energetically efficient as possible for long-distance flight. Only a few dozen species have coiled tracheas, like trumpeter swans. Modern cranes evolved this melodious gift sometime over the eons, as their early ancestors who graced the earth thirty-seven to fifty-four million years ago didn't have a coiled trachea.

The types of sandhill cranes who migrate farthest, lesser sandhills, evolved the smallest body size, yet largest tracheal-to-body ratio. As their migratory paths increased, the longer mileage demanded smaller bodies. But potential mates still preferred larger bodies, and researchers think that's how tracheal coiling took off. The longer windpipe makes the cranes sound bigger than they actually are, appeasing both their mates and migratory demands.

Though they sound like a trumpet or trombone, their anatomy functions more like a stringed instrument. Their spiraled windpipe inside their chest is like the bridge of a violin, which transmits vibrations to a larger surface, the sternum, to amplify the sound.

Like people, cranes rely on language to communicate, and when they can be easily heard, they have an advantage. Their most beloved melody is their unison calls. The cranes duet with their mate, standing side-by-side, for maybe a few seconds or up to a minute. They thrust their heads back as they open and close their bills. They might perform a few times throughout the day to get to know each other, or the calls can be used to claim territory. The melodies are thought to even kick-start egg production in females.

Unison calls require some practice, and older pairs have their routine nailed down while younger cranes' calls are loosely coordinated. The sounds remind me of when Miles Davis shies away from his mellow, smooth tone and lets out a grittier wail during a solo, trumpet pointed to the sky. But instead of one Miles Davis, there's two, playing with exact nuanced phrasing and inflection.

Their communication is a "mix of sounds and sign language," says Gary Ivey, a self-proclaimed "crane-iac" who has studied sandhill cranes since the late 1970s. "I think they can communicate almost as well, or probably better than we can."

Ivey has studied cranes for decades and worked as a wildlife biologist at Malheur National Wildlife Refuge for fifteen years. He now works part-time for the International Crane Foundation, a conservation nonprofit, and is also a Friends of Malheur National Wildlife Refuge board member, another conservation nonprofit. As I sift through Pacific Northwest sandhill crane research, I notice his name on most studies. I ask him if there are other researchers I could talk to who study cranes at Malheur. He pauses and says, "There's no one."

Of his many field observations, he tells me about a time he released a sandhill crane back into the wild in a flooded rice field near Sacramento. "He ran out into the water, and he started calling, and within three minutes, his family came out of nowhere.

"They knew it was him," he says. "They recognize individual voices."

THE JOURNEY

Flying sandhill cranes are like horizontal Olympic divers. The entire length of their body—from bill to toes—are in perfect alignment, seemingly without any effort. Their toes are glued together in a sharp point, necks proudly stretched long, and their massive wings move slowly like a wave, propelling them onward. If they get cold, they tuck their legs into their thick feathers and continue soaring. When they land, they bend their legs downward, and their feet dangle like a parachuter, rocking forward and back with the wind they're patiently navigating to reconnect with the ground.

An estimated fifty thousand sandhill cranes journey from California's Central Valley to scattered breeding sites in Oregon, Washington, Canada, and Alaska. Most of the cranes travel east of the Cascade Mountains and have their own routes and favorite stops in southern Oregon.

Three different types of sandhill cranes grace Oregon and Washington with their presence: lesser, greater, and Canadian. Although they're difficult to tell apart, they differ in size, with lessers being the smallest, weighing up to seven pounds and standing at about three feet. Greaters weigh about twice that, up to fourteen pounds and can stand five feet tall, making them among the Northwest's tallest birds. Canadian cranes are somewhere in-between.

The different subspecies also differ by their migratory routes, breeding, and wintering sites, which have, over the millennia, affected their body size. The Canadian crane population is smaller, about five thousand birds. They take a coastal route to the northwesternmost point of the United States at Cape Flattery as they travel to their coastal breeding grounds in British Columbia rather than follow the greater and lesser cranes' eastern Cascades route. Some smaller groups of Canadian cranes are the birds who spend the winter with us near Portland. Lesser sandhill cranes venture from California's Central Valley—a long stretch of land in the middle of the state from the southern tip of Shasta County to just north of Los Angeles County—to western Alaska to breed. Of the thirty-five thousand lessers, about three thousand stop by Harney County before continuing north. Greater sandhill cranes, which total eight to ten thousand, also venture from California. Some travel to Harney County to breed, while lately more of them seem to go wherever the grain fields are—in Klamath or Lake Counties or in neighboring Washington and Idaho. They have the shortest migration of the three subspecies in the Northwest, which is why they are the biggest.

How much they all differ genetically is still up for debate. Canadian cranes are considered part of the greater sandhill crane subspecies, though Ivey groups them in separate populations since their migrations and wintering sites are different. One theory suggests that greaters and lessers evolved separate genes during the Pleistocene, about 11,700 to 2.6 million years ago. When glaciers covered most of Canada, the lessers were thought to have stayed farther north around the Bering Land Bridge, while the greaters remained south of the ice sheet.

Greater sandhill cranes who breed around the Malheur refuge end their travels after a few hundred miles and stop to try their luck raising young for several months in this bird oasis on the northern edge of the Great Basin.

The more than 187,000-acre Malheur refuge is shaped like a *t* with the shallow and alkaline Malheur, Mud, and Harney Lakes creating the top portion of the refuge. The protected area then follows the Blitzen River south nearly 50 miles through ponds and marshes which welcome more than 340 different bird species to the region.

Basalt plateaus surround an endless expanse of sagebrush and meadows and grasslands and more birds and stars than I've ever seen. At the southern part of the basin is Steens Mountain, a massive yet gently sloping ridgeline formed from 16.7-million-year-old basalt flows. When a fault uplifted the basalt, the thirty-five-mile-long chunk of rock tilted ten degrees westward while its eastern face dropped steeply down a vertical mile. Its summit reaches nearly ten thousand feet. Glaciers later carved its picturesque valleys.

Water levels at Malheur Lake, where some flocks of cranes sleep at night, have fluctuated over the centuries. The entire basin was covered in water several times over the course of nine thousand years. Then, in some years, a drought.

Water. Drought. Water. Drought. A climatic seesaw that lasted, at times, for centuries.

A French-Canadian fur trapper who explored the area in the early 1800s deemed it *malheur*—"misfortune" in French—when trappers couldn't find food, river otters, beavers, or other creatures to kill, even though people have lived in the area for millennia.

Floods in the 1980s altered Malheur's landscape, which used to welcome thousands of cranes, Ivey tells me. More significantly, the refuge used to plant more than one thousand acres of grain for cranes to eat, he explains, but grain farming is nearly non-existent here today. Now, only about three hundred greater sandhills visit each spring.

When they travel here, I wonder if they recognize a particular line of cottonwoods or willows along the river. Can they see the cinder cones or sagebrush dotting the valley? Do they remember the checkerboard pattern of farms, occasional houses, and basalt flows that lead them to their marsh? Do they recognize the sudden expansion of the land that is Steens Mountain and remember where the internal workings of the earth powerfully shot the rock mass upward by a mile? Once they see that, do they know they've arrived?

Birds develop a complex map of the land in their mind, far more intricate than many scientists initially thought, their own internal GPS. Young cranes learn from their parents and know their migratory routes after just a year, Ivey says.

Cranes typically travel during the day, though some choose to navigate by starlight. Ivey tells me that he's observed cranes flying at 10 p.m. "Maybe they've learned the city lights in different areas," he says.

They take off for flight with a bit of a running start. They rise into the sky with a pump of their massive wings, spiraling upwards in wide circles, lifted by shafts of warm air called thermals. They climb maybe a mile high, where they often stop flapping, extend their wings, assume a V formation, and soar thirty-five miles per hour with the support of gravity and wind. They travel two to three hundred miles a day, then find a place to rest and refuel, likely in their preferred corn fields. They'll stay for a few days or weeks and wait for good weather so they can cruise on thermals again, saving as much energy as possible. They continue on.

In late September as the cranes arrive back to their California winter homes, Ivey recalls seeing three hundred cranes "dropping out of the sky, coming down in a big funnel," riding the thermals to land. "They were making lots of sounds and calls," he says.

Cranes call constantly when they're traveling, maybe filling the time like we do on road trips, chatting, and listening to music. They travel with their family and friends and switch off who leads the flock, which is the most physically demanding job that battles the power of the wind.

Their bodies are made for migration. Instead of heavier, flexible lungs like ours, birds have rigid, lightweight air sacs. The apparatus allows air to constantly pass through, which allows birds to inhale and exhale at the same time, perhaps an evolutionary gift from the dinosaurs when the earth had half as much oxygen as today. Even when they're exerting themselves thousands of feet up in the sky, birds are never out of breath.

Cranes travel along what's called the Pacific Flyway, which spans thousands of miles from the Arctic to Baja California. The Flyway is one of four migratory bird routes in North America. Each route—Pacific, Central, Mississippi, and Atlantic—has its own governing council with state, national, and international representatives working together to protect birds while navigating complex land and hunting regulations. The birds nest and rest on whatever plot of land is suitable, regardless of our laws and convoluted bureaucracies. Most of the land that cranes nest on in Oregon is privately owned.

Birds need wetlands to rest during migration. It's like running an ultramarathon or biking across the country with no suitable place to stop and refuel. Malheur is among this critical chain of stops along the Pacific Flyway, though these areas aren't as big and healthy as they used to be, and they're predicted to get smaller and smaller as the climate warms and people develop more land.

Millions of birds, like sandhill cranes, Ross's geese, snow geese, Brewer's sparrows, western meadowlarks, canyon wrens, yellow warblers, black-throated gray warblers, yellow-rumped warblers, Townsend's warblers, western tanagers, lazuli buntings, Lewis's woodpeckers, Bullock's orioles, Rufous hummingbirds, Anna's hummingbirds, Calliope hummingbirds, willow flycatchers, western snowy plovers, long-billed curlews, short-eared owls, greater sage-grouse, bobolinks, common nighthawks, trumpeter swans, green-winged teals, mallards, ruddy ducks, northern shovelers, northern pintails, cinnamon teals, redheads, canvasbacks, lesser scaups, gadwalls, American wigeons, ring-billed gulls, Franklin's gulls, Caspian terns, western sandpipers, long-billed dowitchers, Wilson's phalaropes, American avocets, black-necked stilts, pied-billed grebes, horned grebes, eared grebes, white-faced ibis, great blue herons, black-crowned night herons, green herons, egrets, American white pelicans, red-tailed hawks, rough-legged hawks, ferruginous hawks, northern harriers, American kestrels, bald eagles, golden eagles, and prairie falcons, among others, depend on these lands to survive.

Most of the world's fifteen crane species are threatened with extinction. Sandhill cranes are among the few cranes whose populations are increasing, or stable. More than eight hundred thousand cranes live in North America, including non-migrating sub-species in Mississippi, Florida, and Cuba. Among the world's most stunning migrations—which I hope to see someday—is when six hundred thousand midwestern lesser sandhill cranes gather on the Platte River in Nebraska every spring, near the Sandhills region of their namesake.

LIFE CYCLE

Many birds haven't changed much since the world's climate was more like Costa Rica millions of years ago, teeming with humidity and ideal bird habitats. Many species we marvel at today came into being around this time because Earth was full of perfect places for birds to live, providing endless opportunities for new species to discover their niche. As the earth began to cool and welcome the Ice Age and winter from about 2.6 million years ago to 11,700 years ago, not many new bird species evolved.

Sandhill cranes are among the oldest birds and have likely survived all this time because they're aggressive and big. They also eat whatever they can pluck from the marshy ground with their long bill. They take careful steps with scaly toes and razor-pointed nails reminiscent of their giant ancestors as they eat tubers, camas bulbs, earthworms, berries, rodents, and even baby blackbirds. More recently, they've acquired an appetite for corn. They used to feast on acorns from big oaks that covered California prairies and woodlands, but when European American settlers moved in and replaced trees with grain fields, the birds had to adapt.

Their bill is the perfect tool for prying through mud for roots or for nabbing any mouse scurrying by. All the probing and rummaging through the soil they do helps spread plant seeds and aerates the soil.

Instead of hiding or blending into grasses like the similarly shaped yet smaller and shier American bittern, cranes can see over most obstacles. With protective girth, cranes chase predators, like coyotes, minks, or ravens, with six feet of wings extended, ready to defend their eggs or chicks. Cranes also become combative toward neighboring cranes, especially if their nesting habitats are small and too close to each other. They'll even kill a neighbor's chick.

When the cranes arrive in Malheur, they'll survey the water levels, and if it's not a good year, they won't build a nest. Since they live to be anywhere from twenty to forty years old, or older, they have to raise only two chicks to maintain their population. Cranes who have been together for many years—and most stay together for life, only switching mates if their partner dies—are typically more successful at getting chicks past the pre-flying stage. Like people, they figure out how to be good parents.

Chicks, called colts because of how leggy they are, often don't survive past the first few months of their life, leaving adult cranes to try again next year. And the year after. And maybe the year after until, finally, they have a young one to journey south with.

"Some pairs are pretty good and regularly produce chicks," Ivey says, "and other pairs are dismal failures."

Ivey observed one thirty-six-year-old crane named Sarge who never produced a colt during the fifteen years Ivey worked at Malheur. Cranes typically have better luck rearing chicks when they don't have aggressive neighbors close by in densely populated places like Malheur. Many cranes now choose to nest in isolated mountain wetlands nearby.

When cranes do build a nest, they typically lay two eggs that they keep warm for about a month. Both mom and dad, who are nearly identical in looks and size, rest on the nest, and when the colts hatch, both feed them together for several months.

The colts are puffs of butterscotch fluff on golden stilts with oversized ankle joints and rumps. They look like they're wearing little poofy bike shorts on their calves (what we think of as their thighs) and have receding hairlines, though these will soon develop into their burgundy visors. For the first three to four weeks, they sleep in their mother's wings, a behavior called "tenting." In the evening, the chicks will gently peck their mom, asking for her to lift her large wings, where they snuggle up, sheltered from the rain or the cold. Within three to four months, parents will begin teaching colts how to fly. They'll guide their young ones on hour-long and overnight trips, preparing them for their end-of-summer migration. Colts will quickly grow out of their gangly phase and into their extraordinary adult form by mid-winter. Then they'll try to find a mate of their own.

DANCING

Cranes dance when they're nervous. They dance when they're excited. They dance when they're trying to socialize or mate, and sometimes they dance just because. If one crane starts to move in a group, others will follow, leaping into the air and flapping their wings with contagious joy.

They crouch down, bend deeply at the ankles, and jump skyward, fluttering their wings as they pirouette. Their head bobs up and down and they open their bills, sometimes without making a sound. When they land, they often pick up whatever object is nearby—grass, feathers, moss, or sticks—and fling it into the air at random.

The dances typically involve partners, but never include any body contact. They bow, curtsy, and salute each other, according to the many dances outlined in the "Sandhill Crane Display Dictionary" pamphlet. Several sequences have names, like tour-jeté, which is when a crane jumps three times to complete a full-body rotation, with their neck long, head forward, toes pointed, and legs extended. There's a minuet, when a mated pair circles each other, wings extended. Cranes also perform the "jump-rake" dance when they spring into the air and kick their legs toward their partner.

Some dances display aggression, like the "ruffle-shake, ruffle-thigh-threat." In this dance, cranes fluff their feathers and crimson crown, as their neck is pulled back, tucked in toward their body. The crane might start grooming, while pacing or rocking from side-to-side.

Crane dancing is ancient and complex. "It probably means more than we know," Ivey says. Some cranes as young as two days old dance. The routine strengthens relationships between mating pairs and family. Newly paired cranes dance more than older cranes, and single cranes dance the most.

When dancing leads to mating, the act usually starts simultaneously among both females and males. Sometimes, the male may be 150 feet away from the female and proceeds to walk toward her in what's called a parade march, with his inner wing feathers raised, red crown enlarged, and bill pointed upward, neck stretched almost vertically. He gently purrs. The female observes, judges, and doesn't change her body language much. Afterward, the two might eat, preen, or dance together again.

Cranes are also self-care experts. They stretch in the morning, preen with their natural body oils, and drink. After mating, they often spend hours fixing their feathers, one by one. They pay extra-close attention to the longer body and wing feathers that need to be in tip-top shape for flying. Sometimes, they'll paint their feathers with mud, giving them an earthly tint, which helps them blend in with the grasses. They spend mornings eating any food they can find, and then they search for a comfy spot to "loaf," where they again preen, drink, yawn, and socialize the day away.

MALHEUR

Sandhill cranes used to live in San Francisco, Los Angeles, and San Diego. They were common residents in the South Puget Sound prairies, dancing in vast, open wet meadows awash in indigo camas blooms in spring, their voices carrying across the landscape. They migrated in huge flocks over the Willamette Valley and may have wintered there.

Once white settlers arrived in the West, fueled in part by the Gold Rush in the 1800s, cranes' lives changed. The newcomers needed meat to eat, so they shot whatever animal was plentiful and easy to kill. Cranes became a specialty $20 dinner, Ivey tells me. Hunters could get close to the birds when they were nesting because they boldly stood their ground, protecting their chicks as they learned to do for millions of years.

They'd die there, near their nests.

Cranes stopped breeding in Washington. Just five pairs were left in California. Most cranes remained in Oregon and found safety in what's now the Malheur refuge.

In the late 1800s, an aggressive cattle baron named Peter French operated the region's largest private cattle ranch, called P Ranch, at the southern tip of today's Malheur refuge. He took snowmelt from Steens Mountain and diverted it for his farm, hayed the pristine meadows, and kept anyone else in the area off his land. Because the ranch was open and secluded, save for the cows, cranes started nesting in the basin again.

As the P Ranch empire developed, plume hunters slaughtered egrets at Malheur Lake so women could have feather hats. Ranchers fenced off camas fields harvested by the Wadatika people. With ranchers using so much water, the lake became a desert playa by the late 1920s. People soon introduced common carp into the area, likely for a food source, and millions of the invasive fish have filled Malheur Lake since the 1950s. Carp have been partially responsible for destroying the once pristine lake's flourishing, thick vegetation, which gave birds food, shelter, and protective nesting sites. A landscape where people and birds lived forever drastically changed in less than a lifetime.

By the mid-1940s, about one hundred pairs of cranes lived in Oregon. Federal conservation laws to establish public refuges and hunting restrictions—like the Migratory Bird Treaty Act of 1918, which prohibits the unregulated hunting of cranes and other birds— helped save their populations.

Cranes have recently started breeding again in Washington, but they're still listed as endangered by the state. Lesser sandhill cranes in California are a "species of concern," and the greater sandhills are threatened. In Oregon, the greater sandhills are a "sensitive" species because their habitats are so fragmented and vulnerable to climate change and development. Ninety percent of western wetlands are now gone. Snowmelt from glaciers and mountains that replenishes the wetlands is drying up.

TODAY

Almond, olive, and walnut orchards as well as vineyards are replacing sandhill cranes' California winter homes. The number of chicks that survive is fewer than it was 30 years ago, and about 10 to

20 percent of their wintering habitat is disappearing each year. Cranes run into power lines. They get tangled in barbed wire fencing. There's not much room for them as they're locked into smaller plots of land, most of which are privately owned. They may even be forced to move out of the United States within our lifetime if warming temperatures that are drying up wetlands aren't controlled.

Like us, cranes have a strong fidelity to their homes. They return to their favored sites, year after year, as their ancestors have for hundreds of generations. Their resting sites, though, risk becoming more and more separated from the fields they feed in as their habitat is developed. Since greater sandhill cranes are so large, they don't have enough energy to make long trips to eat every day.

Conservationists and scientists over the years fought for federal laws to ban unlimited crane hunting and legislation to form more public wildlife refuges, like Malheur, in the Northwest. Cranes rebounded. But without strict protections against future development to preserve grasslands and wetlands, they remain at-risk.

What would spring be, after all, without their dancing and poise? Without their voices carrying across landscapes as they have since before anyone can remember to welcome the warmer season of hope?

Yellow-Cedar,

Sgałaan, Callitropsis nootkatensis

Three sisters were busy preparing salmon at their camp. Then, Raven came along.

The great Creator and trickster smelled the fish, saw the young women, and thought, "Hmm, I wonder how I can get some of that salmon." So, he sauntered toward them, asked how they were doing, and then asked, "Aren't you afraid of being out here all by yourselves?"

"Oh, no," they said.

"Are you afraid of wolves?"

"No, we're not afraid of wolves."

"Aren't you afraid of bears?"

"No, we're not afraid of bears."

Raven thought for another minute, then asked, "Aren't you afraid of owls?"

"Ahh, don't talk to us about owls!" the women said. "We're really afraid of owls!"

Raven continued talking for a bit, and then said, "Well, I better be off now. See you later."

He didn't go very far, though, and hid behind a tree close by. Then, he called, "woo-hoo-hoo-hoooo, woo-hoo-hoo-hoo-hooo," mimicking owl sounds as best he could.

The young women dropped everything and ran right up the mountain, leaving their fish behind. They kept running and running, until they got so tired one said, "Sisters, we can't go any further. Let's stop here."

When they stopped, they changed themselves into *ɫaḥmapt*, yellow-cedar trees. This is why yellow-cedars are found on mountain slopes, and why they have beautiful long, drooping branches and silky bark like the three women's long, silky hair.

Ethnobotanist and author Nancy J. Turner tells me this story, which was told to her many years ago by cultural specialist Alice Paul of Hesquiaht First Nation of Vancouver Island. "The story itself is so moving because it tells you that the yellow-cedars used to be people," Turner says. "They're relatives. They're young women."

"That story kind of sums up the relationship that people have had with these trees," she says. Many other stories tell of Cedar Man, or Cedar Boy, she explains to me, and all tell of times people transformed into revered and generous cedar trees.

She shows me a hat by renowned Haida artist Florence Davidson woven with the trees' smooth inner bark. Turner stayed with her during the summer in 1972 on Haida Gwaii, an archipelago off the northern coast of British Columbia where Haida people have lived for thousands of years. She taught Turner how to make her first basket out of yellow-cedar, *sgaḷaan* in Haida.

Turner couldn't find her basket to show me but says it's about a foot tall and looks like a child made it. She's held onto it all these years as a memento and reminder of how much skill and knowledge is required to weave with tree bark.

"When I was in university, people would say, 'Oh, you're taking 'Basket Making 101,' which is like another way of saying that's just a simple course, just a throw away course," Turner says. "To me, 'Basket Making 101' is probably way more difficult than 'Physics 101,' or any other course you could imagine because of the amount of knowledge required to just produce something like this hat," she says, while holding the creation under its wide brim below its long, narrow, rounded top.

"You not only need to know the weaving techniques, but everything else about the material: the plant and where the plant comes from, and how to harvest sustainably; where and when to go; how to process the materials; how to store them until you're ready to use them; and then the whole process of making and using the basket or hat," she says. "It's like a transformation of the tree into something else, something cultural that's important to people.

"I always get annoyed with people who think basket making is an easy, little craft."

A LOOK BACK

Yellow-cedar's outer bark is shaggy and layered like it's been decorated with silver ribbons that are candy to bears. Young trees tend to have flakier bark that reveals a smooth, orangey trunk underneath, almost reminiscent of madrone. The fibrous inner bark is like soft leather that's easy to bend and strong.

The older trees may seem a bit melancholy at first glance, with one hundred feet of gray bark, preferred gray skies, grayish green foliage, and drooping branches, but they are tough. Yellow-cedars, *Callitropsis nootkatensis*, live in the wettest, coldest places, where some other trees can't grow.

Their ancestors knew the dinosaurs. They knew the earth before the continents separated. As proof, their closest relative isn't our familiar western redcedar but a recently discovered tree that lives across the Pacific Ocean in Vietnam, the golden Vietnamese cypress, *Xanthocyparis vietnamensis*.

Their family, Cupressaceae or cypress, appeared some two hundred million years ago in the Triassic period when our Pacific Northwest home was a seafloor. Trees similar to yellow-cedar first appeared in the Miocene about 5 to 23 million years ago, though trees with comparable foliage date to the Eocene, and alike cones date to the Late Cretaceous, geological time frames that range from 34 to 145 million years ago. Fossil records show that close relatives of yellow-cedar were much more common in the Northern Hemisphere than they are now.

Cypress family trees have puzzled scientists because they're extremely old and found all over the world—a living reminder that our continents used to be one giant landmass until it broke up some 150 million years ago. Members of the Cupressaceae family include conifer trees and shrubs that have small, scale-like or lacy foliage and lack obvious buds, like junipers, cypresses, and false cedars. Redwoods and yews are fairly close relatives. Trees within the cypress family are found all over now, from warm and dry landscapes to wet and snow-covered mountain slopes.

Yellow-cedars appeared in Pacific Northwest scientific records five thousand years ago after the ice sheet that covered Canada and parts of northern Washington retreated. Exactly when the trees first appeared in the region is hard to say because their pollen doesn't hold up well in sediment samples from lake bottoms or bogs, which is how scientists study historic plant distribution. The Cupressaceae family is thought to have been abundant by about 7,000 years ago in the region when the climate cooled, not long after the Pleistocene about 11,700 to 2.6 million years ago when the now dry and arid land east of the Cascades was probably more hospitable to yellow-cedars.

Both western redcedars, *Thuja plicata*, and yellow-cedars grow in moist soil, often near streams and wetlands. Unlike redcedars, though, yellow-cedars like high, snowy slopes within northern coastal rainforests, the Cascades, and the Olympic Mountains—a huge range that spans from Alaska's Kenai Peninsula to Northern California. In some areas if it's cold enough, they can grow at sea level. They're the queens of the north, as one traditional basket weaver tells me, and they become rarer in the Oregon Cascades. Within western Oregon tribal basketry traditions, redcedar is queen.

Scientists don't know for sure how yellow-cedars populated the once vast, ice-covered areas of the Northwest. Since the late Pleistocene, as the weather warmed, the trees may have made their slow and steady journey from south to north, like redcedar, to the wet and cold places, where they're most commonly found today. Another speculation is that, during the last Ice Age, the trees may have been growing in ice-free refuges in western areas of the Alaskan Panhandle and British Columbia. Then, when the glaciers melted, the trees spread out a bit more, and moved slightly east.

Another theory is that the first people may have helped distribute the tree. Some scientists wonder whether that could explain why two small groves of yellow-cedars live east of the Oregon Cascades, near John Day, and interior British Columbia by Slocan Lake and Evans Lake, hundreds of miles away from their typical homes.

Whenever and however they arrived, once established, the trees started their slow journey to expand their population. They chaotically traveled by spreading their seeds and pollen, generation by generation, until they found their preferred homes. Seeds that landed in an unfavorable area or got trapped in a bad climate died off. The ones that survived kept the migration going. The trees did this over and over and over again, spanning thousands of generations.

I think of yellow-cedars as the ultimate west-of-the-Cascades Pacific Northwest resident. They seek out the rain. They move to the wettest and coldest places in the farthest northern reaches of the Northwest, choosing challenging terrain where many other trees can't survive.

STRENGTH

They're battered, weathered, and droopy. Although they might not be as massive as their redcedar counterparts, they live well past our sense of time.

If an avalanche comes rumbling toward yellow-cedars, they simply take the hit, bend over, and spring right back up. Their weeping branches provide a natural defense against the weight of snow, and their bark and wood has supplied coastal people with hats, mats, masks, chests, dishes, baskets, blankets, robes, and hearty canoe paddles for millennia.

Both yellow-cedar and redcedar are known to people of the Northwest Coast as the "tree of life." Every part of the tree—bark, wood, branches, roots, and leaves—provides materials for nearly every aspect of living, from musical instruments, clothes, and medicines to houses, canoes, and fishing gear. Babies first greet the world on cedar bark mats and blankets within a cedar root cradle. When people die, they're placed on a cedar bark mat within a cedar burial box. Acclaimed Haida artist Bill Reid once wrote about the trees:

"If mankind in his infancy had prayed for the perfect substance for all material and aesthetic needs, an indulgent god could have provided nothing better."

No other Northwest tree has been so giving, so renowned, as the cedar.

They're among the oldest living trees on Earth, though it's hard to know exactly how old because the ancient trees' centers are often rotten, erasing evidence of their lifespan. Some trees with relatively small trunks could actually be hundreds of years old because they're so slow growing and live on less nutritious soil, which stunts their growth. On average, yellow-cedars live for about 500 to 750 years—nearly twice as long as spruces and hemlocks.

Several yellow-cedar groves in the Olympic Peninsula are home to Washington's oldest trees, with one tree still living after more than two thousand years and boasting a diameter of twelve feet—perhaps the largest yellow-cedar in Oregon and Washington. These groves are accessible by road and trail but aren't well known. At least in Oregon, yellow-cedar doesn't seem to be as revered as their fellow old-growth counterparts, like Douglas-fir and Sitka spruce, maybe because of their spotty range in the Cascades, and maybe because people mistake them as redcedar. From Deer Lake to Sol Duc Park in Olympic National Park, my partner and I hiked through more yellow-cedars than we've ever seen on a cool late August afternoon. They even joined us all the way to the High Divide trail at just over five thousand feet. We slept next to them every night.

To our Northwest standards, they're a medium-tall tree, reaching heights of 66 to 115 feet, on average, though some grow to 170 feet. When spruce and hemlock die, their trunks eventually fall, providing habitat for forest floor creatures and plants, while yellow-cedars can remain standing for up to one hundred years after they die. Without their foliage, they provide more light to the forest floor rather than cluttering it with more decaying wood. They give shrubs and flowers sunlight to grow.

Yellow-cedars' internal chemistry is built for longevity. Instead of putting more energy into growing faster to compete with other conifers, they produce powerful internal antifungal chemicals that sustain them for centuries, preventing rot and insect infestations. The natural world, though, is complex, and yellow-cedars tend to have fungi-caused "heart rot" or "stem decay" as the trees age even when they're generally rot-resistant. It's a paradox that has puzzled forest scientists for years. One theory suggests that the fungi are cedar specialists and have figured out how to make a living inside otherwise decay-resistant wood. Researchers are even studying one chemical found in cedar trees to see if it could be used in a natural mosquito or tick repellant.

Because of these chemicals, redcedars and yellow-cedars are fragrant trees, though they smell differently from each other. Yellow-cedars have a spicier, bitter smell, and several Indigenous words for the trees refer to their aroma. Ditidaht people call the tree ch'ukwtłapt—"chupał" meaning "smelling of bad odor." The Makah call them bachłapbap, a name which also references its pungent scent.

Young trees are snacks to deer, elk, and moose, which is likely one reason why their regeneration is slow—they keep getting eaten before they grow large enough to escape browsing.

Unlike big Doug-firs and ponderosa pines, whose thick bark protects them from fire, yellow-cedars have thin, flaky bark since they live in wet, typically fire-free forests. They're built for cold Alaskan coastlines or alpine environments. And their wood is strong. Really strong.

"I challenge you to try to pull a branch off of a yellow-cedar tree," says Richard Cronn, a US Forest Service geneticist who has studied the trees. "I won't say it's impossible, but I have had three adult men on the end of a rope, yanking, trying to snap a small branch that was half an inch around, and you can't break it. It's unbelievable."

Because of the wood's strength, First Nations peoples use it for canoe paddles, while redcedar is typically used to make dug-out canoes. Yellow-cedar's soft, even-textured wood is prized for carving, as it doesn't split as much as redcedar. The tree's rot-resistant wood also doesn't require chemical preservatives, which makes yellow-cedar valuable for building ships, boats, yachts, patios, door panels, bus stop shelters, benches, and play structures.

THE HARVEST

The right tree is the one you can hug. It's not too large or too old that you can't wrap your arms around, but it's also not too small and young.

The sap should still be running, usually early summer is best, depending on the location and elevation. The tree's lower branches should be higher up because you want to harvest a nice, long strip of bark. If you find the right tree, sometimes you can pull off a strip that's thirty-two to forty-nine feet long.

"Before you do anything, you'd talk to the tree, and ask before you take its bark, and say how you're going to use it, and you give an offering," ethnobotanist Turner says while describing some harvesting techniques, though they vary among different cultures. Now, people may give something of value, like tobacco or a coin, as a thank you.

Then, very carefully, harvesters start about four or five feet up the tree, make a horizontal cut, not too long, maybe one-fourth of the tree's circumference. Gently, they pull the bark away from the cut with even tension as they step back from the tree.

"And as you're walking backwards, you'd pull the strip, and it goes up the tree, and when it gets to the top, it's tapering, so eventually it tapers, and if it hits the branch way up there, you can give it a jerk, and it would come right down," Turner says.

In late spring or early summer, weaver Ariane Xay Kuyaas remembers traveling with her family to their harvesting site on Haida Gwaii, where she lives. They'd make a day out of it and bring a picnic. "It's a lot of work, but it's pleasant," Kuyaas says. "A lot of people really look forward to it."

Kuyaas is the great-granddaughter of artist Florence Davidson, who taught Turner how to make a basket. Already at thirty-one years old, Kuyaas is an accomplished cedar and spruce-root weaver.

After they pull bark from the tree, Kuyaas explains, little kids sometimes run around, swinging on the bark to try to get it to fall. Once it does, she coils the bark, then gets more, depending on how many pieces they pull that day. They clean the silvery outer bark and break it off with a knife. Then, they gather the fibrous inner bark in long bundles.

They might harvest from ten trees, enough to make quite a few hats, baskets, and mats. It's a gentle process, Kuyaas tells me. "If you take cedar bark from one tree, then you wouldn't take any more, and you'd let it recover," she says.

"We treat it like it is a living spirit because it is a living thing," she says. "It's a friendship to maintain, a kinship. I'm not sure if it's the same for everybody else, but that's what I was raised to understand."

Kuyaas's harvesting sites on Haida Gwaii are a one- or two-hour drive away from her home, but she's camped before, sometimes for ten to twelve days while harvesting spruce roots. Her brothers harvested enough cedar bark for her several years ago that she hasn't had to gather any more since. In the old days, Turner says, some Nuu-chah-nulth women weavers would take off and stay by themselves for up to two weeks.

Once the outer bark is off, getting the inner bark into thin strips for weaving takes days. Sometimes, Kuyaas will put the bark through a stripper to get the pieces small enough—a millimeter or two—depending on what it'll be used for. Then, the bark is dried out for storage, typically up to a year before it's woven. Some people dry it flat on the ground, turning it regularly, while others spiral it and hang it to dry.

When the bark is ready for weaving, Kuyaas explains, it needs to soak in water so it becomes pliable. She weaves with it damp, and once the bark dries again, it'll stay in whatever shape she creates. She works with both redcedar and yellow-cedar, which are overall similar, but she says yellow-cedar is more popular and less brittle than redcedar. Yellow-cedar, though, shrinks more compared to redcedar. "You could have a basket going, and think, 'Oh, this is the right shape,' and then you let it dry for a day, and it's smaller, and the lid might not fit. It's something to keep an eye on," she says.

Because redcedar bark has more structure and won't shrink as much, people have started using its bark for the vertical warp, which creates the foundation of a piece. Then, with yellow-cedar, they'll weave horizontal weft parts, which are woven around the warp, using both trees for a basket.

Thousands of yellow-cedars and redcedars along coastal mountains have been used sustainably like this, with long scars running up their trunks, known as culturally modified trees. They're found all over, from Oregon's Cascades to the Kodiak Archipelago in Alaska. The bark will heal, curling in on itself to eventually regrow. They're partially harvested at a time during the growing season when the tree can regenerate.

People observe seasonal signs to gauge when yellow-cedar bark is ready for harvest each year, like the blooming of a certain flower, or the appearance of a certain bird. There's only a small window of time to harvest easily off the tree, and people know exactly when to harvest, so they don't waste a trip halfway up a mountain.

One of Turner's friends, Helen Clifton, a ninety-six-year-old Gitga'at Nation elder, says to never harvest redcedar bark, for example, before harvesting seaweed. Her village is on a small island south of Prince Rupert on British Columbia's northwest coast. When you harvest bark from redcedars, Clifton told Turner, it often causes rain because nature brings a healing mist to the trees whose bark has been peeled. Since it's unsafe to harvest seaweed when it's raining, you wait to gather redcedar bark until after you've finished drying and processing the seaweed, typically in May.

Like Kuyaas's family, people develop relationships with the trees. "Just as you wouldn't think of going and trashing your grandmother's living room, you would treat their home places very carefully, and you'd be respectful and grateful for anything they give you," Turner says. "You don't just go and pull the bark off any old tree."

Turner has worked closely with coastal First Nations peoples for decades to help preserve their knowledge of native plants, which earned her great respect and friendships among the people from whom she learns. She's written dozens of books and published nearly one hundred scientific journal articles, many of which she co-authored with elders.

She views her work as a personal act of reconciliation in a country whose government forced more than 150,000 First Nations,

Inuit, and Métis children into residential schools to "kill the Indian in the child." Thousands died from starvation and disease, and others ran away from physical and sexual abuse by school authorities. The government denied them the chance to learn from their families and banned the use of their languages and cultural traditions.

TRANSFORMATION

Kuyaas remembers when her sister wanted to be a veterinarian growing up. Other kids wanted to be architects or chefs. "And I always said, 'I wanna be a weaver!'" she says, proudly. "And people were like, 'OK,'" as she imitates their reactions with one eyebrow raised in confusion. She remembers clearly when her great aunt and acclaimed Haida artist, Delores Churchill, patiently taught her how to weave her first cedar-bark basket when she was four or five years old.

Her mom is a weaver. Her aunt is a weaver. Her grandmother, great-grandmother, and great-great grandmothers were weavers. One wide-brimmed hat created in the late 1800s by her great-great grandmother Isabella Edenshaw is meticulously made from spruce roots. Chevron woven designs zig zag across its brim, providing texture underneath a black frog painted on top by her husband, Charles Edenshaw, also a famous Haida painter and carver. The frog's face is painted where the hat starts to taper, lips red, tongue black, while the animal's legs extend across the largest part of the hat. At the very top, Edenshaw painted a four-pointed star that's also black and red.

"I don't know how many generations back, but there's always been cedar-bark and spruce-root weavers in our family, so there's been an interest for my whole life," Kuyaas says. "I've always just been weaving."

She shows me yellow-cedar bark intricately woven into a small, golden basket with a knob-top lid in the Haida weaving style that's distinct among other coastal weaving techniques. Traditionally, Haida weavers make baskets and hats without a mold, shaping their creations to support themselves, she explains. They weave baskets starting from the bottom, spiraling from left to right in what's called a "z-twist" pattern. The more intricate side of Haida baskets are on the inside, so you see more details when you look in, she tells me.

Her nieces love coming to her house because they say it smells like yellow-cedar. "I think I'm kind of nose blind to it at this point because I've smelled it my whole life," she says, laughing. "My house is filled with cedar, so I don't notice the scent much anymore."

She makes headbands, baskets, aprons, and robes and has studied for years with family. She now takes on complex and intricate traditional coastal textile-weaving patterns called Ravenstail and Naaxiin, or Chilkat, where yellow-cedar, wool processing, and weaving patterns can take years to complete an item. The work that goes into making a Ravenstail robe—made by Haida, Tlingit, and Tsimshian people—is comparable to a carver creating a totem pole. "People don't really understand the whole effort," she says.

The robes are striking. Cedar bark is woven into them vertically, giving support to geometric designs in a beautifully refined color palette, often canary-yellow, teal, black, and cream. The perfectly sharp lines, which can feature various shapes and animals, are paired with an elegant fringe that outlines the blanket and flows especially long in the back. The fringe sways gently as a dancer drapes the robe over their shoulders during a ceremony. Yellow-cedar suddenly becomes something new.

Bark for Chilkat weaving needs to steep in a pot of water for four days to draw out all the saps and oils. "That's when it starts to come into the thin layers, and you split them, very narrowly, almost like grass, and spin them into the wool," she says. "It takes quite a while to get to the point of even starting to weave because of all the processing."

Kuyaas grew up in a Haida village in Old Masset on Graham Island within the Haida Gwaii archipelago where weaving was passed down in her family of renowned artists. Traditional techniques haven't been accessible to all Native people after colonists banned cultural traditions, like weaving. Haida people were beaten and forbidden from living and creating art as they had done forever.

Kuyaas recalls a time when she was nineteen and tried to buy a book written by a non-Native scholar who studied weaving from coastal elders. The book detailed Ravenstail and Chilkat designs and techniques but was out-of-print and sold for $1,500. So, she started making her own designs and creating her own style. Now, people want to learn from her. The award-winning artist shows her art in galleries and privately commissions pieces.

Weaving is traditionally passed down matrilineally. Kuyaas's aunt, Isabel Rorick, has three sons, so she passed her weaving knowledge to Kuyaas, who hopes to pass her skills on to future generations, either through children of her own or relatives. Weaving is becoming more popular again, she says, and she wants it to be taught and accessible.

"We are still here. We are still weaving," she says. "Even through all of these different changes throughout time that were imposed on us, it's still carried on."

TRUE CEDARS

Some people call them Alaska-cedars, though more of the trees grow in British Columbia. Others call them Nootka-cedars or Nootka cypress, after the Nootka Sound area of western Vancouver Island where they were "discovered" by white people. Some say Alaska cypress, yellow cypress, canoe-cedar, or Sitka cypress, but no matter what you call them, it's all confusing and often technically wrong.

Despite their name, yellow-cedars aren't true cedars, as defined by Western scientists. Redcedars are also not true cedars and neither are incense-cedars. When my partner and I started learning about trees in our neighborhood, we couldn't identify one type that was seemingly on every block near our Northeast Portland home. Their needles grew in bundles like a larch, but their barrel-like cones sat upright on the branches like a noble fir and similarly crumbled immediately upon any contact.

The trees are Himalayan (or deodar), Lebanon, and Atlas cedars, all in the pine family, and are native to the regions of their namesake.

Once you notice one in the city, you'll notice them everywhere. They seem more common than the "false" cedars whose home is here and not across the world.

What we in the Northwest consider "cedars" are trees within the cypress family that have lace-like foliage made up of tiny, elegant leaves and small cones, like junipers. True cedars, in the genus *Cedrus*, belong to the pine family, have needle clusters and upright cones, and aren't native to North America. All this confusion, scientists say, may have been because of the trees' wood. Romans called trees with aromatic wood "*Cedrus*," and since our "cedars" also have fragrant wood, maybe that's where it all went wrong.

Those in the timber industry called the tree "yellow-cedar" because of the color of the wood. When cut open, yellow-cedar heartwood is the color of spaghetti squash stuffed within a creamy tannish sapwood.

Different First Nations peoples call the tree many names, and Turner provides me with a lengthy list. Tlingit people refer to the tree as *xáay*; Gitxsan people say *wil*; Kitasoo/Xai'xais people say *wàl*; Heiltsuk people say *díw'ás*; Wuikinuxv people say *diìw'ás*; Kwakwaka'wakw people say *dixw*; Nuu-chah-nulth people say *ʕaɬmapt*; Nuxalk people say *iixɬp*; Comox people say *tíixway*; Squamish people say *q'eɬmáy'*; Stl'atl'imx people say *páxlaqw*; Nlaka'pamux people say *kwátɬp*, which is the same word used for redcedar. All the different languages also have variations of these words and include different words for yellow-cedar bark blankets, the bark itself, and young yellow-cedars, such as the Heiltsuk people, whose word for the bark is *díxw*, and young yellow-cedars are called *ɬískw's*.

Proper English spelling of false cedars requires a hyphen or prefix, like "western redcedar," or "yellow-cedar," "incense-cedar," or "Port-Orford-cedar"—which are the four Northwest "cedars." Similarly, the proper spelling of "Douglas-fir" is with a hyphen because they're not true firs.

To add to the confusion, yellow-cedar's scientific name has been up for debate for some time. The tree was initially a part of the *Cupressus* genus, or true cypresses, in the 1800s, and then botanists changed it to *Chamaecyparis*, or false cypress family, because the trees looked similar to others in this genus. Then, botanists reclassified the trees as *Callitropsis*, which is a separate genus among the true cypresses. And then, more confusion. Scientists in 2001 identified a new and closely related tree species in Vietnam, which spurred more analysis of what exactly is a yellow-cedar. Some scientists argue that the tree belongs in this new genus, *Xanthocyparis*, based on its genetics, while others say it should remain in its current genus, *Callitropsis*. And some scientists think that the new golden Vietnamese cypress should join yellow-cedar in *Callitropsis*. The International Botanical Congress, which formally oversees all these names, was set to decide whether to change yellow-cedar's genus to *Xanthocyparis* in 2011. The proposal, though, was never brought to the committee, and the trees are left with their *Callitropsis* first name.

Even more, all species within *Xanthocyparis*, *Callitropsis*, and western North American *Cupressus* share a common lineage, and may trace back to a common ancestor from thirty to fifty million years ago.

ALDRICH MOUNTAINS GROVE

Not far from the sagebrush, where lizards dash into tiny crevasses within eastern Oregon basalt cliffs, where the orange bark of ponderosa pines warms hillsides, and where the rush of city life is as far away as rain clouds, the moisture-loving yellow-cedar calls this land home.

They're more than one hundred miles away from any of their kin, tucked within a steep alpine slope where freshwater bubbles from the earth, a postcard from their more typical climate farther north and west.

On the short, secluded, one-mile trek to the grove, my partner and I see a medley of trees—ponderosa pines, grand firs, Doug-firs, western juniper, western larches, and a mountain mahogany.

I first notice the sound of the creek and then the cedars' silvery, shaggy bark that glowed against the browns, reds, and oranges of their neighbors. In this twenty-six-acre grove, called the Cedar Grove Botanical Area, in eastern Oregon's Aldrich Mountains, a sub-range of the Blue Mountains about thirty miles outside of John Day, yellow-cedars somehow survive. The trees are the only ones in the country that grow here, far east of the mountains that divide the state into wet and dry lands.

In the heat of summer, when the surrounding landscape is scorching, the shaded, cool grove provides a welcome relief to occasional hikers, or cows that are allowed, though discouraged from grazing within the grove and surrounding forest.

A series of small springs merges to form the frigid Buck Cabin Creek at about 5,740 feet elevation. From the springs, the grove extends downslope for about a mile, where the land becomes steeper and narrower and stays moist and cool enough to trick the trees into thinking they're in Sitka, Alaska.

Thunderstorms often sweep through the area, with lightning igniting fires in the hot, dry summer. The grove's average annual rainfall of eighteen inches is nearly what cedars in their normal range see just within the month of October.

Yellow-cedars aren't built for fire. Their thin bark can't tolerate heat, which is what makes their persistence in this area so puzzling. It's thought that the surrounding dry mountains burned from lightning and Native-set fires every ten to twenty years, on average, before white settlers arrived in the 1800s.

When the US Forest Service banned all Native-set fires in the early twentieth century and worked hard to suppress any natural forest fires, some Forest Service officials who managed the grove grew concerned in the 1990s that the unburned, extensive underbrush would fuel a severe fire that could wipe out the unique trees. And in 2006, it kind of happened. A lightning-caused fire ravaged the Aldrich Mountains, burning twelve thousand acres in a day, becoming one of the largest forest fires in the Pacific Northwest that summer. A giant plume of smoke reached thirty thousand feet and created its own weather. An official within the Forest Service decided to set a low-intensity burn to try to save the cedars from the hotter natural fire nearby, despite advice from fellow employees who recommended otherwise. The natural fire burned only the northernmost part of the grove, while the intentional fire killed 90 percent of the trees, including one that sprung from the earth in 1428. The fire was the first to scorch the cedars in 135 years—the longest fire-free period since the mid-1500s.

As my partner and I make our way up the creek that runs through the grove, we step on and over fallen yellow-cedars who didn't survive the blaze. Hardy trunks support us as we try to avoid remnants of the season's now-melting snow. Many of the trunks are charred and most have lost their graceful and ornate foliage. Just a ways up the creek, though, where the springs begin, a pocket of living trees with mesmerizing layered bark welcomes us, their pendant-like branches blowing in the crisp alpine wind. A few are still living. They look the same as their relatives would have thousands of years ago.

Grand firs now take up more of their fair share of the Blue Mountains and threaten to crowd out cedars in the grove. The Forest Service wants to remove some of them before they grow too large and potentially take over. The agency also planted some cedar seedlings sourced from the grove after the fire, but natural regeneration has so far outpaced the plantings. Dozens of young, tiny yellow-cedars sprout from the damp soil hoping to survive as their elders have for centuries in this secluded refuge. We notice yellow-cedar and grand fir seedlings next to each other, and I pluck the grand fir to give yellow-cedar a chance.

Although the grove hasn't been thoroughly studied, some scientists have questioned if the area's first people may have planted the trees. Retired Malheur National Forest archeologist Don Hann says that's possible, but he isn't aware that people from the nearby Burns Paiute and Umatilla tribes used the grove, even though they likely knew the trees were there. Weaving and carving materials vary among tribal cultures based on what plants are abundant and close by. Burns Paiute weavers typically use willows, tules, sagebrush, and hemp. For other Oregon tribes closer to the Cascades, redcedar, not yellow, is more commonly used.

Not too far from the grove, Hann found an obsidian flake, a volcanic glass that was commonly used for tools and projectiles. Thousands of scattered artifact sites found within Malheur National

Forest show that people heavily hunted and foraged within the area since at least 11,200 years ago, though they likely didn't venture to the mountains until the climate warmed about 8,000 years ago, when the Blue Mountains' glaciers melted. People then used the high ridgelines as travel routes from the John Day River valley to big upland meadows to the south.

Most clues lead scientists to believe that the grove is a relic of the Pleistocene, when eastern Oregon was cooler, tundra-like, with spruce and likely more yellow-cedars.

Scientists call the grove a climate refugium—a little spot within the landscape where plants survive despite being outside of their usual habitat. Several moss varieties more common in western Oregon and Washington old-growth forests, like *Sphagnum* and *Hylocomium splendens* or "stair-step" moss, have been found in a similar north-facing refugium nearby.

The grove is also a fire refugium because it burns less frequently than the surrounding area. These unique habitats are typically found in drainages. Trees here are sheltered from solar rays as they face north on a steep ridge, hiding in the shade of mountains, and avoiding direct sunlight that southern facing slopes take on. The trees are also protected by the creek that may have barricaded them from fire over the years.

Though they're a fire-sensitive tree, they've experienced more flames here than in any other place where yellow-cedars grow. From 1560 to 1890, researchers say twenty-three fires swept through the area, while just seven went through the grove, in a slightly shorter timeframe, from 1650 to 1871. Fire was two and a half times less frequent in the grove than the surrounding area, and research found two seventy-year periods where no fires spread into the grove at all.

CLONING

Richard Cronn noticed a curious straight line of young yellow-cedars along a wet slope covered with cushy *Sphagnum* moss while doing research in coastal Alaska. After walking a bit upslope, the Forest Service geneticist turned to look back down and noticed that under the thick blanket of moss was a sixty- to seventy-foot-tall downed yellow-cedar. When it hit the ground, the tree didn't die. Instead, the canopy of branches formed roots sprouting hundreds of new trees, thanks to what Cronn describes as the always moist and perfect planting conditions in Alaska.

"We were standing on the hillside, and I thought, 'Wow! That is awesome,'" Cronn says, enthusiastically. "Imagine that happening over a period of thousands of years, where one of those trees will grow up, and it, too, might fall over," repeating the same cloning cycle. "It raised a question of how expansive these clones might be in Alaska. The connections between these trees could be quite extensive, all connected to some parent tree that goes back in time, who knows where."

Yellow-cedars can reproduce both sexually, through spreading pollen and seeds, and asexually, through cloning. New, small, cloned trees look more like a bush and form roots while still attached to a parent plant. They later separate from the parent, with whom they share the exact same genes.

Doug-firs and pines can't clone themselves. But yellow-cedars, western redcedars, Port-Orford-cedars, and redwoods have developed the sci-fi seeming superpower. Cloning gives yellow-cedars an advantage against other trees by taking up more space and using more resources. It also allows trees to grow in areas where it may be difficult to reproduce sexually. Yellow-cedar seeds are extremely slow to germinate, and only a few baby trees will grow big enough to replace the next generation, so they need all the repopulation help they can get.

With clones, however, trees grow closer together, which increases the likelihood of self-pollination, which then increases the local rate of inbreeding and may cause reduced fertility or early death. Scientists don't yet know the long-term implications of self-pollinated yellow-cedar trees.

In Echo Basin off of Highway 20 near Santiam Pass in Oregon, Cronn suspects that two massive, possibly five-hundred-year-old trees growing sixty feet apart could be clones, or they could be siblings. "These could be sister trees from a common mom," he says.

The trees in Echo Basin are massive. Their silver, layered, and shaggy bark speckled with mint-green lichen affirms that they've been here a long time. They're in a wet, alpine environment, and they grow like they're in Alaska, not in Oregon's central Cascades. Some trees might be hundreds, or thousands, of years old. "They're mammoths," Cronn says. "They're just monsters. They're wonderful."

We visit the grove and have lunch with a tree known as "Big Momma," because she's, well, very big. She has a split, moss-covered base that divides two mammoth trees, each boasting branches that are as large as a reasonably sized tree trunk. Two of her clones grow nearby. She's been here, growing, as the world around her has drastically changed over the centuries. We enjoy her grounding company and shade on the hot July morning.

ROOTS & NITROGEN

I know anything with "nitrogen" in a title is not catchy or appealing, but I hope you'll bear with me. Both redcedars and yellow-cedars have pretty interesting ways to find nutrients, and I promise to spare you the fine details, as they include words like "spectrofluorometric," "osmolarity," and "cytoplasm," the latter being a word I thought I was done with after my biology class in college.

Redcedars and yellow-cedars grow in wet areas with low nitrogen where other trees can't grow well. It's not that they necessarily want to be there—in fact, cedars grow to their largest potential on sites that are better suited for big trees—but they're forced into less ideal homes from their competitors, spruce and hemlock. Both trees hog sunlight and are faster growing.

Cedars root shallowly in the ground, likely because they needed to find a way to get nutrients in nutrient-poor sites. It's hard to study something underground, though, and all scientists know about their roots is inferred, based on other clues, like their chemistry and behavior. Their knack for living in wet soils requires shallow roots to get any nutrients, says David D'Amore, a Forest Service soil scientist and yellow-cedar researcher based in Juneau, Alaska.

Cedars are hard workers, staying essentially awake through all seasons. They're always ready to grow at any moment to take advantage of any nutrients that are available, and once temperatures start to warm, they'll go to work. Other conifers, like Doug-firs and pines, enter a deep sleep in the colder months and start their growing season when the days become longer.

It's long been known that members of the Cupressaceae store more calcium than other conifers, but scientists didn't know exactly why. They store so much calcium that if they didn't send it to their foliage, it would become toxic.

"I asked myself, 'Why would they need so much calcium?'" D'Amore says. He couldn't find an answer from colleagues or from research, so he kept thinking about it. "It's almost like this urban legend that cedars need calcium to grow."

D'Amore authored a 2009 paper hypothesizing that the trees absorb so much calcium because it's their way of finding essential nutrients, mainly nitrogen, to grow. They convert calcium into a usable form of nitrogen.

"This whole paper emerged when I woke up one night and said, 'Wait a minute. They're not after calcium. They don't need calcium. They need nitrogen,'" he says.

Two nitrate ions can hitch a ride on one calcium ion. From there, yellow-cedars reduce the nitrate to gain access to nitrogen. During that reduction, a toxic chemical is spit out that then bonds with the calcium, which is sent to their leaves and safely stored. I wrap my head around it by thinking of the calcium as a conveyor belt, bringing helpful nutrients to the trees that take what they need, and send the rest to their leaves.

"It makes sense," D'Amore says, "because in that way they can get a foothold in those really marginal environments where trees have a hard time growing. They thrive in crappy habitats."

This process is not the most energetically efficient and most other conifers don't bother, D'Amore says. They have their own, easier way of finding nitrogen through ammonium. Redcedars also store high amounts of calcium in their leaves, but not as much as yellow-cedars.

Because of this nitrogen adaptation, cedars can alter the chemical make-up and microorganism communities in soils and watersheds. When their calcium-rich leaves drop, the nutrients are cycled back into the forest floor, enriching the soil, and helping to maintain proper stream balance so the water isn't too acidic.

WARMING

Deep green, weeping silhouettes that covered swaths of coastal mountains are now skeleton forests. These long-lived, resilient trees are dying within more than half a million acres of their home.

Yellow-cedars are freezing to death in our warming world.

The trees can't keep up with climate change. In some pockets, more than 70 percent of them are gone. The die-off stretches along six hundred miles of Earth's largest coastal rainforest, with dying trees now found on the more temperate Haida Gwaii.

Paul Hennon spent his career, beginning in 1981, studying the trees' decline, thought to have started in the late 1800s. With help from other scientists, including D'Amore, the now-retired Forest Service plant pathologist discovered that yellow-cedar's unique knack for rooting shallowly puts their roots at risk of freezing. Because most roots don't go deep into the ground, they need snow to insulate them, especially the fine roots that are one to two millimeters in diameter. As the areas where they live become warmer and more rain falls than snow, the roots are left without any protection and can freeze in early spring if temperatures drop.

When the roots are injured, they can't send nutrients and water to the rest of the tree. Younger trees might still be green, though all their roots are dead. "It's as if the seedling was in a refrigerator," Hennon says. "You can cut crops, and they'll stay green in a refrigerator, and then they'll start to wilt. So, it'll take months sometimes before the top dries out and there's evidence that the tops are done."

The older trees, who may have some deeper roots, often endure several freezing injuries for multiple years before they eventually succumb. The trees die from the inside first, and then out, Hennon tells me, hanging on for maybe ten to fifteen years. Their lacy foliage yellows, and their crown starts drying. Lesions form where roots feed into the base of the tree. "By the time you see those in the lower part of the tree, there's very little green left in the canopy, and it's kind of hanging on by a thread sometimes," he says.

Less snow could also affect their reproductive rates, Hennon explains. During heavy-snow winters, deer aren't around as much to feed on seedlings. But during low-snow years, it's thought that deer feast so much on young trees that many don't grow large enough to survive.

Yellow-cedars in the past have migrated to better climates, but the climate is changing too quickly, and some populations can't move to a more suitable home in time. Trees at the edge of their northern range near Juneau, Alaska, have plenty of suitable habitat, but they don't appear to have moved much in the past two hundred years. Few seedlings survive.

If carbon emissions continue to rise rapidly, trees at higher elevations near their northern range limit may be at-risk of freezing by 2070, causing some researchers to weigh moving yellow-cedars to snowier areas to try to save them. Mortality within populations, though, is never 100 percent, Hennon tells me, and some trees survive, though he's not sure exactly why.

Logging also threatens trees in the Tongass National Forest, and conservationists petitioned the federal government to list yellow-cedar under the Endangered Species Act. The effort was rejected in 2019 because the US Fish and Wildlife Service said the die-off isn't significant enough to threaten the tree's survival, since it's killing trees only within 6 percent of their habitat.

Cedar's value has fluctuated in Alaska's timber industry, from unwanted to being the region's most valuable wood. It was favored in the 1800s for ship-building in Sitka, Alaska, and trees were logged until the cedar supply was exhausted. In the 1950s, the Forest Service wanted to grow Alaska's timber industry and saw an opportunity to send trees—mostly western hemlock and Sitka spruce, but also redcedar and yellow-cedar—to Japan, which was rebuilding after World War II.

Yellow-cedars initially avoided the saw because they generally don't grow near the more sought after hemlocks and spruces in the Tongass. When regulations prevented loggers from cutting down trees on those sites, they turned to areas where yellow-cedars grow abundantly and started cutting. Most high-quality yellow-cedar logs are still sent to Japan and are used to build marinas, temples, and shrines. Their light-yellow wood is prized for its resemblance to the largely unavailable Hinoki cypress.

On Haida Gwaii, Kuyaas says, clear-cutting is decimating the northern part of the archipelago, where the trees aren't protected. "You won't really find much where you can make a canoe or totem pole," she says. "Nobody really wants to bring politics into everything, but it does affect art, and it does affect lifestyles."

Haida Nation members made international headlines in the 1980s when they fought logging companies over cutting down the beloved trees. People blockaded logging roads on the archipelago, and elders dressed in ceremonial blankets were arrested. The protests led to a new national park and heritage site on the southern part of the archipelago to protect red and yellow-cedars. The protests also inspired similar fights for forests and Indigenous rights in British Columbia. Haida people continue working to preserve cedars.

Root injuries haven't been found yet in Oregon and Washington yellow-cedars. For trees here, the threat is likely competition from other trees and shrubs—or fire.

Extreme drought conditions in 2021 were more widespread than at any point in at least twenty years. As I'm writing this in late June 2021, Portland is 116 degrees: the hottest day ever in the city. The year before, the West saw its worst fire season on record with massive blazes blanketing Eugene and Portland in toxic smoke, turning the sky an ominous orange. I couldn't go outside for two weeks without wearing an N-95 mask.

The future's not good for yellow-cedars at the southern end of their range, or those living within the Aldrich Mountains. We may lose some of these groves.

The heat wave scorched trees and shrubs around the Portland area, leaving large chunks of Doug-fir needles and redcedar leaves orange, particularly on southern facing branches that bore the brunt of the solar rays. Hennon shows me several redcedars on Reed College's campus whose tips are dead from the heat, but surprisingly, yellow-cedars in the area—including one in his backyard—show no damage. He's not sure why. Tip damage on redcedars looks similar to what acute freezing injuries on yellow-cedars in Alaska look like, he tells me.

Yellow-cedars have been challenged before, though. The climate has warmed and cooled countless times over millions of years. They've had to move and migrate to more suitable habitats, and maybe they've similarly died off. But this time, our way of living threatens them at a pace they haven't yet seen.

Talking to experts who have studied the trees for longer than I've been alive gives me a deeper perspective. Many yellow-cedars are doing just fine. A good proportion of trees, even within the die offs, still survive. The conifer calendar is much older than our sense of time. We're not here long enough to see the whole pattern.

The trees may grow somewhere else, but they won't be gone.

Western Bumble Bee,
Bombus occidentalis

I spent hours as a kid running around barefoot in my North Portland backyard, chasing butterflies with a net on warm July afternoons. My mom often yelled at me to "come quick!" whenever enormous dragonflies landed on our fence, and we both observed their mesmerizing metallic emerald bodies. I was particularly interested in bees, though, especially bumble bees. I even dressed up as one for Halloween in first grade. Compared to other insects who looked less cuddly, bumble bees' round velvet bodies intrigued me. I wanted to know how soft they were to touch.

My older cousin caught bumble bees in her hands. She showed me how she carefully scooped them up without getting stung, and I followed her lead. I remember catching one, putting them in a Mason jar, and studying them. Once they, sadly, died in the jar, I tried to dissect them with Popsicle sticks still red at the tip from my summer treat. I tried to pull out the stinger, hoping to better understand these creatures I admired.

One quick, painful moment changed my relationship with bees forever: I finally got stung. I probably stepped on the yellow jacket who assaulted me, but I felt betrayed by my flying friends, even though it wasn't even a bumble bee who attacked me.

Two decades later, and I'm still terrified of bees. I've had my share of horror stories, too, in my defense. I've found yellow jackets in my bed on Guemes Island, had a handful of bees get into my house somehow, and one even journeyed into my mouth while I was running. When I worked as a newspaper reporter in Eugene,

I had to write about the arrival of four million honey bees packed in a semi-truck at a local bee company's annual "Bee Weekend." I'll jerk quickly, look from side-to-side in horror, and scream in soprano tones awkwardly mid-conversation if I hear even a buzz, until whoever I'm talking to assures me that it was just a fly.

Although I think I've gotten better, my behavior has caused multiple people to ask if I'm allergic to bees, and I almost wish I had that excuse. So, perhaps this essay is my way of rectifying my relationship with the creature who never did anything wrong to me, who's still cute and fuzzy and fascinating, and whose lives are worth learning from and protecting.

BUMBLE BEE HUNT

"What do you think?" a US Geological Survey employee asks, while securing a decently sized, mostly black bumble bee in a plastic vial underneath a net. "It looks a little different, right?"

Jeff Everett takes hold of the net and the plastic vial, carefully transferring the bee to a better vial with a lid.

"Nicely done," she says to Everett. "It's like you're a bee person."

Everett, a US Fish and Wildlife biologist who works with native bees, hands me the vial, and I peer down at the bee, who's buzzing and trying to find a way out to hurt me, I initially think, then I gather some composure and compassion in front of these bee experts.

"It's fuzzy all over," Everett says. "Shaggy, almost."

"Could it be a *melanopygus*?" she asks, referring to the bee's Latin species name.

"Mm-mmm," Everett says, shaking his head from side-to-side while studying the bee. "No, it doesn't have enough orange or yellow."

He turns and hands the bee off for someone else to try to identify. "I got another one for ya," he says. "It's either a cuckoo or a male. I think it's a male."

The woman looks at the bee, mumbling "T4 and T5," the scientific names for the different segments on the bee's abdomen, what we think of as their back.

"The shoulders look almost a bit white, too," Everett says.

"Yeah, he's a male," she says, after inspecting the creature for a few moments, describing the long antenna and "wedge-shaped" abdomen that are apparently characteristic of male bees.

"So *mixtus*?" Everett asks, referring to a common bumble bee in this area on Mount Ashland in southern Oregon.

"I think it's *insularis*," she says. "And we've been seeing tons of female *insularis* too."

I try to find my identification guide to sort through all these Latin names and to see how on Earth they're identifying this bee, but my sheet has only female bees, who often look different from males. I laugh to myself as I think about standing here around bee biologists and enthusiasts holding a bee identification guide in one hand and a three-foot-tall butterfly net in the other. I even started to pick up on their Latin species names and convinced my sister to join me during her vacation, to wake up early and find bees by 9:00 a.m.

We started our trek to Mount Ashland on a warm mid-July morning, assured by the Prius behind us that we were, indeed, headed in the right direction. Several bee researchers joked that it was the "biggest bumble bee hunt ever," as forty-eight adults—mostly federal Bureau of Land Management and US Fish and Wildlife employees—circled up in earth-toned clothing, nets in hand, determined to find rare bumble bees to help scientists understand and, hopefully, save these creatures.

Lots of jerking, many careful steps through bee-covered clovers pretending as if everything is OK, and several awkward trying-to-be quiet screams occurred throughout the six-hour day. With my sister's moral support, I successfully caught two yellow-faced bumble bees who, thankfully, wanted nothing to do with me and swiftly resumed their foraging after I released them.

Fire smoke blanketed the Siskiyou Mountains, hiding what would normally be a view of Mount Shasta, but the area was still stunning. More bumble bees than I've ever seen—or heard—darted around picturesque, wildflower-laden meadows, their orange hind legs dangling heavily, weighted down by freshly collected pollen to feed their colony. Neon-green lichen decorated giant mountain hemlocks scattered among impressive rock outcroppings, reminding me that we were over six thousand feet.

The US Fish and Wildlife Service organizes this bumble bee blitz, as Everett calls it, every year to try to find three, now-rare Northwest bumble bees: the western bumble bee, Suckley's cuckoo bumble bee, and Franklin's bumble bee, which hasn't been seen since 2006 at our location at Grouse Gap, where the Pacific Crest Trail cuts through the meadow. Franklin's bumble bee has the smallest range of any bee in North America, possibly in the world. They live only in southern Oregon and Northern California between the Coast Range and the Cascade-Sierra Mountains, but they're thought to be extinct now.

A dedicated group of bee scientists and enthusiasts have surveyed the area since 2000 to understand the bees more. Though scientists have studied bumble bees for decades, little is known about some native bumble bees' behaviors and where exactly they live, like the western bumble bee. "The most important thing we can do now is to find them," Everett says.

These sugar-loving creatures that weigh less than a gram are animals, too, with a brain and a heart in their tiny, furry bodies. Their early ancestors survived the asteroid that eliminated most other living things off the earth sixty-five million years ago. They inspire us with their tenacious work ethic and provoke intellectual debates about human economies through their ancient, social way of living. We tend to lose our child-like curiosity once we deem their lives less worthy than our own, even as they continue to feed us and pollinate plants that sustain our world.

POPULATION

Western bumble bees, *Bombus occidentalis*, are tough. They live in the frigid alpine, coastal forest, sagebrush, and desert. They have a huge home range, from the Alaskan tundra to our Cascades and east, to North Dakota's Great Plains, even reaching as far south as the cacti in Arizona and New Mexico. Their luxurious fur coats and unique ability to keep themselves warm by shivering allows queens to start their season early, in February or March, depending on where they live, while honey bees are still in their nests drinking honey. They continue to forage until November, when newly anointed queens begin their hibernation before assuming their duties to carry on the next generation.

Western bumble bees used to be among the most common bumble bees in the West. They feasted on camas blooms in the Willamette Valley's vast prairies before the landscapes were plowed. They foraged on flowers in our backyards and gardens thirty years ago, and I probably admired one as a kid.

We're not too interested in what's common, though. We deem raccoons as pests despite their high levels of creativity and problem-solving abilities and dismiss the sheer brilliance of crows just because they're loud. Similarly, the western bumble bee wasn't studied much because it was so common. Not a lot of researchers wanted to study the bee equivalent to grass, or dandelions.

"It's there, but you don't give it special attention because it's just kind of cosmopolitan," says Lincoln Best, Oregon State University's native bee taxonomist. "People are always drawn to the more rare things. And rarity is a type of charisma."

When honey bees started to die off suddenly sixteen years ago, in what's known as colony collapse disorder, people started to care more about bees. "Save the Bees" stickers are now common on Hydro Flask water bottles, computers, and cars. Most non-bee people know about their important role in pollinating plants and the food we eat. Honey bees, though, are the face of this campaign, which is a little strange because they're not native to North America.

Honey bees are, essentially, livestock. They're here for us. European colonists brought them here in the 1600s. They pollinate our food and give us honey and are no doubt important to our landscape now, but the "bee friendly" marketing for gardens and flowers tends to leave out the bees we should care most about—native bees.

Bumble bees are more effective pollinators of native flowers than European honey bees, especially in cold and high-elevation places where honey bees can't survive. Some flowers have even evolved their shape and size to perfectly suit the long tongues of many bumble bees looking for nectar and pollen. They're so good at living in cold temperatures thanks to their ancestors who thrived in a cooler climate some fifteen to twenty million years ago. One bumble bee fossil found in eastern Washington is estimated to be twelve to twenty-one million years old.

Bumble bees start their day once it's light out and, in the summer, will work from dawn to dusk gathering nutritious and protein-rich pollen for food, which they store on their legs like they're wearing orange cargo pants. Pollen is basically plant sperm, and since plants can't move, bees make plant sex much more convenient by bouncing around from flower to flower, transferring pollen attached to their specialized hairs onto other flowers.

They love all types of flowers and need a variety of blooming plants to sustain themselves throughout the several seasons that they're alive. Western bumble bees are particularly drawn to thistles, goldenrods, willows, rabbit brush, and a smattering of other things, like asters and lupines, depending on the location. I look extra close at these plants now whenever I'm in the alpine where the westerns live, hoping to catch a glimpse.

IDENTIFICATION

Western bumble bees look like their rears have been dipped in sugar. This classic, white tail sets them apart from other native bumble bees, who may have just a black, yellow, or orange tail. The color patterns vary, though, among western bumble bee queens, workers, and males, the latter of which typically have more yellow on their bodies. But, in general, westerns are black with yellow shoulders and white tails.

To a non-bee person, most bumble bees look alike. I'll notice slight color variations if there's orange or red stripes on the bee's back, but I likely won't get close enough to inspect all the differences that make these creatures unique.

More than thirty different species of bumble bees live in our Northwest landscapes. Oregon alone has about two dozen different types of bumble bees—part of the seven hundred native bees that live here, including many that are new to science. Our native bumble bees seem to have endless color patterns and variations despite our childlike way of drawing their stripes as evenly alternating between black and yellow. Bees' coloring is found on their heads, midsection, and different segments on their back, or abdomen.

When you look closely at a bumble bee, you can count these segments. Females have six, and males have seven. Females also have a stinger, which is an extension of their egg-laying apparatus. She can sting as many times as she wants, unlike the honey bee who dies after the deed. Male bumble bees might pump their abdomen and thrust their rears forward and back, as if they're about to sting, but it's all for show. Only females have the venom.

Some bees have yellow heads and shoulders, with a band of yellow just above their rear. Some have mostly yellow backs, while others will have a black spot on their yellow backs. Some will have an orange rump while a common backyard bumble bee, the yellow-faced bumble bee, *Bombus vosnesenskii*, has a yellow head and often a yellow stripe near the rear, on the fourth abdominal segment.

I get flashbacks from my childhood as I peer down at a bumble bee in my yard using a cheap magnifying glass, hoping to get a good look at her black and yellow and red coloring to try to identify her. I reference my Pacific Northwest bumble bee identification guide and think she might be a black-tailed bumble bee, *Bombus melanopygus*, but I'm not sure. They're common around here, like westerns used to be.

The first step in identifying a bumble bee is figuring out whether the bee is male or female. Among different species, though, the coloring can vary between females and males—who also differ by antenna and abdomen length and leg size—and coloring can be different among the female workers and queens and can vary by region, which makes it seem all the more hopeless to properly identify these fuzzy creatures.

Then, there's a chance the bee is not a true bumble bee but a cuckoo bumble bee. Cuckoo bees are vagrants. They're robbers that sleep late into the season, waiting until true bumble bees have labored for weeks to establish their colonies. Then, they break in, kill, or subdue the queen with force or with pheromones, eat some pollen, lay their eggs, and leave. They sometimes usurp the queen and take over, "enslaving" her workers while they simply kick back and get fed for free.

These larger and shinier bumble bees prey on specific types of true bumble bees, like the Suckley's cuckoos that target western bumble bees. Since their host's population has declined, Suckley's have only been seen a few times over the last few decades.

LIFE CYCLE

Illustrations and graphs online explain the bumble bee life cycle clearly and in good detail but hearing bee taxonomist Lincoln Best walk me through it reminds me of its complete jaw-dropping insanity. It's like a matriarchal science fiction movie that is fundamentally different from the honey bee's multi-year life cycle, let alone our own.

Bumble bees are social bees, meaning they form hives or colonies with divisions of labor, cooperative baby bee care, and overlapping generations. Social living is relatively rare in bees and occurs within only 10 percent of the 20,000 bee species in the world. This communal way of living is also one of the major evolutionary transitions of life on Earth and happens more often in insects than any other animal.

Bumble bee colonies are made up of queen bees, female "worker" bees, and later in the season, male bees. Unlike honey bees who hibernate together as a hive, bumble bee queens go at it alone in an almost lifeless state underground over winter. To protect herself from getting too cold, she produces an anti-freeze-like chemical to keep her tissues from bursting.

Queens emerge from their slumber in early spring in dire need of nectar and pollen to refuel. The queen searches for early spring flowers for food, while also plotting her nest site, which is typically underground, maybe in abandoned mouse burrows, dead tree cavities, or in rock crevices because she doesn't dig her own nest. She'll search tirelessly for a new home that's in a good location, close to food and in a safe place away from predators, like cuckoo bumble bees. Sometimes she'll take two weeks or more of daily house hunting before finding a suitable site.

Once she selects a nest, the queen will construct thimble-sized honey pots made of wax that she excretes from glands on her belly. She regurgitates nectar stored in her special "honey gut" and fills the pots with the sugary drink, which will be used for food until enough pollen is collected. Honey pots are also used for extra food on rainy days when the bees prefer to stay cozy at home. The queen will then begin to forage for pollen, which is packed with protein, vitamins, and minerals, and she'll mold the pollen dust into a Play-Doh-like mound. Because she's still fertile from last season, she'll start laying her eggs on top of the pollen clump and will have her first adult workers in a few weeks.

By summer, the queen produces enough worker bees for them to take over foraging. She'll then stay home to begin her "queenly duties," as Best describes it, which means continually laying eggs to generate more and more workers. The colony numbers peak by mid- to late-summer depending on the species, and where they live. Colony size ranges anywhere from fifty to five hundred bees—much smaller than a typical honey bee colony of fifty thousand bees.

Workers live for just several weeks and develop specialties, like helping tend to young bees, cleaning, defending the nest, and regulating the temperature of the nest, which can involve the workers—and sometimes even the queen—moving their wings like fans in front of the nest site to help air move through. More so than other bees, bumble bees can be quite aggressive with each other, and fights break out between the queen and her workers, who will sometimes eat the queen's freshly laid eggs. In some large colonies, the queen might keep her workers obedient by sending a chemical through the colony to tranquilize them.

The queen is an "expert economist," Best says, and knows exactly when things dry up in mid-summer. Once she notices a decrease in the amount of pollen and nectar coming in, she'll switch from producing female workers, to producing the next generation of bees—males and future queens.

Perhaps the most royal power given to queens is their ability to choose which eggs become female or male. Instead of sex being determined by the presence of sex chromosomes during fertilization like in humans, a bumble bee's sex is determined by fertilization itself, a process called haplodiploidy. I look at Best with a furrowed brow when he says that word, almost thinking he made it up, and we both laugh. Other creatures, like ants and wasps, do this too. If sperm is added to an egg, the young bee will become a female, and if an egg is left unfertilized, it'll become a male. So, male bumble bees never have a dad.

What's more, the queen uses the thousands of sperm stored in her sperm-storage chamber, called a "spermatheca," from last season to fertilize her eggs. "Which is crazy," Best says, laughing.

If a colony is successful, full of food and workers, the queen will produce lots of future queens and males. Researchers don't know if there's a standard male-to-female ratio for the reproductive caste of bees, though colonies seem to have a male bias, because males are cheap. The more males a queen produces, the greater likelihood they can pass along the colony's genes to the next generation.

Males are not as big as queens, so they don't eat as much, but they also don't help out much either, other than with mating. They don't collect any food for the colony, and once they leave the nest to find a virgin queen, they don't come back. They sleep on flowers and will often be found in their petal beds snoozing at dawn and dusk.

Future queens at birth are exalted with a larger body and the queenly gift of being able to mate and produce female worker bees, who can lay unfertilized eggs that become male. Only queens can pass down their genes to daughters.

By the end of the summer, once males fly away and mate with future queens, they start to die off. The old queen and all the workers eventually die, too, leaving it up to these newly mated queens to fatten up for hibernation and continue the cycle next spring.

One of the big unknowns in the bumble bee life cycle is how and where queens spend their winter. No one has found a hibernating western bumble bee, or one of their nests, though the hope is that citizen science programs can get enough willing adults to chase around queens in late summer and fall to find their nests, and, hopefully, their wintering sites.

From lab observations, researchers know that bumble bees are messy and, for the western bumble bee, even a little smelly. Some bee colonies give off a sweet smell, like Hunt's bumble bee, a Northwest native. Western bumble bee colonies, though, are musky, and I imagine their nests smell more like a locker room with air thick of pollen, nectar, fermenting honey, and bee feces combined to create a unique stink.

"If you look at the way that they live in the nest, it looks like a teenager's bedroom," says Liam Whiteman, a graduate researcher at Ohio State University, who's studying with James Strange, a leading bumble bee researcher and chair of Ohio State University's entomology program. We spent a day together around Mount Hood in July collecting bees for Whiteman's thesis research, which looks at pathogens that make bees sick.

"Everything is haphazard," Whiteman says of the bumble bee nests he's observed in the lab. Their pollen clumps aren't organized, and everything is strewn about, which makes me think of the massive pile of laundry that haunts me in my bedroom, and I feel more connected to these animals. "It's not like a honey bee colony, which is intricate with a meticulously created frame of hexagonal cells, and they keep fastidiously clean," he says. "Bumble bees live in this very organic way. They just leave everything."

FLIGHT

Bumble bees aren't built to fly, but bumble bees don't know that, according to bee folklore. Scientists in the 1930s claimed it should be impossible for bees to fly because their wings were too small for their plump bodies. This supposed lack of aerodynamics, though, has not been a problem for bumble bees for the millions of years they've been flying and has proven to be just a myth. Though they're tumbly and heavy and a little awkward, bumble bees are, indeed, built to fly.

"They're pure muscle," says Whiteman, who's dissected plenty of bees for his research. He turns his head quickly. "Oh, that was a chonk," he says of the graceful linebacker who zoomed past us in the snow-free, now wildflower-covered hillsides near Mount Hood Meadows.

"Their thorax is packed with flight muscles," Strange adds, as he continues catching and identifying bees faster than seems humanly possible. "They're fit, like they're spending time at the bee gym."

Instead of moving their stained-glass-like wings up and down using a specific wing muscle, like dragonflies or mayflies, bumble bees and most other insects twist and rotate their wings during flight, allowing for more control over speed and direction, almost like a kayaker moving and rotating their oars quickly while navigating whitewater. This allows bees to scoop themselves up in the air and generate enough lift—basically creating mini-hurricanes under their wings—to get their fuzzy, hefty load airborne. Their wings move incredibly fast, about two hundred times per second, and they're never out of breath, thanks to a highly efficient respiration system. The buzzing sound they generate comes from these rapid wing maneuvers, and their genus name, *Bombus*, fittingly means "booming, buzzing, humming."

Bumble bees, like all insects, have three main body parts: a head, thorax, and abdomen. They fly using two sets of vertical and horizontal muscles in the thorax, where their two pairs of wings are attached. When one muscle flexes, the other naturally stretches, similar to how when we flex our bicep, the tricep naturally lengthens. When the thorax moves, the wings move. Their thorax is basically their flight motor.

Bees do have muscles directly attached to the base of their wings that allow them to control how much up-and-down body movement happens during flight. These muscles serve a similar function to the little flaps on the back of an airplane, though bumble bees are more like helicopters, as they always fly straight up whenever they leave a flower.

Bumble bees' beefy flight muscles also allow them to survive in cold temperatures. We move around when we're cold to get our blood flowing, and bumble bees do the same thing. They relax a small muscle in their thorax that detaches their wings from their flight-powering muscles, so when they start to warm up and move, their wings stay still. By using these powerful thorax muscles to shiver, they can control their body temperature, allowing them to fly in the cold and keep their nests warm.

BUZZ POLLINATION & NECTAR ROBBING

Most flowers produce sugary, energy-rich nectar as a bait to lure bees in to spread their pollen, and most flowers make it easy for them. They stash their pollen outside of their tubular anthers, the bright-yellow male part of the flower, and when a bee visits, the tiny, dusty pollen particles scatter on the bee's body and spread onto other flowers they visit.

Eight to ten percent of plants, though, have their pollen hidden, tucked deep inside narrow anthers only accessible through a pore at the tip. The way to get it out is to shake it vigorously, kind of like a saltshaker.

To get the pollen, bumble bees firmly wrap their legs around the petals, chomp down on the anther, and activate their mighty flight muscles to start shaking the pollen out that eventually spills all over their bellies. Their sheer power causes the bee's entire body to vibrate rapidly, creating a high-pitched, loud buzz, and giving this process—buzz pollination—its name. The bees' vibrations produce a gravitational force so strong that it's close to the record for what humans can endure.

Plants like tomatoes, cranberries, blueberries, eggplant, potatoes, bell peppers, among others, all have their pollen tucked away, which is why bumble bees are second only to honey bees as the top insect contributor to our global food economy.

Some bees have to learn how to do this. Videos online from University of Nevada, Reno professor and biologist Anne Leonard show a bee's first encounter with such a flower. She moves all around it, confused, clinging onto the petals to investigate, desperately trying to find some way to access the food. After more than two minutes, she starts noticing the flowers' anthers, but gives up. On her second visit to the flower, she heads straight to the anthers and starts to buzz, figuring out where to put her legs and latch on, but she can't get any pollen out. By her third visit, she's attacking the anthers, and finally, succeeds.

In addition to buzz pollination, western bumble bees have another way to get food, through what's called nectar robbing. Westerns have a petite face and short tongue, compared to other bumble bees, so they prefer plants with wider, open petals. Some flowers, though, stash their goodies in narrow, tube-shaped petals, and if those are the only flowers available, the westerns will get creative. They'll chew through the petals and stick their tongue in to sip up the nectar, without actually collecting or delivering pollen to the flower, perhaps their way of critiquing the plant's inconvenient petal evolution.

THREATS

Western bumble bees are now hard to find. What used to be one of the most common bees in the West has now declined by 93 percent in the last 20 years. Other bumble bees throughout the country are also struggling.

In the previous eight years of the Mount Ashland bumble bee hunt, the crew found just six western bumble bees. We searched a north-facing meadow just west of Mount Ashland's summit where surveyors spotted two western bumble bees last year. Tons of other bumble bees still live here with plenty of flowers to dine on, but the westerns are missing. No one saw Franklin's or Suckley's in the area this year, either, but the group did find three western bumble bees nearby several days after we looked—the most they've found in a few years. During the several hours I spent bee hunting around Mount Hood, we didn't see a western.

Tons of western bumble bees lived in the Coast Range fifteen years ago, but they're not around anymore. "They might be somewhere, maybe a little relic population of small numbers," Oregon State University's Best says, "but with wide-scale sampling of thousands and thousands of specimens, we haven't seen a single one. It's this extremely dramatic and precipitous decline."

The bees loved cranberry bogs in Long Beach and Bandon, and now you can't find them at all. You won't see them in Portland or Eugene anymore.

The late bumble bee expert and professor Robbin Thorp regularly surveyed Mount Ashland in the late 1990s to document Franklin's bumble bee for the US Forest Service when the agency was tasked to learn about special species in old-growth forests during the northern spotted owl controversy. Seemingly overnight, Thorp noticed both of the closely related Franklin's and western bumble bees disappeared. In 1998, he recorded 102 western bumble bees. The next year, he found nine. The year after that, he found one. He saw none from 2003 to 2007. Thorp last saw a Franklin's bumble bee on Mount Ashland almost two decades ago.

Western bumble bees likely got sick with a disease spread from commercially raised bees. Packages of four to five hundred bumble bees are shipped today all over to pollinate tomatoes, peppers, blueberries, and cranberries, among other plants that keep our multi-billion-dollar agricultural industry afloat.

Western bumble bees were first bred commercially in 1992. The US Department of Agriculture soon after allowed a distributor to send western and common eastern bumble bee queens to European rearing facilities. Then, the colonies were shipped back to California. Within a few years, the commercial bees became sick with a fungal disease, formerly called *Nosema bombi* but recently renamed to *Vairimorpha bombi*. The bees stopped mating with each other in captivity, and they couldn't produce the next generation of queens and males, which nearly wiped out all western bumble bee commercial hives.

Given the timing of the sickness with declines of wild bees, Thorp hypothesized that the bees caught the disease in Europe and spread it to wild populations. Worker bees from commercial colonies were found to have foraged outside of the greenhouses, likely because they preferred pollen and nectar of wildflowers over pollen from the tomatoes that they were forced to pollinate with their high-energy buzzing.

Researchers haven't found evidence that a European strain infected the bees, so they don't know exactly how the commercial bees got sick. Regardless of where the disease came from, scientists think that highly infected western bumble bees likely did escape from commercial facilities and infected wild bees. The disease is thought to have spread from commercially reared bees on the East Coast, as well, and likely caused dramatic declines of yellow-banded bumble bees and rusty patched bumble bees, the latter of which is one of just two federally endangered bumble bees. The US Fish and Wildlife Service recently listed Franklin's as an endangered species—the first bumble bee here in the West on the list—and the agency is in the lengthy process of listing western bumble bees, too.

Oregon bees have been especially hard-hit. Sick bees have been found in southern Oregon, and it's thought that their disease caused Franklin's bumble bee's dramatic decline. The bees ingest the pathogen on a flower, or maybe off their nest, and pass it to their young. Then, when infected bees go out and forage on a flower, where maybe dozens of different bees visit, they spread the disease, Ohio State University professor James Strange tells me. He specializes in bee health and genetics and has studied *Vairimorpha bombi*.

The disease is a slow killer. Spores proliferate in the bees' guts, eventually filling their bellies and causing distended abdomens. Males who get sick can't fly, which means they can't find queens to mate with to continue next year's colonies. "They're just stuck there," Strange says.

Some bees continue foraging even if they're heavily infected, until they eventually succumb, he says. Queens might even have a harder time surviving over winter, but scientists don't know exactly how the disease affects hibernating queens in the wild.

Though western bumble bees are not used commercially anymore, you can still buy packages of hundreds of common eastern bumble bees and yellow-faced bumble bees, a common backyard visitor, especially on the lupines in my backyard and lavender plants in my neighborhood. The industry is largely unregulated, experts and conservationists say, and they've worked for years to try to get the USDA to set some sort of standard. Commercially raised bees have more pathogens than bees in the wild, and research shows that they regularly escape greenhouses, which is easy to imagine, given their small size and agility.

Oregon has now banned the import of non-native commercially raised bees. Washington is considering a similar law, and California requires that commercially sold non-native bumble bees be used only in contained greenhouses, though some bees will likely still escape. The non-native common eastern bumble bees have now established populations in the wild in Washington, and Strange expects they'll move south to Oregon in the next few years. "That's the reality," he says.

To prevent a possible disease from spreading in commercially raised bee colonies, Strange says companies need regular testing and inspection protocols, among other regulations. "We should make sure these colonies that are coming out of commercial production are healthy and well-maintained and are not at a danger of spreading pathogens everywhere," he says. "We really, really need to do that. It's critical."

Beyond the dangers from commercial facilities, bumble bees face a host of other challenges, from pesticides, cattle grazing, and honey bees, to farms and housing crowding out what used to be their homes.

"It's a death by a one hundred cuts situation, where you've got a lot of threats being thrown at these animals," says Rich Hatfield, senior endangered species conservation biologist with the nonprofit Xerces Society for Invertebrate Conservation, based in Portland. "These threats are also interacting with each other."

If we're exposed to a virus when we're stressed, we're more likely to get sick, and for bumble bees, it's similar. Toxic pesticides are killing bees and habitat fragmentation is making it harder for bees to find food and mates. Honey bees are forcing some bumble bees off of flowers, which causes them to change their feeding habits. Sharing flowers with honey bees also puts native bees at risk for potential disease. Shorter seasons from climate change are altering the blooming cycle for plants, which puts pressure on bees' life cycles because they need food from early spring to fall to sustain their colonies. "And you just put all those things together, and it becomes a toxic soup that one can't survive," Hatfield says.

Homeowners have a wide variety of pesticides to choose from and might not think about the potential lives lost, in exchange for fewer aphids. These chemicals are most heavily used in neighborhoods.

In 2013, between 45,830 and 107,470 yellow-faced bumble bees from hundreds of colonies were killed in Wilsonville after a landscape company applied a toxic neonicotinoid pesticide, called Safari, on blooming European linden trees in a Target parking lot. The bumble bees were foraging on the flowers and died rapidly. It's the largest known pesticide bumble bee kill in North America, and researchers say it's likely that even more bees died than they estimated.

Western bumble bees still have some stable populations in mid- to high-elevation sites at Mount Hood and in the Cascades, Olympic Peninsula, Blue Mountains, Colville National Forest, and in the Rocky Mountains, but they're scattered and vulnerable. Researchers don't know whether they've survived the disease, or whether the disease has yet to arrive. And all it would take is a powerful wildfire to rip through their homes and devastate their population.

US Geological Survey ecologist and Utah State University PhD candidate Ashley Rohde is doing extensive work to understand western bumble bee populations. For her dissertation, Rohde is studying twenty-five hundred specimens of the bees from all over their habitat range, collected largely from universities and museums. Rohde's research will likely give insights to which populations are more vulnerable to extinction. "We want to know who are the individuals losing genetic diversity," Rohde says. "And we need genetic diversity for the bees to be able to respond to a changing environment."

Scientists at Oregon State University are enlisting the help of volunteers to track these bees, and all of Oregon's native bees, to learn about their lives through the Oregon Bee Atlas program. "Bees have become a popular narrative," Best says. "It's in the public sphere and people care. We have 150 people with butterfly nets, running around the state of Oregon, camping in remote mountain ranges out in the middle of the desert for weeks, swinging butterfly nets, documenting all this incredible biodiversity of all these incredible relationships between the bees and their native plants.

"And fifteen years ago, I could find maybe one person who would listen to me," he says. "We've come a long way."

Coastal Tailed Frog,
Ascaphus truei

We walk less than two miles in five hours, brushing away deer-flies, avoiding yellow-spotted millipedes and prickly salmonberry stems, maneuvering over massive fallen logs, and trying not to slip on moss-covered rocks along a steep streambed where the cold water looks clean enough to drink in the ninety-degree July heat. Crouched down, we flip over rocks, one by one, ready with nets in hand to catch whoever was home.

At first, I notice only ferns, mosses, and sorrel living near the stream. I hear occasional varied thrushes perform their brilliant one-note songs that pierce through the hemlocks and redcedars. As I quietly peer down into the clear water, I see camouflaged young giant salamanders scurry across rocks and shy torrent salamanders frozen still with perfectly spiraled tails, and the aquatic community of creatures comes alive.

I nearly step on a slimy critter, not much bigger than the fallen fir needles they blend in with.

"Dang, a western redback salamander!" Oregon State University graduate student Mark Leppin says with as much enthusiasm as an NBA announcer recapping a phenomenal dunk. The amphibian, as the name suggests, has a striking rust-colored back and chocolate body.

Leppin's socks and Tevas are already soaked once I turn around with my net, ready to step into Parker Creek, one of dozens of streams that navigate down Marys Peak, just a bit southwest of Corvallis. He's studied young coastal tailed frogs' unique mouth parts in several of these small streams that decorate the mountain like a spiderweb. He's observed them so much that, if given enough tadpoles to compare, he could tell where each of them lives in their Pacific Northwest mountainous homes simply by the structure of their mouth, which he's found may also be a symbol of their genetic identity.

The frogs like it here, tucked within a steep, small stream lined with towering trees, away from the summer heat and clear-cuts that surround this wet coastal mountain landscape.

Under the first rock Leppin flips over, a handful of dark-gray tadpoles emerge, desperately trying to find new shelter. Several use their suction-cup-like mouths, underneath their flat head that resembles a stingray, to hang onto the slippery rock bottom so they won't wash downstream. They're adapted for fast-moving water and are the only frog in the country who can cling on to a rock with their mouth like that.

Within five minutes, Leppin has us with flashlights and head-lamps hunched over in a small culvert looking for adult frogs, but no luck. He's been interested in coastal tailed frogs, *Ascaphus truei*, since he was a teenager, after a friend said he had a hard time spotting them. "It became kind of like a mission to just learn how to find them," Leppin says, while periodically and methodically turning rocks and reaching his hand down into the muck to see what he can find.

"Oh, crap!" he yells, after lifting a rock and losing track of the adult male frog who hops away. We find him, carefully scoop him up, and Leppin proceeds with the glamourous work of measuring, basically, the frog's penis.

He gently flips the frog on his back and whips out a blue tape measure, mumbling numbers while the small, olive-green and light-brown amphibian stretches his arms and legs, trying to wiggle himself free from the quick, but intrusive, procedure.

Coastal tailed frogs and their Rocky Mountain tailed frog siblings are the only frogs in the world to have this tail, which isn't really a tail but is the male's reproductive apparatus. They're a long-living frog and among the most primitive, branching off some 250 million years ago from their ancestors, who lived well before the dinosaurs. Joined only by their closest relative in New Zealand, *Leiopelma*, these frogs remain in their own separate lineage apart from all other frogs in the world, making them a sister species to every frog. Their ancient ways don't always quite fit in with their relatives, like their true ribs and nonfunctional tongue. They also can't hear, speak, or execute a "frog kick." Even their biological order, Anura, isn't fully inclusive, as the name means frogs and toads "without a tail."

They're found nowhere else in the world, living only here in these crisp, fast-moving, small Northwest streams where rivers begin in the Coast Range, Cascade Range, Columbia River Gorge, Olympic Mountains, and Klamath Mountains. Their homes have been bulldozed, driven over by massive logging trucks, sprayed with chemicals, and their lives are often overlooked and ignored in these once ancient forests that now function like corporate farms.

We observe one young tailed frog whose vertical pupils remind me of their nighttime preference, and I think of my sister when I peer into their tiny copper slit eyes. Growing up, she had a collection of stuffed animal frogs, displayed on her bed. We'd spend maybe more time looking for frogs at the pumpkin patch on Sauvie Island than we did searching for pumpkins. I remember hiking with her in the Coast Range when we were kids, running up and down a trail somewhere near Lincoln City, investigating the damp, mossy rocks, looking for frogs. We found some kind of salamander instead.

Nearly every few hundred feet, Leppin and I venture over another waterfall, wider than it is tall, where the stream looks professionally landscaped and gently flows over smooth volcanic rocks that were once far out under the Pacific Ocean but now supply these frogs and their fellow amphibians with safe homes.

COAST RANGE

I wonder what the view was like in the centuries after Kalapuyans took refuge on top of Chantimanwi, now Marys Peak, when the great floods burst through the valley. I imagine seeing the Pacific Ocean on a clear day to the west, with vast bunchgrasses and camas fields covering the space between these mountains and the Cascades to the east. Scattered white oaks would have had enough room to grow branches so big they'd look like tiny tumbleweeds from the nearly 4,100-foot-peak.

What would it have been like, just a few hundred years ago, seeing mountain slopes of unlogged Douglas-firs—some reaching heights of four hundred feet—with branches weighted down by moss garlands that comforted nesting marbled murrelets? With bark thick enough you could stick your hand into cracks that stretched across the trunk too large to wrap your arms around even half of its diameter?

Now, from the top of Marys Peak, I see white squares of meadowfoam fields, green squares of non-native grass fields, and congeries of clear-cuts.

Ancient forests once spanned the entire Pacific Northwest coastline—two thousand miles, from Northern California to southeast Alaska, of trees and shrubs and streams that supported more life than we probably know. Some slopes would have been patchy from natural or Native-set fires, but surveys from 1933 to 1945 show that half of Oregon, Washington, and California forests were old-growth, a category early surveyors based on tree size. Two-thirds of Northwest forests were at least eighty years old. Just 3 to 7 percent of those forests are left.

Oregon's Coast Range is now more like a tree farm, a checkerboard of public and private land where Wall Street investors (who have probably never heard of tailed frogs) get to buy prized forests, treating them like stocks. Trees grow at the same height for acres and acres in monoculture plantations next to naked hillsides, exposing the contours of each ridgeline, which should be blanketed under a canopy of green.

Timber companies in Portland and Astoria in the late 1800s sent massive Doug-firs to the Midwest, East Coast, and to other countries where they had cut so many of their own trees that they ran out and needed our coastal timber. Old photographs show loggers transporting trees with trunks that were taller and wider than their trucks. During the post-World War II baby boom, home construction increased, as did people's preference for bigger buildings and houses, which was satisfied by big Doug-firs taken in massive clear-cuts from private and, increasingly, public lands.

HOME

Like most Pacific Northwest frogs, tailed frogs are brown, tan, olive green, red, and pink—a combination of colors that allows them to blend in with rocks, fallen leaves, dirt, and whatever else lurks on the streambed or forest floor. Their toes are wider and more wedge-shaped than other frogs' "noodle toes," as Leppin describes it.

The adult male we meet in Parker Creek boasts colors of brown, mint green, black, tan, and taupe all blended together and speckled, like the rocks he was hiding under, away from daylight. He had a striking black stripe along his eyes like extended eyeliner.

The tail is a big give away. If you're not lucky enough to see an adult male—who is the only one with a tail, although females can have small nubs—it feels challenging to an untrained eye to tell them apart from other Northwest frogs. Another clue is wart-like bumps on their back and behind their eyes that form distinct stripes, as Leppin describes. "I can usually tell pretty quickly, right off the bat, by looking at their backs," he says.

Coastal tailed frogs are found within coastal and Cascade mountains from British Columbia to Mendocino County in California. Other animals and plants are thought to have arrived in their current Northwest homes after continental ice sheets started retreating about ten to twenty thousand years ago, but tailed frogs may have been here earlier. They've lived in the Northwest for so long that scientists theorize they split into inland and coastal species some five to ten million years ago after giant slabs of earth collided to eventually form the Cascade Range.

It's thought that the frogs evolved with plants and animals from the Miocene, five to twenty-three million years ago, when the Pacific Northwest was moderately moist with deciduous and evergreen forests that weren't much different from the current places the frogs like today. They're so good at surviving massive geologic change that they were thriving in the blast zone just five years after Mount St. Helens erupted in 1980.

Rocky Mountain tailed frogs, *Ascaphus montanus*, now live east of the Cascades in Idaho, Montana, southeast British Columbia, parts of northeastern Oregon, and a tiny bit of southeastern Washington.

STREAMS

On our way to Parker Creek, we pass a huge chunk of brown, treeless mountainside. I've gotten so used to seeing clear-cuts in the Coast Range from our many family trips to Rockaway Beach growing up that they almost seem more natural than a hillside full of life.

The creek begins near the summit of Marys Peak in the noble fir forest on the north slope and winds down southwest from the top, over Parker Creek Falls, and eventually, to the Pacific. It's one of dozens of fern-lined streams that meander down the mountain, some choosing a western coastal route to meet the salt water at Newport, while some head farther south to Florence. Others take an inland journey, providing a bit of drinking water to Corvallis residents before entering the Willamette River, taking its time to meet the Columbia, and finally, the ocean.

Maps of streams that originate in these coastal mountains, like Marys Peak, look more like the branches of bronchioles in our lungs. They're everywhere in these mountains, and even though some may be only a yard wide, they're aquatic cities full of life and diversity that provide healthy homes for salmon and trout downstream.

Biologists for decades have noticed that tailed frogs disappear from forests after logging. Herpetologist Helen Gaige found in 1920 that the frogs weren't living near streams in logged areas around Lake Cushman, on the eastern part of the Olympic Peninsula. The frog was a relatively new species to white scientists exploring the area, and other researchers after Gaige made similar observations. No laws protected these animals, and mountain streams were regularly bulldozed and used to store or send freshly cut logs to trucks, like a true log ride downstream.

Tailed frogs need cold water to survive. They've lived in fast, rocky streams for millions of years and are thought to have among the lowest known temperature tolerance for amphibians in North America: forty-one to sixty-five degrees.

Scientists found that when tailed frog tadpoles were in seventy-two-degree water, they started to die after a day, and all adults died between eighteen and thirty hours. Their eggs, which they lay under stream rocks in the summer, die if water is warmer than sixty-five degrees.

In the Coast Range, one small stream's temperature increased fifteen degrees after a clear-cut took away the canopy that kept the water at fifty-seven degrees. Without those trees, a pool within the stream even reached eighty-six degrees. Other scientists reported seventy-five-degree stream temperatures in the Cascades after logging and logging road construction.

These streams didn't return to their natural temperatures until fifteen years later—about the lifetime of tailed frogs—when trees grew back and protected them from the sun.

Logging makes the land more like a washout and clears hillsides of plants that hold the soil together, bringing gunk into streams, and mudding the waters. When aquatic creatures can't see who's nearby through murky water, they risk being eaten. Logging debris also clogs streams with sediment that fills good hiding spots for frogs. When logging roads cut through these streams, culverts that used to be less sturdy sent even more eroding dirt and debris into the water.

Tailed frogs are among the toughest creatures, having evolved with volcanic eruptions and continental plate collisions that carved our landscapes, but clear-cuts during the last century present a new, foreign challenge. Scientists think the frogs are slow to move back into logged streams, and if entire watersheds become brown and barren, they might not be able to survive.

Until the 1980s and 1990s, scientists didn't know exactly how many species relied on old-growth forests, which were being cut down at a rate of two-square-miles per week. After years of protests and lawsuits from environmentalists, old-growth forests on federal lands finally earned some legal protection from clear-cuts in the monumental 1994 Northwest Forest Plan, thanks to the charismatic northern spotted owl whose home, and livelihood, was decimated from logging. In the years leading up to the legislation, which set rules for more than a dozen Northwest federal forests, scientists named thousands of species that need ancient and healthy forests to survive, including more charismatic characters like salmon, and smaller, less revered creatures, like tailed frogs. The Forest Plan shifted the government's way of thinking about trees in forests, from just a crop to cut and sell, to a larger ecosystem that supports a multitude of non-human life. "It was on the tails of owls and fish when greater recognition started happening," says Deanna Olson, a US Forest Service research ecologist who studies amphibians in headwater streams, like those on Marys Peak. "We're still in an age of discovery for amphibians in this region. Every couple of years there's a new species being identified or recognized."

Logging companies could blow through small streams on federal land before the early 1990s. The Forest Plan, though, required that, on federal forests, they leave a strip of green along streams without any tree cutting, known as streamside buffers. Current rules require wider buffers for streams where fish live, and smaller buffers where they don't, which leaves tailed frogs and other amphibians in those small streams relatively less protected.

With the convoluted patchwork landscape of private and public ownership throughout the Coast Range with different rules for different lands, rewritten laws, loopholes and caveats, corporate money, lobbyists, and not much oversight, the amount of protection for these animals depends on whose land they're on. A bare mountainside cluttered with cut trees near a stream may be next to or downstream from a lush, shaded area. Corporate-owned forests cover a large chunk of the Coast Range, and currently Oregon doesn't require any tree protection on small streams without fish, in state or private forests, even though these streams can make up a majority of river miles within some watersheds. Buffers range from zero protection to fifty feet or five-hundred feet depending on who owns the land, and who lives in the stream.

To further complicate things, sometimes buffers mean no tree cutting at all on certain lands, while other times they may simply mean that no machinery is allowed near the stream. Aerial photos show these buffers as little curving lines of green bounded by brown mountain sides of stumps. "You'll see lots of different practices," Olson says.

Olson's research shows how amphibians live, how they respond to logging, and why we should care about these small mountain streams that are full of plant and animal life and are more connected with each other than scientists initially thought. Her work earned her a national award for being an "unsung hero" for amphibian conservation.

Northwest stream-breeding amphibians, like tailed frogs, need streams to lay their eggs, but they don't spend all their time in the water. Once they develop legs, ditch their fin-like tadpole tail, and become a froglet, tailed frogs venture out of their childhood stream and explore their new forested home. They are especially eager to look around beyond their streams after coastal clouds release moisture in the mountains during fall and winter nights. Some will even travel up and over ridgelines into nearby watersheds. "We don't know how they move from place to place, but we do know that they move," Olson says. "They're all highly connected across those neighboring headwater basins."

In their search for food, some frogs may scour the dark landscape from only a few feet to several-hundred feet from their stream. They breathe through their skin, which is similar to the material of our lungs, a trait that allows air to pass through easily when their skin is moist but makes them vulnerable to dry forest conditions or to absorbing chemicals like herbicides sprayed on nearby forests. The frogs feast on anything from beetles and moths to stoneflies, snails, and millipedes. Because their primitive tongue doesn't shoot out as effortlessly as other frogs, they lunge forward, mouth open, to eat their prey.

Olson is part of a group looking at how to bridge these landscapes when neighboring streams and forests might be logged and pose a challenge for amphibians to safely forage or travel. They're researching ways to add more downed wood to a logged area as a refuge for traversing creatures, or ways to create a corridor of trees that would connect two neighboring streams so animals can travel safely. Prior forest policies focused only on where amphibians were breeding, leaving out other habitats needed for the rest of their life cycle.

Other creatures like small mammals, snails, slugs, and fungi also use streamside areas as a travel route. When the surrounding area of a stream is logged, I imagine it's like trying to drive on the freeway with a section of road destroyed. "Think of these streams as the I-5 of the forest," Olson says. "These areas have a function that we hadn't realized before.

"Just like the owl was the emblem of [old-growth] forests of the Northwest, I feel tailed frogs are one of the emblematic species for how these stream corridors are functioning."

BELLY FLOP

Tailed frogs never gave up their salamander-like trot swimming style in favor of the synchronized leg kicks that every other type of frog developed, which includes more than seven thousand species worldwide. Because of this ancestral lack of motor skills, when it comes to jumping, they can't quite stick their landing. They leap, like other frogs, with a powerful kick and extension of their legs, their arms dangling off to the sides like an airplane, and just when others would pull in their legs to land, tailed frogs keep theirs extended as they crash down, belly first, skidding to a stop.

The adult male we observed in Parker Creek was surprisingly graceful and seemed to be more of a mild belly flopper. If the jump was reviewed in a slow-motion video—like the handful that exist on YouTube, including a few posted by Leppin—evidence might suggest otherwise.

Scientists studied the mechanisms of their ungraceful landings and believe that frogs perfected their jumping skills in two steps: first the take off, and then the landing. Frogs likely evolved the gift of jumping to quickly escape predators. Since the earliest frogs may have just been jumping into water, a little splash landing isn't all that bad and may be a decoy for a quick get-away. It's when they land on rocks where it seems a bit painful.

A variety of belly flop techniques exist among tailed frogs. They might land nose first, while the rest of their body collapses on rocks. Or, they sometimes land on their belly and legs at the same time. Or, their legs might collide with rocks first, thrusting their upper body and head clumsily forward and sliding to a stop.

These frogs are built for their belly flops, though. They're small enough, about one to two inches, that they don't risk injuring any bones during the hard landings. It's thought that they have a large, shield-like cartilage guarding their lower parts and ribs, unlike other frogs, to protect their insides and soft tissues.

Had they been gifted the advanced evolutionary motor skill to draw their legs in before their bodies smash to the ground, tailed frogs would land like any other frog. That landing skill allowed all other frogs to switch between jumping and swimming, which likely helped them find more food and avoid predators.

FINDING A MATE

They can't hear, and they can't vocalize. Tailed frogs move around streams without these seemingly essential survival traits that most other frogs possess, but they do just fine.

Because they live in relatively noisy water they don't need to hear or call, so males simply march along the bottom of streams in search of a partner. Scientists don't know exactly how they find females, though. Some research suggests they might use some kind of smell or taste, and one study found that tailed frogs in Washington sensed mates nearby through their waterborne chemicals.

Males crawl with their tail pointed forward and, perhaps getting a little too excited, embrace any frog who comes near them, even if it's another male. They'll soon realize their mistake and continue the search. Once they do find a female, they'll grab hold of her and may even cuddle her for an hour—or more. They're the only North American frog to fertilize eggs internally with a penis-like tail, likely because the swift-moving streams they live in would otherwise carry away their hopes of a future generation.

After their pelvic embrace, the frogs can't seem to get enough of each other, and they stay coupled anywhere from seventy hours up to seven days. Pairs have been seen hugging underneath rocks or floating while still clutching each other.

Leppin has found that tailed frogs may mate anytime from December to June in the Coast Range, but females don't lay their large, pearly white eggs until months later. It's thought that they store sperm through the year for the next summer and lay their eggs around July or August. Gaige, the early twentieth century herpetologist, described their eggs as "laid in a rosary-like string twisted about to form a large circular mass" that attaches underneath stream rocks with adhesive jelly.

Tailed frogs take their time with a lot of things during their fifteen to twenty years of life. When their eggs hatch in the water, the tadpoles' journey lasts one to four years, depending on where they live. Most other Northwest frogs complete their full-body summer transformation into a froglet, called metamorphosis, in just three months. Tailed frog tadpoles enjoy their childhood, feasting on algae underneath rocks thanks to their unique flat and wide sucker mouths that protect them from getting swept downstream while eating. They prefer to be under rocks for most of the day, safe from the giant salamanders, American dippers, or any fish lurking nearby.

LOGGING

Environmentalist Doug Heiken remembers a four- to five-hundred-year-old Doug-fir with a massive, curved trunk that extended into a small stream in an old-growth forest west of Eugene. Rhododendrons grew so tall that their pink blossoms created a secondary canopy underneath the evergreen giants. Heiken filmed a northern spotted owl. Chinook and coho salmon spawned just downstream.

A curious, fancy brass plaque hung from the Doug-fir with information about coastal tailed frogs that lived in the stream.

Heiken had just joined Oregon Wild, a nonprofit conservation group, and the Clinton Administration had passed an exemption to the Northwest Forest Plan—a year after the initial plan was adopted—that ordered more logging in old-growth forests. Protestors tried to protect the trees, but the federal Bureau of Land Management sold the forest, called Roman Dunn, and timber companies clear-cut fifty-eight acres.

"We came back after it had been logged and it was just complete, utter devastation," Heiken says. "And I couldn't even find the stump where the brass plaque was because it was such a mess."

The stream was wiped out and indistinguishable among the logging debris. "You could barely walk around," he says. After a few years, non-native invasive species like blackberry, thistle, and Scotch broom covered the ground. Then, timber companies replanted trees of the same species so close together that Heiken still couldn't walk around.

The last time he visited, he says it was "an impenetrable thicket of Christmas trees.

"I stopped going back."

Healthy federal forest lands could serve as stepping-stones for animals to travel and live in the Coast Range and beyond, Heiken explains, but logging continues to fragment these landscapes. Heiken says that agencies were initially on the right track with less logging and surveying for rare or at-risk species, but those surveys and annual reviews to see how species are doing proved too expensive, and federal agencies stopped doing them. Logging churns out most of Oregon's carbon emissions and rules and regulations ebb and flow with waves of politicians and money, leaving the lives of tailed frogs and salmon and spotted owls and marbled murrelets and Doug-firs, among hundreds of other species, hinged on who's in power.

I think about scientists' tedious and painstaking efforts to document the importance of these critters and their forested homes, one paper at a time, often showing that taking too many trees and destroying an ecosystem, does, in fact, have consequences.

Local journalists found that the Oregon Department of Forestry—whose budget relies on logging revenues—stopped publishing numbers from the growing list of 242 plants and animals listed or at-risk of being listed under the Endangered Species Act and deleted previous reports. The forestry agency is responsible for making sure vulnerable aquatic species are protected through properly sized stream buffers.

Tailed frogs are listed by the Oregon Department of Fish and Wildlife as a sensitive species and are second on the agency's "top-five priority species" list in the Coast Range because their populations are likely declining from logging, though the agency uses terms like "disturbance" and "habitat change" instead of logging. No one really knows, though, how the frogs are doing because there aren't any recent or historic population estimates, and the agency doesn't have any active research projects. The frogs are among 109 other amphibians, birds, mammals, and reptiles that the state says it's monitoring with small or declining populations.

In the 1990s, Olson started researching different stream-buffer widths on plots of federal land that were clear-cut and are now second-growth forests. Twice the researchers removed some trees (but not all) to observe how animals responded. Ten years after the first forest thinning, they noticed some salamander populations were slow to return, with fewer of them along streams with the narrowest, 20-foot buffers. She found more animals, though, immediately after the second thinning in 50-foot-wide buffers, and even more animals five years later within 230-foot-wide buffers.

Hotter and drier summers will likely make life harder for amphibians living in mountain streams, which are expected to warm up. Some streams are already running smaller and even drying up completely within their upper reaches.

"I do have this inner feeling that these animals are highly resilient," Olson says. "And if we provide the right conditions, they can make it. And in some cases, they will find it," she says, of suitable streams for frogs to live in.

"If they can get there."

Huckleberry,

Wiwnu, Vaccinium membranaceum

The berries can't be picked right away. Once bear-grass goes to seed, after camas plants dry up in the meadows down below, when the sun sets earlier, and alpine snowmelt unveils fields of violet and magenta blooms, that's the time, when the small fruits turn deep purple, nearly black, and gently release themselves off the stem, one by one.

Elaine Harvey began the season in Carson for two weeks when the first berries at lower elevations ripened in July. Then, following her grandma's lead, Harvey, her aunt, brother, and two cousins moved on to Trout Lake for another few weeks before heading up to Surprise Lakes where Pahto, who we now call Mount Adams, watches over the fields. They camped near the lakes to gather these high-elevation berries in August.

"Every summer, probably since I was born, I've been there," says Harvey, a fish biologist and member of the Kah-miltpah band of the Yakama Nation. For up to two months, her grandmother led the family from Goldendale to all the good berries in southern Washington's Cascades. She knew exactly when they ripened each year.

They'd pick and pick and pick, every day, except Sundays. For hours, they'd work until their gallon-and-a-half cedar baskets were full of perfectly sweet and tart huckleberries, called *wiwnu* in Sahaptin. Harvey's grandmother could fill five gallons a day. "She had all those baskets tied around her and one on her back, and that's how she picked," Harvey says. "And she made us pick. I think about those times, and all the different areas that she took me and that whole area, from Trout Lake all the way to Indian Heaven."

They followed the same path that Kah-miltpah people took for generations from their villages near the Columbia River in Rock Creek every summer to gather the revered fruits. They'd pick together in the once boundless berry fields, thousands of acres among the millions of acres of land that belonged to Columbia Plateau tribes and bands.

Once they filled their baskets and headed back to camp, Harvey packed water from the lake to help cook, tend to the fire, wash dishes, and clean the berries at night. "That was all work and all discipline," she says of picking with her grandma. "As a kid you wonder, 'How come I have to do this?'" she says. "It's like a labor job. But, really, it was teaching."

Every spring, Yakama people celebrate the first salmon harvested with a feast to give thanks and commence new seasons. They line up foods throughout the year, starting with salmon, suckers, and lamprey, then deer and elk, followed by different roots like camas and wapato, and finally, the berries. "We honor all of them," Harvey says. "And we're not allowed to go fishing and root gathering until we attend our feast every year. That's our unwritten law. When the berries are ready, we have a huckleberry feast with the other berries, and we're not allowed to go gather berries until that feast happens."

Her grandma arranged her own huckleberry feast each year. They celebrated and thanked the summer fruits together before heading to the mountains to pick a year's worth that they'd can and freeze to save for weddings, funerals, and other ceremonies.

This area, within and around what's now called Indian Heaven Wilderness in Gifford Pinchot National Forest, has gifted people with huckleberries since anyone can remember. The shrubs extended across the volcanic landscape in fields kept mostly clear of conifers through people's regular fires and care.

The plants are still here. They cover hillsides near Surprise Lakes and provide the US Forest Service with thousands of dollars in huckleberry permit sales. But they aren't cared for in the same way. They don't have as much room to grow. Views of Pahto from the lakes are now obstructed by trees that inch taller as each decade passes without fire. Huckleberries can live to be one hundred years old, and as I meander through the fields, I like to think that some of these shrubs may have sprouted from the earth before this area was inundated with outsiders looking for profit. With proper care, sunlight, and water, perhaps plants in fields now overgrown can flower and fruit again.

BERRIES

Huckleberries aren't actually huckleberries. It's similar to our cedars not being true cedars, all according to Western scientists. Common plant names can be misleading. Huckleberries are blueberries. They're in the genus *Vaccinium*, which is the same biological category of all our commercial blueberries. True huckleberries, in the genus *Gaylussacia*, grow only on the East Coast. "People get confused," says Bernadine Strik, a professor emeritus and berry crops specialist at Oregon State University. "Especially people who come from the East."

The plants look similar, though the fruit of our Northwest huckleberries is packed with dozens of unnoticeable tiny seeds, while true huckleberry fruits are larger with ten conspicuous seeds inside, Strik tells me.

The word "huckleberry" is likely American, thought Henry David Thoreau, who wrote about the plant in *Walden* and in his aptly titled essay "Huckleberries." The name is derived from "hurtleberry" or "whortleberry," known as European blueberry, perhaps explaining the true huckleberry's name and why white colonists from the East Coast confused our blueberries as huckleberries.

The Pacific Northwest has more varieties of native *Vaccinium* than anywhere else in North America. Twelve different types of the edible plants grow prodigiously all over mountain slopes in Oregon and Washington, and hikers in the Cascades or Olympics often see, and taste, a handful of the most common varieties, though most people probably don't notice much of a difference between the species. "They have slightly different habitat requirements," Strik says. "They're slightly different in leaf morphology and fruit shape and color, but their ranges overlap a lot."

Mountain or black huckleberries, *Vaccinium membranaceum*, prefer land that rises eighteen hundred to six thousand feet above sea level. They're the most prized and popular species whose large, deep-purple, luscious fruits are supposedly the most delectable, though I find them all delicious. On a hike along the Sol Duc River to Seven Lakes Basin and the High Divide trail in Olympic National Park, maybe five different species in endless supply carpeted hillsides with their green, purple, and red leaves and fueled us all along the twenty-mile loop. We slept next to yellow-cedar and what I think was oval-leaf huckleberries, *Vaccinium ovalifolium*, speckled with welcome rain drops at Deer Lake. Dwarf huckleberries, *Vaccinium caespitosum*, who, as their name suggests, like to grow close to the ground, provided vitamin C to our morning oatmeal before we headed to Lunch Lake, where several black bears feasted on the fruits until the sun set. Red huckleberries, *Vaccinium parvifolium*, stood out against the greens and browns of the lower elevation dense forest. Their strikingly bright fruit is more tart than sweet, yet still refreshing. They're the most common huckleberry within Oregon's Coast Range and grow at low to middle elevations. *Vaccinium deliciosum*, another common type, is distinguished by their glossier fruit and leaves that turn red before other plants in late summer, which may protect young leaves from harsh ultraviolet light in their preferred high elevations.

Our native bees, particularly bumble bees, give us voluminous berries. Flowers on mountain huckleberries are small and bell-shaped, like mountain heather. Huckleberry flowers aren't appealing to many pollinators because of their tricky shape, and they don't have as much nectar compared to other berry plants, like native blackberries, Strik tells me. Huckleberries require several visits from a pollinator, ideally a bumble bee, who would engage their beefy thorax muscles to buzz pollinate and vigorously shake the pollen out of the flower. When lots of bumble bees visit flowers and transfer pollen to fertilize female parts, it's more likely that those parts become seeds, which leads to bigger berries. "And that's one of the reasons, too, when people who go to stands and keep going back to the same place, they'll see a variation from year-to-year in berry size," Strik says. The number of seeds a flower can produce is also affected by weather. "If it's too hot or too cool we can lose that window of opportunity while that flower is open to get a good seed set," she says.

The elegant plants grow just a few berries on their delicate stems. Usually one or two per leaf. They prefer fields mostly to themselves because they're not too good at competing for sunlight or water. Fire reinvigorates them. They thrive in stony, acidic soils. They love the frigid alpine, subalpine, and foothills, tucked under a thick blanket of snow for most of the year before supplying people, black bears, cedar waxwings, varied thrushes, white-crowned sparrows, golden-mantled ground squirrels, and coyotes, among others, with their fibrous, antioxidant- and potassium-rich berries. Just one cup of their fruit provides half of our daily recommended vitamin C intake. As my partner and I make our way to the Sawtooth Berry Fields in mid-August, we see a buoyant black bear run across the dirt road, maybe also in search of the fruits.

DRYING

Cheryl Mack knew huckleberry drying sites had to be everywhere around Indian Heaven. The once massive, open berry fields covered the landscape with juicy, almost black fruit in late summer.

The now-retired Forest Service archeologist and huckleberry researcher spent hours in the early 1990s looking for inconspicuous trenches in the ground that Native women created to dry their berries. As the berries lay out in the sun for two or three days, women searched the fields for a suitable log that was dry enough with just the right amount of decay to maintain a smoldering fire. Once they found their preferred log, they'd dig a three-foot wide and thirty-foot long trough, tossing dirt off on the opposite side of the log to create a mound where they first laid out bear-grass, placed tule mats on top, and then spread out the berries. They lined the bottom of the trench with rocks to hold the mats in place, lit the log, and let it smolder for hours to heat and eventually dry the fruits. Women, usually grandmothers, spent entire days stirring berries with an eight-foot-long, oar-like cedar paddle, called *su-xaash*. They'd tend to the fruits until they became like raisins and could be stored for a year.

Tribal elders and their grandchildren told Mack about these sites, recalling berry camps scattered everywhere in this high-elevation landscape, especially near lakes or streams. Forest Service photographs show women from the 1930s drying their berries in these fields, with cedar-root baskets strapped to their hips decorated with elegant chevron designs. Other photos show a camp somewhere near Surprise Lakes and reveal the same view of the White Salmon glacier on Pahto that we enjoyed while picking, but more ice covered the mountain back then. Another photo shows a woman sitting among the huckleberry bushes gathering fruits with both hands and two baskets strapped to her waist. She's laughing and smiling from ear to ear.

One man told Mack about a site where his grandfather remembered seeing tipi poles tied in a tree near a berry camp on a section of the abandoned Cascade Crest Trail. "I'm wandering all over this place in the wilderness and asking, 'Why aren't I finding these?'" Mack says. "And I moved forward, and I tripped over a rock and looked down and there was a straight line of rocks. And I look in front of me, and there's a log, and it's burnt on the bottom, and I'm standing in a trench. I was standing in the absolute best example of a trench I'd ever found," Mack says, still enthusiastic and smiling about it decades later.

Berries haven't been dried in the trenches since the Forest Service restricted their use in the early 1930s and as canning became the preferred method for preserving the fruits. The logs have now decomposed, and the rocks and dirt mounds are mostly covered with new soil and plants, which makes it hard to notice them. Early archeology on national forests like Gifford Pinchot was scant, and scientists never searched for these sites until the early 1980s when they surveyed the land before logging and trail reconstruction. Once Mack realized what they looked like with their new growth and with the help of Yakama elders like Harvey's grandmother, she started to find them regularly. "It takes you a while to get a feel for the landscape," says Mack, who worked in Gifford Pinchot for thirty years. "You can walk right over all kinds of things and just not be aware of them."

"They're all over here. There's a whole bunch back there," she says, pointing northeast toward Pahto. "Those ones are in the trees now."

Mack spent years searching for these sites, using historical forest fire maps to give her a glimpse of just how expansive the fields were. Peeled cedar trees are often clustered near old berry fields that have been converted into thick forests. When women filled their baskets full of berries, they'd gather cedar bark close by and make baskets to pick more, she tells me. She found at least six thousand of these trees—one of which was peeled in the early 1700s—all throughout the forest.

In the 1990s, Mack took a large group of Yakama elders up to some of these sites on horseback to see if they remembered camping at any particular place as kids. They told her stories of guarding sun-drying berries from birds or squirrels and fetching water for the drying trenches in case the flames got too high. But they didn't remember this camp where Mack found her first trench. "They were frustrated because the trees had all grown in," Mack says. "They were looking around going, 'We can't see anything; we can't recognize anything.' I felt like if it hadn't been so closed in, perhaps they would have remembered that place. They could have camped there as children."

Mack shows my partner and I one trench near Surprise Lakes, on the side reserved for Native people to pick berries and camp, east of Road 24. The trench is part of a campsite, and maybe it's among those featured in old photographs. To most people, it would seem like just regular uneven ground. "If I had a probe, you'd find a straight line of rocks, and we can see just a couple of them here," she says, bending down to touch the exposed rock, now nearly embedded in new soil and grasses that have grown since they last held berry drying mats in place one hundred years ago. "And the log would have been here, but it's completely gone."

We stay near this trench for a while. Red crossbill calls and occasional nearby berry pickers' chatting cut through the alpine silence. Here I am, a fourth-generation Oregonian and product of colonialism, standing in this trench among these fields that Yakama people have always cared for and preserved. I think of the women who would have dug out and worked at these trenches each summer, providing for their families, and maybe also enjoying bird songs, the pink evening glow on Pahto, and the last long, warm days of the season.

Mack and her husband Rick McClure, who is also a retired Forest Service archeologist, have urged other national forests to search for these drying trenches, but none have noted them, except for one similar site in the Mount Baker-Snoqualmie National Forest. They exist wherever people gather berries, like Mount Hood and Mount Rainier. "They are likely there, just nobody has found them," Mack says.

THE FIELDS

The plants grow everywhere in open spaces. Their thin branches spread across the sloping hillsides, and their oval-shaped, burnt-orange leaves gently sway in the warm August breeze, almost ready to release to the ground within a few weeks. Trees, mostly of the same height, border the fields, while dozens of young firs squeeze in between the berries and bear-grass, making the land look like a haphazard Christmas tree farm. Patches of new forests farther east toward Pahto form rectangular indents on the hillsides, reminding me of all the clear-cut logging in national forests not too long ago. Just two hundred years ago, the fields extended, unrestrained, across this landscape. A few pockets of mountain hemlocks, subalpine firs, and burned tree snags would have provided just enough shade for huckleberries to grow in one of the Northwest's most prolific fields.

We pick until our fingers turned magenta like we'd been cutting beets, and our lips and teeth stained like we'd enjoyed a bottle of wine. We step over several downed trees, cut to try to keep these fields open. Three-foot-tall bear-grasses—thought to be a huckleberry competitor—are everywhere, and I often hit a dried stock, spewing seeds like confetti into my Tupperware that was never as full as I think despite the hours we picked. We spend the afternoon in one of the largest remnants of traditional fields where Yakama mothers, and their mother's mothers, gathered. Colonialism is more obvious to me now on these seemingly natural landscapes. I just needed to learn how to notice it.

Forty different groups of people from all over the area gathered huckleberries every summer in what's now Gifford Pinchot National Forest, including members of the Yakama, Cowlitz, Warm Springs, and Umatilla tribes. The Twin Buttes picking area, southwest of Pahto and just north of the Sawtooth fields, covered twelve thousand acres in 1920 but was a third of its size by 1996. Without maintenance, it's predicted to be gone by 2040.

Huckleberries have been on this land since glaciers started receding here some eleven thousand years ago. Charred berries that date to six and eight thousand years ago were found in caves within the forest. The late renowned Yakama elder and tribal cultural expert Johnson Meninick always reminded Mack that his people have been here since time immemorial. She'd consult with Meninick about a site she was going to test for artifacts, and he would, again, tell her that people have lived here forever and that she would find something. "And when we did find artifacts, they were thousands of years old," Mack says of the projectile points, "and I called him up so excited, and he was like, 'Yeah, that's what I told you,'" she says. "To him, it was no surprise."

Meninick was the great-grandson of Chief Meninick, who was among the fourteen people to sign the 1855 treaty with the US government that created the Confederated Tribes and Bands of the Yakama Nation. He testified in front of a federal court during what's known as the 1974 landmark *Boldt* decision, which strengthened the concept of tribal sovereignty and forever changed state and federal governmental relations with tribes.

Although I've chosen several notable foods to write about, Native people have a wealth of knowledge about all plants and animals on the landscape. Meninick said in 2010 that "everything on this land is important. There is nothing that is unimportant." They gathered food in all kinds of ways, he told Mack, and ate things that people today don't even realize are food, like black lichens that are high in iron. At one huckleberry site, Mack says they found an additional roasting pit likely used for lichens.

Many roads and trails we use in the forest today were created by Native people to get to the berry fields. The Middle Trail, which used to start where the Pacific Crest Trail cuts through the Sawtooth fields, extends through Surprise Lakes and down to Trout Lake and has "berry camp after berry camp all the way along it," Mack says. The trail is now heavily used by ATVs and takes a beating.

When European Americans first saw the berry fields, several remarked on the sheer abundance of berries, while one noted that the forests had been burned by the Indians and "lay waste large sections of the country." Forest Service fire reports from the early 1900s accused Native people of being careless and setting fires when they dried their berries. A report found that half of the thirty-two fires set in 1904 and 1905 were caused by Native people, and the fires were set mostly in mid-September when rain and snow would soon quash the flames. The forest supervisor at the time never acknowledged that the fires—set under specific conditions every few years—maintained the huckleberries. Rangers often scolded Native people for burning.

Indigenous fire management shaped every ecosystem in the Northwest and the rest of North America in some way. Prairies, oak savannas, and subalpine parklands were largely created by Native people through regular burns that determined which types of plants flourished, like camas and huckleberries, giving people a regular source of food. Fire speeds up seed production in huckleberries, creates space for the plants to get enough light, and keeps them well-pruned and pest-free. Traditional fires burned less intensely, and the year after a burn, huckleberries grew vigorously

For decades, white land managers feared and banned these fires they ironically characterized as negligent when our western skies now regularly turn orange every summer as mega-fires burn out-of-control, fueled by years of overgrown underbrush, in part, from these fire suppression policies. In 1910, after a massive wildfire burned millions of acres in the West, destroying communities in Idaho, Montana, and eastern Washington and killing eighty-five people, the public suddenly supported national fire protection policies. Gifford Pinchot, the first chief of the newly created US Forest Service in 1905, lobbied for more money and employees for the young agency. After the 1910 fire, and with a public now weary of forest fires, the agency received more funding to aggressively fight and prevent fires in forests they managed for timber. The 1910 fire, known as the Big Burn, wasn't as devastating on tribal lands, which were managed with traditional burns that kept the underbrush clear of excessive fuels.

Scientists have questioned whether Native people maintained resources through fire, and other traditional practices, saying that it's difficult to find supporting evidence, even as Native people themselves speak of their land management. Many old and new scientific articles quote white people's first observations of the Northwest, rather than elders' knowledge.

Yakama leaders have complained since at least the 1910s that the huckleberry fields were being destroyed. Even a 1972 Forest Service report urged officials to protect the dwindling fields in both Oregon and Washington, though, not because of their cultural significance but because of their economic importance. Since the Forest Service didn't take much care in the fields after fires were banned, the report warned that many fields could be gone within twenty-five years. They blamed lack of knowledge and money for the negligence. "No one really knows how to manage northwestern wild huckleberries," the report said.

Now, most of the fields are gone.

"Listening to our elders about the way that the land was and being able to apply that to adaptive management plans or restoration plans is critical," says Emily Washines, a native plants, food, and Yakama War scholar and Yakama Nation member. She speaks and writes about food sovereignty, treaty rights, and murdered and missing Yakama women and girls. "Because if you don't listen to the knowledge of elders, you're ignoring the oldest data set of the land. And how do scientists just ignore that? It's a really weird dynamic to face."

For her master's thesis, Washines wrote about how Yakama Nation members restored wapato in the 1990s to wetlands degraded by agriculture on the reservation. Their work combined modern science with elders' knowledge and brought the plant back from a seventy-year absence. Washines is not a biologist or scientist, but she wrote about tribal knowledge and what happens when it's used in land management. Her paper has since been adapted for restoration projects in several cities in the Midwest and for the Hanford Site, a decommissioned World War II and Cold War-era nuclear site in southeastern Washington.

"Tribal knowledge is passed down in bits and pieces," she says. "Sometimes it's in ceremonies and it's very lit up and you know when you're gonna hear it, but sometimes you're randomly driving and your father's sharing historical knowledge about the river, and what it used to look like, and the species that were there."

Using this knowledge can be simple, Washines tells me, and it's often the cheapest land management tool.

"My great-grandparents were photographed by Edward Curtis, but their knowledge and their wisdom and words that they shared about the resources that were passed down through generations was not quoted by him," Washines says. "I think about how readily accessible those images are, and how readily accepted those images are. But why is there so much resistance with those Native peoples' words in management plans?"

WILD

As much as Western scientists tried, huckleberries don't want to be tamed. People attempted to domesticate them for commercial use in the early 1900s, and one University of Idaho researcher recently studied them for more than two decades before retiring without any luck.

Huckleberries make us wait three or five or seven, or more, years before fruiting, and once they do produce berries, they gift us only single fruits per leaf rather than bunches. We pick for hours to fill just a half gallon, which explains why they're priced at $9 for half a pound at my local farmer's market.

Demand for huckleberries boomed in the 1900s when newcomers realized the abundance of traditional berry fields all over the Pacific Northwest. They picked berries not just for their family or community, but for profit, especially during the Great Depression. Pickers used rakes, which are now illegal, that sped up the process but damaged the plants. One worker in the early 1930s quit his job when the berries ripened and picked the equivalent of $7,230 in today's dollars in just two months. A storekeeper sold 4,200 cases of fresh berries for $9,450 or $170,850 today. One forester in 1933 even wondered if land managers should "lay stress on the growing of timber or if huckleberries may be the more profitable crop."

Small towns near good picking sites, like Randle and Trout Lake, sell huckleberry pie, milkshakes, jam—huckleberry everything. Large companies like Tillamook also buy the berries for their ice cream. Any successful attempt to domesticate these plants would yield huge profits. Professor and plant genomics expert Amit Dhingra realized the folly of his efforts to try to grow the special fruit at Washington State University. "I was working with Native American students at that time, so I got some education through the elders that this is not something to be conquered," Dhingra says. The shrubs have developed their own ecological niche in high-elevation mountains for thousands of years and don't do well out of their natural environment. They love a good, thick insulating snowpack, high humidity, and volcanic soils. Plus, it's not feasible to have a commercial farm on the hillsides of the Cascades.

Lowbush blueberries, for example, grow in the flatlands of the Atlantic provinces and Maine, where farmers can easily clear the trees, fertilize, irrigate, and manage the fields in the berries' natural habitat, berry expert Strik tells me. "But here, where huckleberries are native," she says, "it's not practical. And then when you bring them down to the valley, their yield is so low, you could never make any money growing them."

Dhingra is now concocting a cross between mountain huckleberries and commercial blueberries. Plants that grow commercially have domesticated genes, which make tomato plants, for example, grow larger fruit with fewer seeds than their wild counterparts. These types of genes for tomatoes are different from those in huckleberries and blueberries, though, and scientists are trying to figure out how to introduce them from blueberries into a huckleberry plant to make the fruits bigger, grow in bunches, and flower quicker. "That knowledge is something being worked on now," Dhingra says. "It's not something available to us."

Dhingra, who grew up in India during a time when nutritious food was scarce, said he hopes to create a blueberry-huckleberry hybrid to make a more nutritious berry readily available and affordable. Huckleberries have four times more anthocyanin than blueberries, which packs lots of antioxidants into the fruit and gives them the deep-purple pigmentation that stains your fingers, teeth, lips, and tongue. Anthocyanins are found in the skin of the fruit, and since huckleberries are so tiny compared to commercial blueberries, the skin-to-pulp ratio is much higher, which is why they're more colorful, nutritious, and delicious.

They're taking the research slow, though, and have a few hybrid plants growing in greenhouses. Traits that help plants survive in the wild are dominant and huckleberry genes are, overall, overpowering the blueberry's domesticated genes. "As we do further breeding, we may be able to bring out the blueberry traits as well," Dhingra says. If nothing else, he adds, the plants could be a new addition to someone's backyard.

TREATIES

Washines still remembers the way her uncle's camper smelled when they gathered berries together in the Mount Adams area. She remembers her father letting her fall asleep on the long drive.

"There're a lot of family memories connected to the gathering time," she says. "It definitely was a happy time and place."

Washines describes sitting at a ceremonial table as a child and learning about native foods. "We would be taking in different knowledge about the foods in front of us," she says, "the way the food was gathered, where it was gathered, treaty rights. I remember at a very young age, when I was four, as I grew up, I saw the differences in other ethnicities sitting around their dinner tables on TV, thinking, 'How come they're not talking about the history or treaty rights or policy or legal battles?' They're just talking about homework, or what some friends said in the hallway."

Between 1778 to 1871, the US government signed 370 treaties with Native nations. These documents have the same legal status as those between the United States and foreign nations because Native tribes have always been considered sovereign. So, when the US government set its sights west, officials needed to either negotiate a treaty with the tribes or wage war before they could own the land.

Not all tribes have treaties, though, and during the mid-1800s, the government negotiated more than sixty treaties with Pacific Northwest tribes, and many, including twenty in Oregon, were never ratified by the US Senate. Others were ignored, changed, or revoked. The government ceased treaty making in 1871.

Treaties required tribes and bands to give up their land for continued tribal sovereignty. Treaties secure rights that Native people already had. Many guarantee land; peace; on- and off-reservation hunting, fishing, and gathering; and federally provided health care, education, and housing. In exchange for these rights, many of which the government never provided, tribes were left with just a fraction of their homelands and forced to live far away, often in undesirable locations. In subsequent years, the government terminated more than one hundred tribes of these rights, stripping people, like those of Grand Ronde, of their land and resources for several decades.

Isaac Stevens negotiated ten treaties, which were nearly identical, within a year and gained title to most of Washington, Idaho,

Montana, and parts of north-central Oregon. Stevens, who was the Washington Territorial governor at the time, declared just twelve days after signing the Yakama treaty in 1855 that all ceded lands were available for white settlement. People from fourteen different tribes and bands—Yakama, Palouse, Pisquouse, Wenatshapam, Klikatat, Klinquit, Kow-was-say-ee, Li-ay-was, Skin-pah, Wish-ham, Shyiks, Ochechotes, Ka-miltpah, and Se-ap-cat—whose territories extended across Washington, Oregon, and Idaho became the Confederated Tribes and Bands of the Yakama Nation. Their treaty wasn't ratified until 1859.

Tribal leaders preserved future generations' rights to access traditional foods, including berries, in their treaties. The US government promised to protect access to treaty resources, which was, and continues to be, how the government acquired tribal land. These rights, however, have never been guaranteed by the government or white property owners and were challenged through decades of assimilation policies, termination, and legal battles.

Many of the lands ceded by the Yakama—nearly one third of the state—are now owned and managed by federal agencies, including the Forest Service that oversees Gifford Pinchot National Forest. Although these agencies have a legal responsibility to uphold tribal rights, they had little interest over the years in Native gathering places, traditions, or ecological knowledge. Under the Forest Service's management, most of the berry fields are now gone. Berries are hidden under 120-year-old forests or on steep mountain slopes away from roads and not easily accessible for elders. Many Yakama people stopped going.

For decades, Yakama leaders have held officials accountable through regular meetings and complaints, which changed berry picking rules forever. Raking berries off branches—which damages both the leaves and branches and clears the shrubs of all their berries, leaving none for late-pickers or bears—is now illegal. Anyone who wants to gather berries must also apply for a permit. Commercial pickers are only allowed to buy a permit on the second Monday in August to allow tribal members to gather berries for their first foods feast. In the 1930s, Native pickers also earned exclusive picking rights in part of the Sawtooth fields. "I look at the actions that our people have taken to protect our treaty rights and the costs that have had toward them," Washines says. "Their kids were taken away. They were killed.

"And to be able to stand up to say, 'I have a long-standing and treaty-protected right to gather this food, and I will risk everything for it for future generations,' there's something very beautiful and sad in bringing the full awareness of that."

HANDSHAKE AGREEMENT

Yakama Chief William Yallup of the Kah-miltpah band told the forest supervisor in 1932 that in the last two years "whites as thick as the needles on the firs have driven our tribal women from the berry fields. Our young men, too, are arrested for hunting the deer. Yet our treaty, signed in 1855, gives us the right to hunt, fish, and gather berries for all time in our usual and accustomed places. So let the white man leave. This is our land."

During the Great Depression when the region's timber and mining industries collapsed, thousands of white people flooded the berry fields to find work. "It's hard to even describe what it was like," Mack says. "Literally there were little communities of people living up here, and they set up a commercial store to buy and sell berries in one of the campgrounds here. They'd drive them to Yakima or Portland to sell the berries. People were basically making a living during the Depression doing this."

Traffic between Twin Buttes and Smokey Creek was so congested that it took two hours to travel sixteen miles to Trout Lake.

With so many pickers taking more than they needed, damaging the bushes, and letting thousands of sheep graze the fields, Yakama leaders told the Forest Service their treaty wasn't being upheld. The Forest Service, surprisingly, agreed. In a meeting with Chief Yallup at Cold Springs in what's known as the "handshake agreement," the agency set aside twenty-eight hundred acres of land and three campsites for Native use only during huckleberry season. The agreement is now written in Gifford Pinchot National Forest's management plan and signs along the Sawtooth fields remind visitors to respect the rules.

The handshake agreement fields, though, were reduced to just seven hundred acres in the 1990s and are even less now. Yakama Council Chair William Yallup Sr., grandson of Chief Yallup, pressed the agency in 1993 to clear the undergrowth. Workers started restoring the fields in the 1990s and 2000s, but Mack tells me that it's been inconsequential. "That's what it feels like," she says. "We've done numerous projects, large and small, and they feel like a drop in the bucket. And I look at it now and just think, 'What are all these trees doing here?'"

Tribal and Forest Service crews manually cut some trees and sold timber to thin traditional fields, like Pole Patch in the northwestern part of the forest. "We've done a lot, but one thing we haven't done is burn," Mack says. "The tribe wanted us to simply set this all on fire and burn it like they did."

The tribe and agency burned ninety acres in the Sawtooth fields about ten years ago. But without setting fires regularly and on a larger scale, the trees keep getting taller and more and more keep sprouting up, robbing the berries of needed sunlight and water.

The agency wanted to burn in Pole Patch, but that hasn't happened yet, says Jessica Hudec, a Forest Service ecologist and fire specialist who wrote a recent huckleberry restoration report for the agency. They planned to burn Mowich Butte, but that didn't happen either, she tells me. Officials have to balance a myriad of state and federal rules and air quality regulations. As the region gets hotter and drier and more fires burn out of control after years of fire suppression policies, prescribed burns become less of an option. "Ecologically, it's tough," Hudec says, "because Native Americans would have burned in the fall after everything is super dry and we haven't had any rain yet. We have not been, and we won't be allowed to put a match on the ground. That's just not gonna happen."

With warming temperatures, huckleberry habitat is predicted to decline by anywhere from five to forty percent in the Northwest by the end of this century, with plants at lower elevations affected the most. Berries may even fruit one to two months earlier. An invasive fruit fly is also damaging the berries and native bee declines, like those of the western bumble bee, may affect plants' fruit and genetic diversity.

Harvey's family, including her uncle, Freddy Ike Sr., regularly met with the Forest Service to protect these gathering grounds. Those relatives have since passed, and Harvey is now in these meetings. She's complained for years about commercial and non-Native pickers wreaking havoc on the fields. Some pick before tribal people have gathered for their first feast. They leave garbage and beer cans scattered and still use rakes, she tells me. Some even block the roads with their cars.

One year, a group of seventy to one hundred churchgoers came up to the fields to pick. They brought an ATV and cruised through the area as the berries were ripening. They built an obstacle course around the fields and shot paintball guns. "You guys have a church," Harvey told them. "Well, this area is like our church.

"When we were kids, we were taught that you don't scream in the mountains," she says. "You don't yell, and you don't act obnoxious because you have to have respect. There are wildlife that live here, and they're not used to that," she says. "They don't want us coming in every year, screaming, yelling, and tearing up the forest and being disrespectful. And these people are doing that."

Harvey says that the ATVs would fly through the fields at thirty miles per hour when children were close by. They'd cruise through the historic Middle Trail. "I kept complaining about it, year after year," she says, until she convinced the Forest Service to ban ATVs in the Sawtooth fields and Surprise Lakes area.

Harvey picks some years at Pole Patch where the late berries ripen. Commercial harvesters at one point took over the whole area. "Tribal people didn't want to go anymore," she says. "It's so disheartening."

The Forest Service says it doesn't have enough law enforcement officers to make sure commercial harvesters are taking their fair share and not picking too early or bypassing rules and selling berries to buyers in the fields. "Our law enforcement is stretched really thin, and at the end of the day, people stealing berries might not be their highest priority with everything else going on," Hudec says.

A large interpretive sign in the Sawtooth fields explains the handshake agreement and cultural significance of these lands. The agency and Yakama Nation installed the cedar sign in the 1990s that features photos of women drying berries in the early 1900s, framed next to Native carvings of huckleberries and other first foods. A quote from Harvey's uncle, Chief Frederick Ike, Sr., featured on the sign reads: "The Creator made the Mother Earth, the mountains, streams, trees, animals, roots, and berries and made it sacred. May the future generations honor and respect the work of the past leaders in working in harmony to create the treaty."

Over the years, the Forest Service has had several district rangers come and go. Harvey says she and other Yakama leaders have to continually teach new rangers—and other agency employees—about their traditions and treaty rights. In the past, one district ranger said no to nearly every one of their requests. She even stopped servicing the bathrooms and garbage at Cold Springs Indian Camp.

In recent years, the agency seems to be listening to tribal concerns. Rangers now talk to and engage with the tribe more often, Harvey tells me. "We're working with people who are what I would say compassionate for us and our rights," she says. "They're working with us to help us."

TRADITION

Harvey's family didn't move to the reservation after tribal leaders signed the treaty. She still lives in Goldendale near their village site. "We didn't wanna move because this is our area," she says. Colonists wanted Native people to become farmers and Harvey's family, led by Chief Yallup, resisted. "We're tied to this land, and we're tied to this river," she says of the Columbia, called Nch'i-Wána in Sahaptin. Harvey's most recent work looks at how dams along the entire Columbia River basin affect salmon. "It's ingrained into us. We have to stay here because it's a part of us."

Harvey's grandmother, Louise Billy, never went to school, and instead learned from her parents. They hid her from federal government workers who took all her siblings to boarding schools during violent assimilation efforts. Billy learned Kah-miltpah ways of life and language. "All the ceremonies and the songs, she knew all of them," Harvey says. "She knew so much."

Harvey describes spending hours cutting tules with her in a storehouse that Billy built where she shared stories and knowledge. She didn't like electricity, TV, or radio, so they'd cut the plants with just the windows open for light. Harvey remembers hearing other kids playing outside while she worked. Billy knew all the native foods, like camas, and how to care for them. "You don't just throw camas in a pot," Harvey says. "You need to cook that in the ground, and you've got to have certain plants to go under with it, and there are even certain words you have to say when you're cooking it, traditional words. It's not just like 'Well, I'm gonna go dig camas and cook it in the oven.' No, you have to cook it in the ground, and there's a process for everything.

"She knew everything. She was the smartest person I could say I knew in my whole life," Harvey says.

Recently, Harvey met with Forest Service officials to map out areas to bring huckleberries back. She identified five locations that were once traditional picking sites but are now overgrown with trees. With a bit of thinning, the land would welcome huckleberries again. "In our belief, the Creator gave us these foods for a purpose," she says. "So, we have to honor those foods and treat them with respect because if those foods weren't here, we wouldn't be here. Our ancestors wouldn't have survived to this point where we're descendants of them."

Over the years, Harvey kept saying no to the Forest Service when they asked her to help select restoration sites. "I was so upset at the commercial pickers competing with us and being obnoxious that I didn't want to create huckleberry sites for them," she says. "I didn't want to open up land for them to push us out."

With a son, daughter, and now grandchild, Harvey realized she needs to protect areas for future Native generations. "If I don't say anything, my daughter is not gonna come here because there will be no berries, and my grandson, and all the generations in the future," she says. "They won't be able to come here and gather here.

So, I'm gonna do it for them, and that's it. My grandma took me to these places for a reason."

When gathering traditional foods, Harvey learned to work with a good heart and mind. You shouldn't gather when you're mad or upset, she tells me. "You have to be in a good spirit," she says. "Because if you aren't, you're gonna take that food home, and you're gonna feed your family or your longhouse community, and those people will get those bad feelings. That's our teaching."

Harvey made sure commercial harvesting won't be allowed at the new gathering sites. Once restored, the fields will welcome only Native and non-Native individual pickers.

With fewer people in the fields picking for themselves and not for profit, Harvey's family will again have a quiet place in the mountains to be with the berries.

"We want to go there and hear the birds sing," she says. "We want to have peace."

Olympic Marmot,
Marmota olympus

They lived on little islands surrounded by ice. Among steep sandstone cliffs, thousands of feet above the sea. I imagine them exactly as they are today, their stout bodies and short legs bumbling over jagged rocks and stopping every few feet to look around and sniff lingering scents in the crisp evening air. I picture them poking their dark, round noses over ledges and looking down on valleys encased in ice sheets half a mile thick that turned the lowlands of the peninsula pastel blue and glowed like magic under a full moon. The marmots have been up here in the Olympic Mountains since glaciers covered most of the region thousands of years ago. They could tell us when ice dams blocked salmon from the Elwha River's upper reaches and when glacial melt unveiled a newly sculpted landscape. I bet they were happy in their ice world as long as they had full bellies. Would their piercing whistles, which soar to the highest notes, have even more resonance and cut through the frozen silence? Did they have much company up there?

I walk as quickly and safely as I can along a steep section on the Seven Lakes Basin Loop trail that probably would give me vertigo if not for my hood that also functions as blinders while keeping me dry. My partner, his dad, and I enter a part of the trail that transforms from meadow slopes covered in wildflowers and huckleberries to a massive sixty-foot chasm. This ridge high above the Hoh, Bogachiel, and Sol Duc Rivers is ripping apart. Gravity is slowly pulling it in half. Couch-sized boulders lay scattered around, some split down the middle.

I look up and see her perched. Fifty feet above us, she stands tall on the highest rock in the area, her fur still wet from the late afternoon August rain. Maybe she was drying off as the sun poked through swift-moving clouds that looked close enough for us to touch. We walk a few dozen feet farther and see another perk up on a rock then lumber across the trail in front of us, showing off her bushy tail and butterscotch coat with blotches of dark brown. Perhaps she just woke up from her usual afternoon nap.

She stumbles across the still damp boulders and nearly slips on one rock, then takes a few steps before stopping to look around. She scurries a bit further, stops and again looks around to be safe, a typical day for an Olympic marmot, *Marmota olympus*. We're close enough that I can see her slender brown paws and fingernails manicured into a pointed shape for digging her burrow, where she'll soon snuggle up until next spring.

The marmots are perfect here—chunky, furry, and friendly house-cat-sized rodents living and playing in treacherous landscapes that people experience only briefly or wonder about in photographs. They've been here, away from their Pacific Northwest marmot cousins, for so long that they evolved unique genetics, calls, tawny fur coats, greetings, and a love for wide porches that lead down to their burrows and provide a space to relax and enjoy the sunrise. They might even have their own species of flea. Their ancestors lived on ice-free rocky islands in these mountains on the Olympic Peninsula, once separated from the rest of the region by ice and now separated by salt water on three sides and a river valley to the south. Their earliest ancestors might even remember a world before our mountains fully formed when tundra-like grasslands, similar to their preferred mountain meadows, covered more of the landscape. They've lived through a changing climate many times, but they now struggle to keep up with our human-caused changes that have brought a new predator to their home.

HIBERNATION

Marmots spend most of their lives underground. As summer days grow shorter and food becomes scarce, they're ready for a dark, cold winter.

Their heartbeats slow. Their blood cools, and their metabolisms shut down. They weigh twice as much as they did a few months earlier. They've worked for this moment, when their hard-earned chubby bodies power them through seven or eight months in their burrows, nearly lifeless.

They're safest here, away from coyotes, cougars, and golden eagles, huddled with family from September through May, while the ground above them freezes and harsh alpine winds scatter freshly fallen snow. Not a single draft enters their winter homes.

Their laziness peaks in August. Even before they've entered their burrows for a long winter sleep, their metabolisms slow, so they can conserve as much energy and fat as possible. They lay around on their wide, dirt porches or survey the alpine world from inside burrows, until the time comes for deep sleep sometime in September or October. They hibernate with family on a thick bed of grass and wildflowers, as they've done every fall and winter for millennia. I think of them as the weather cools, knowing they're still in the mountains where we last saw them, when the meadows were colorful and the sky was blue. They know winter is a time to slow down.

Marmots are the largest members of the squirrel family and the largest animals to truly hibernate. When it comes time, their breathing slows to an extreme. Their hearts beat just three times per minute, and their body temperatures drop to less than forty degrees. They don't store any food or water inside their burrows and rely entirely on fat reserves for months. Bears, by contrast, keep their temperatures relatively high: eighty-eight degrees at the lowest. Since their bodies aren't as shut off as marmots', they awaken from hibernation quickly if startled.

Six species of marmots live in North America and prefer our western landscapes. Most have a blend of brown, tan, gray, and red underfur that's soft and protected by longer, coarser "guard" hairs that are typically light brown or gray. The mix of colors and textures gives their coats a salt-and-pepper finish. All marmot species have stocky builds, silvery muzzles, bushy tails, short legs, tiny ears, and stout necks that are essentially indistinguishable from the rest of their bodies. They can live eight years, grow up to two feet in length, and can weigh ten pounds or more.

Hoary marmots, who have a striking silver-gray back and shoulders, live in high elevations and are found throughout Washington's Cascades. They live as far east as western Montana and the Rocky Mountains, and their habitat stretches north through British Columbia to the Yukon Territory and Alaska. Brooks Range marmots live in the northern Alaskan mountain range of their namesake. They have a dark face and rump and much softer fur compared to their hoary relatives. The Vancouver Island marmot flaunts a chocolate-brown coat and is found only on the British Columbia island just north of the Olympic Peninsula. Yellow-bellied marmots are common throughout the Rockies and eastern and central Washington, and they are Oregon's only marmot species. They prefer drier landscapes and lower elevations than hoary or Olympic marmots and have earlier hibernating seasons since the snowpack isn't as heavy. They're a distant relative to Olympic, hoary, and Vancouver Island marmots. They have a grayish brown face and back, and unsurprisingly, golden bellies.

Just one marmot species, the woodchuck or groundhog, lives in low elevations in the eastern part of the country and has the widest habitat range of any marmot. Woodchucks are found all along the East Coast, throughout eastern Canada, in some parts of the West, and as far north as Alaska. They're the least social of the marmot family and largely refrain from showing off their vocal range, unlike the rest of their western counterparts. They're also the only animal to have their own holiday, Groundhog Day.

For all marmots, life largely revolves around winter. They've developed the remarkable ability to lose about half of their body weight during hibernation and regain it over just a few months—an unusual feat for most mammals. Olympic marmots gorge themselves on fresh glacier lilies, lupines, paintbrush, and other vegetation blooming in Olympic Mountain meadows throughout the summer. Their plump bodies and energy-saving habits allow them to survive in mountainous terrain, where food is scarce most of the year.

Growing a hefty enough body takes time—about three years for Olympic marmots—so they've adapted to live in family groups, or colonies, while their young become big enough to reproduce and survive winter on their own. Colonies, which can vary in size, usually consist of a male, two females, a couple of two-year-olds, a few yearlings, and several newborn pups. Different marmot colonies can live near each other within a meadow, with each colony constructing multiple burrows throughout the open fields.

They stay underground and don't reemerge until the sun sets later, usually in May. Snow still covers the ground, as their wakeup process begins. Their hearts beat faster and their blood warms. Revitalizing energy shoots through their bodies. Initially, they're lethargic and not fully awake. They use nearly all their stored fat to slowly come back to life, inching closer to the finish line of their winter journey.

When the time is right, they crawl up through several feet of snow, and, finally, poke their heads out from their burrows. They look around, blinking, while slowly adjusting to the bright world.

David P. Barash, who has studied marmots extensively in the Olympics, remembers seeing one first emerge from hibernation in late spring near Hurricane Ridge. She popped her head out, while accompanied by a small cloud of flies that must have found their way down into the burrow, he recalls. "It must have been quite a shock because it was a beautiful day," says Barash, a University of Washington professor emeritus. He researched marmots all over the world for several decades and earned his doctorate after observing and detailing Olympic marmot behavior for three summers in the 1960s. "The sun was shining, and this animal had been under several feet of snow when it must have been very dark, if not totally dark. Not only is it daylight, but it's bright sun and white snow all around. You know what it's like when someone suddenly turns the lights on."

As much as I like to think that they'd be a dream to cuddle, they're smelliest in spring, after being hunkered down with flies and fleas for months. They plug their burrows with a mixture of grass, dirt, and feces that they have to crawl through before breaking free for the season. They're not able to groom themselves or groom each other while they're hibernating, so it's understandable that they're not fresh after spending more than half a year underground.

They regain strength slowly and mostly stay near their burrows during the initial days back above ground. They eat snow. They stretch their paws forward, arch their backs and yawn, exposing two pairs of long characteristically rodent teeth in a dramatic display that reminds me of my cat. Their bodies must restore the lining of their guts, which diminishes during their sleep, before they can finally have their first meal. I imagine they immediately resume play-fighting after eating, standing on hind legs to box each other and roll around. I envision fresh tracks all over the glittering ground.

Marmots can sleep so hard that they forget where they are. Barash once trapped and released two about twenty-three feet from their burrow. Normally trapped marmots dash right back to their burrows during the summer from even as far as fifty feet away, but these marmots that Barash caught, fresh out of hibernation, seemed confused and walked around aimlessly for fifteen minutes. They flattened themselves against the snow, maybe in an overwhelmed surrender to an unrecognizable white landscape that they needed to relearn.

PERSONALITY

Stumpy was a pushy guy. He weighed twenty pounds and lived near Hurricane Ridge. He chased other males away from his colony and growled. He kept all the marmots in check.

"He was forward. He was the boss, and he knew he was the boss, and no one was going to forget it," Barash says. "He was a big, dominant male. Not that I'm a big, dominant male, but maybe that's why I found him intriguing. I named him Stumpy."

Stumpy provided Barash with more data than probably any other marmot because he was fearless and often out, making the rounds and keeping watch for any intruders.

Stumpy loved to eat but especially loved the peanut butter that Barash would leave in cages as bait to trap marmots so that he could tag their ears, and know who's who for his study. Barash would often find Stumpy, though, in the cage again and again, licking his chops. "I had already marked him," Barash says, laughing. "I already knew who he was. I wanted to catch someone else."

So, each season Barash began hauling an extra fifteen-pound cage up a steep, trail-less ridge, often in eighteen-inches of snow, just for Stumpy to enjoy the salty peanut-butter treat. "I kind of resented having to carry one just for him, for God's sake," Barash says. "I remember saying to myself, 'Shit, there's Stumpy again.'"

Barash's work is still the most comprehensive look into the lives of Olympic marmots, nearly sixty years later. He documented their daily routines, mating patterns, greeting rituals, alarm calls, mother-to-pup relationships, colony behavior, and lifespan. In his book, *Marmots: Social Behavior and Ecology*, Barash has charts and graphs detailing exactly what time of day adult males, females, yearlings, and pups feed; when adults look out of their burrow; what time of day that they're in the burrow; and how often they play fight. He created flow charts of sexual behaviors of females. He has photos of mother marmots nuzzling their young and photos of adolescent marmots wrestling each other that are blurry from movement.

Not many researchers choose to study Olympic marmots, let alone spend entire summers observing them for countless hours like Barash did. Organizations that dole out money for research don't seem to value them. That has left aspects of their biology and ecology relatively unstudied in recent years, even though these unique, charismatic mammals found only in the Olympic Peninsula, have declined in population by an estimated 40 to 50 percent since Barash first began studying them. Many colonies in the park are now gone. Researchers aren't sure of their exact numbers, but it's thought that only one thousand, or fewer, marmots remain.

When Barash attended graduate school in the 1960s, he wanted to study how evolution affects behavior. At the time, evolution was thought to influence animal anatomy and physiology, but relatively little research applied evolutionary thinking to daily routines, mating, or sociality. He knew he wanted to study mammals but needed to find closely related animals with a variety of species in different environments so that he could study how natural selection may have influenced their behavior relative to their environments. Mammals are a bit tricky to study, though, because they tend to be nocturnal and move around a lot. "Marmots came to my attention," Barash says. "I'm not sure exactly how."

They quickly became an ideal group to study—there's just one genus, *Marmota*, which represents about fifteen different species worldwide. About half of all marmots live in North America, while the rest are found in Asia and Europe. They're active during the day, relatively sedentary, and hibernate during the academic year. "Which is very convenient, so I know I'm not missing anything in December, January, February, March and so on," Barash says. Plus, they live in meadows above timberline overlooking spectacular mountain views. They're also relatively unbothered by humans. "I could go sit in a meadow maybe one hundred feet away from the animals I was studying, and they would come out of their burrows and be hanging out pretty much right there."

Barash found that marmot species living at different elevations matured at different ages and evolved reproductive cycles and social structures that corresponded to their environments. Marmots living at the lowest elevations, like woodchucks, sexually mature faster. Since these marmots have easier access to food and don't live in harsh alpine cold, they live solitary lives. Marmots in high elevations take longer to grow large enough before they can sexually mature, which takes three years for Olympic, hoary, and Vancouver Island marmots. They were initially thought to reproduce every other year because the growing season is so short in the mountains, but recent research has indicated Olympic marmots may reproduce annually. More studies, however, are needed to definitively know their reproduction cycle. Such information would also help researchers better understand colony structure because the number of marmots living in a given burrow is determined by how often they reproduce. Researchers have observed one to six marmots of different generations living together, sometimes in a meadow with other colonies, which Barash describes as "colony towns."

Part of science is to generalize, to be able to sum up an animal's behavior neatly, so scientists can research hypotheses and come up with insights about why animals behave the way that they do. But in doing so, we can lose the color and richness of individual personalities, like Stumpy's, or nuances to their everyday lives. Barash became fond of certain individual marmots, whom he got to know, and who, in turn, got to know him. Initially when he approached a new colony, the marmots gave off alarm calls. But after spending a few days around them, they stopped calling and grew accustomed to their observer. Stumpy wasn't the only marmot Barash named. There was Forehead, named for the large white patch across the marmot's forehead, and Blackback, who haunts him somewhat.

Blackback was out eating not far from her burrow one afternoon near Hurricane Ridge. She had just given birth to pups, who were still too young to leave the burrow and were dependent on her milk. Barash observed Blackback often. On this day, he noticed a cougar, about 100 to 150 feet away, but Blackback didn't see the big cat.

Blackback put her head down to eat some more. The cougar inched closer.

As Blackback looked up, the cougar crouched down in the high grasses, or hid behind a clump of subalpine firs. Blackback again put her head down to eat. The cougar crawled even closer. "I was really tempted to stand up and make noise," Barash says. "It was a heavy debate, as you can tell because I still remember it more than fifty years ago. And so, I took the scientific route, if you will, and I did nothing. I just watched."

The cougar pounced. The cat grabbed Blackback behind her neck and shook her, likely killing her immediately. He never saw the babies. "I felt really shitty about it, and in some ways, I still do," he says. "But I was following my scientific sensibilities."

If he had the chance to relive the moment? He's quiet for a moment. "I think I would have scared the cougar away, to be honest. The reality is, though, if I think it was a female cougar, she may have also had kittens, so who am I to decide who lives and who dies?"

Barash saw several golden eagles and coyotes, but the cougar hunt was the only successful predation of marmots he witnessed. He remembered one coyote approaching a colony and all of the marmots hurrying into their burrows. The coyote approached one of the burrows, and a nearby marmot popped his head out and gave an alarm call. The coyote lurked around before checking out a different burrow. Each time the coyote neared, another marmot would stick her head out and let out a scream, sending the coyote back again to the first burrow. "That went on for a little while," Barash says. "I remember describing it as coyote ping-pong."

Other researchers told me stories of curious marmots crawling inside their car engines when they were parked on Obstruction Point Road, not far from Hurricane Ridge. One marmot hitched a ride a few miles down the road, while some marmots have been known to regularly ride in car engines from Hurricane Ridge down to Port Angeles, nearly twenty miles away, and Olympic National Park staff must retrieve them. Maybe the marmots want a quick glimpse of the outside world.

In California, one yellow-bellied marmot even made a two-hundred-mile trip to San Jose from Yosemite National Park. She crawled through storm drains and scurried across manicured lawns but was eventually returned to her natural habitat. A few yellow-bellied marmots were recently spotted in Sequim on the Olympic Peninsula, far from their eastern Washington homes, leading some to wonder if they're also hitching rides.

Yellow-bellied marmots are infamously known for chewing brake cables and radiator hoses in Kings Canyon and Sequoia National Parks. In one instance, they chewed the brake cables off a man's car, leading to his death. The man unknowingly drove down a steep, windy road from White Mountain northeast of Kings Canyon, without working brakes. The National Park Service recommends hikers in the areas wrap the entire bottom halves of their cars—tires included—in tarps held together with ropes or bungee cords, to marmot-proof the car. In the Spokane area, hundreds of yellow-bellied marmots ravaged the city, chewing transmission and radiator lines, pooping on doormats, and tearing up lawns and flowerbeds.

The first marmot I ever saw—a hoary—was far less active. He lay flattened across a huge boulder on a too-hot July day, just up from Paradise on Mount Rainier. I liked them immediately, while observing their shameless laziness and apparent protest to the heat. Several other marmots kept us company, as we looked down into the Nisqually Glacier, ate our lunch, and played backpack-sized bocce ball. I've seen marmots in the Cascades and a yellow-bellied friend at Crater Lake. I witnessed another hoary stand up on a rock ledge overlooking Hidden Lake in North Cascades National Park, surrounded by the most rugged mountains I've ever seen. Our presence might have aggravated her, though, as she tucked her paws in, leaned back, dropped her jaw and let out an impressive scream that carried across the entire ridge.

GREETINGS

Every morning just after sunrise, Stumpy would run around to different unoccupied burrows and wait. He cheerfully bolted toward the first marmot passing by, rubbing his nose against theirs, a sweet "good morning," Barash recalls.

Sometimes, he'd stop there, or he'd extend the salutation by stroking his nose against the other marmot's cheek. The two might interlock their long, yellow teeth, depending on their moods. Once they finished their hellos, Stumpy would move on to another burrow, awaiting the next colony member he saw. He repeated this until he seemingly wished everyone in the colony a good day. Then, he would return to his burrow for a few hours to rest before repeating the greetings later in the day.

Marmots are social. They rub noses. They nuzzle and groom each other. They growl, chirp, and chatter their teeth. They have meals together. They somersault through idyllic meadows. They push and shove each other, all in good fun, with their tiny, squirrel-like hands. Their thick fur coats provide a cushion when they tumble and fall during the playful scuffles. They're friendly because they don't have time to be mean. They need each other to survive.

Olympic marmots and their close hoary relatives prefer togetherness. They've developed these elaborate greeting rituals that they repeat every morning, afternoon, and evening before returning to their chambers. The greetings aren't to prove dominance, and they aren't restricted just to their home burrows. The marmots make the rounds through the entire meadow colony to simply say "hello" to all.

The greetings can sometimes go too far, though. Each marmot prefers to be the initiator, often enthusiastically approaching a fellow marmot who does not reciprocate the cheer. The receiver sometimes ignores the welcome, or holds rigidly still, putting up with it, albeit reluctantly.

Usually, greetings begin and end with a quick nose-to-nose, or nose-to-mouth touch. If the initiator tries to test their luck by sneaking in a nibble on the receiving marmot's ear, let alone attempting a neck chew, the receiver communicates that a line has been crossed. They'll nip or growl.

Barash observed and documented hundreds of these greetings. Of the 467 nose-to-nose encounters, 11 percent resulted in a nip or growl. Of 18 ear-chewing episodes, 61 percent ended in a scolding. All nine neck-chewing encounters Barash watched ended with aggression. Males are most enthused earlier in the season, perhaps because they're eager for a mate. Then, by August, females and pups conduct most of the salutations. The youngest marmots are especially energized. As summer progresses and the heat drags on, they all eventually tire of socializing, and greet each other just briefly, so they can keep focused on eating and gaining as much weight as possible before fall.

Yellow-bellied marmots, by contrast, are reserved and more subdued. They typically don't make contact when they greet each other. They simply sniff and prefer to stay several feet away.

MEADOW LIFE

Some marmot burrows are fifty years old. They're multigenerational homes used by colonies for decades. About eighty percent of marmots' lives take place in these burrows. Inside, they nap, shelter from bad weather, give birth, and enter their deep winter sleep. Marmots make sure they're cozy, functional, and aesthetically pleasing. They like wide porches and landscaped grass-like sedges surrounding the entrances. These qualities make me think of the inviting, early 1900s craftsman houses in my neighborhood with covered porches and neat lawns. Marmots create separate chambers for bedrooms and bathrooms. They make cushy mattresses of lupines, grasses, and other meadow wildflowers, stacked ten to fourteen inches, for sleeping.

Other smaller burrows are scattered throughout the meadow and serve as a quick escape from predators. Scientists aren't exactly sure how far down or how wide burrows extend, but one analysis found that these smaller burrows were typically a few feet deep. Burrows made by other marmot species were found to be about 200 to 250 feet long.

Olympic marmots prefer to live in sloping meadows rather than rocky terrain, where their hoary and yellow-bellied relatives are typically found. They create numerous burrows throughout a meadow and, in doing so, alter the landscape. Downslope from the entrance of their home, Olympic marmots build porches of dirt and rock left over from excavating their burrows. The porch elevates the marmots slightly. They use them to look out over their territory and lounge during mornings and evenings. Their extensive digging and bathroom habits affect soil structure, as dirt samples from their tunnels are higher in carbonates, sulfates, and chlorides. Their feces and urine also give nutrients for tufts of tall sedges to grow around their homes, shading the marmots from the sun as they easily get stressed by heat.

Landscapes are sculpted, in part, by the animals who live in them. Even the smallest creatures, like insects, can change where plants grow. What seems like a natural, untouched meadow is one designed by animals.

"They're ecosystem engineers," says Maia Murphy-Williams, a wildlife ecologist who studied the marmots and their meadow habitats for her 2020 master's thesis at the University of Washington. "They change their environments and certainly affect the plant species that grow in the alpine meadows."

Marmots' extensive excavations create opportunities for a variety of plants, especially weedy and unpalatable species, to grow. Since marmots eat the common, tastier plants, like lupine, paintbrush, mountain buckwheat, and avalanche and glacier lilies, they control which species dominate a field, giving other, less sought-after, uneaten plants a home. Soon after emerging from hibernation, marmots might eat fresh succulent leaves under melting snow, giving those plants a helpful prune and boost to the start of their season.

Trees stop growing in dense forests at an elevation around five or six thousand feet in most mountainous areas in the Northwest. Olympic marmots prefer to be in eight or more acres of open meadow with few trees or rocky outcroppings that block their view of predators. Most of them now live in the northern part of the park where these open meadows are found. Boundless heather and huckleberry meadows around Lunch Lake and Heart Lake are dotted with patches of mountain hemlock, subalpine fir, yellow-cedar, and probably too many young seedlings of all three species. Though these trees take much longer to grow large in the harsh alpine, scientists worry that as the weather warms, more and more trees will take over mountain meadows, pushing out marmots and other specialized alpine species who have nowhere else to go.

Drier and warmer summers may also change the growing cycle of meadow plants that marmots feed on and use for bedding and shelter. Once marmots reach two or three years old, they may move out of their home meadow and travel to other colonies to start their own families. But as trees inch farther up the mountains, these travel routes may become overgrown and threaten their ability to reach other meadow colonies. "Now, you see more connected burrows in the northern areas," Murphy-Williams says, "and a lot less in the south. They're kind of these clusters that aren't very close together."

Marmots prefer traveling along ridgelines and meadow edges, not through trees. "They're a lot more likely to get predated in deep forests," she says. "It's not their habitat."

If marmots can't travel safely to other meadows for food or mates, they risk getting cut off from other marmot populations which could lead to inbreeding and subsequent genetic problems that would threaten their health and survival.

WHISTLES

Olympic marmots effortlessly sing, or more accurately scream, at the highest pitches. The fundamental frequency of their voices is around 2,500 Hz, or just about the highest E on a piano. This is the same note that Mariah Carey hits in her own famous whistle tone at the end of her 1991 song, "Emotions." Yellow-bellied marmots hit even higher notes, to a frequency of 4,000 Hz, which is basically the highest note, a C, on the piano.

When they sense danger, they bolt up, drop their jaws like they're on a rollercoaster, quickly draw in their bellies and thrust air up and out of their mouths with such powerful resonance that it shocks me every time I hear them.

Marmots are versatile in their vocal abilities, except for the woodchuck, who has only one call. Yellow-bellied marmots can produce two types of calls: a short, powerful whistle, and multi-note trill, which sounds somewhat like a bird singing. Hoary, Vancouver Island, and Olympic marmots, meanwhile, possess the widest range and can produce four different calls. They have a quick ascending whistle where the pitch rises at the end, like a question, and a descending call that falls at the end. They have a flat, unchanging whistle where the same note is held steady the entire time, and they have a seldomly used trill, which involves moving rapidly between two different notes.

They call to alert fellow marmots of danger. Scientists studying their different calls haven't found particular vocalizations to be directed at specific threats. However, Olympic marmots do call more frequently when they see a ground predator, like a coyote, rather than an eagle. Hoary and Vancouver Island marmots have also been found to call at higher pitches and for longer durations after seeing a ground predator, as opposed to an aerial one.

They call when humans are nearby too, as marmots have been hunted before. People of the Olympic Peninsula tribes frequented the high country for food in the summer long before national park policies prohibited tribes from hunting and gathering on their own land. The paths they walked to visit alpine meadows with mountainous views are many of the same trails we continue to use to admire the same sights.

ISOLATION

The Olympic Mountains are elusive. Although you can see their silhouette throughout the Seattle area and from ferries, their geography confused me for years, probably because I never hiked far into the park. But I was drawn to them.

I always hoped for clear skies on days when my dad bought us tickets to see the Yankees play the Mariners in Seattle. I wanted to avoid Seattle's rain so the stadium's roof would stay open, but I also wanted to see from the city's waterfront the most jagged, rugged mountains I knew. My experience with the Olympics stayed there, at a distance, for many years, a faraway glimpse into the high peaks that looked like the way a kid would draw a mountain range.

The mountains here aren't in a neat line. All the peaks are relatively the same height without any one prominent mountain visible from the lowlands like the Cascade volcanoes. The Olympics are instead composed of several ranges and steep river valleys within a conglomerate of sharp peaks. No roads cut across the park and, aside from views at the Hurricane Ridge Visitor Center, you're only blessed by Mount Olympus if you put in effort. It took hiking nearly eight miles and climbing three thousand feet to see the park's tallest peak, and a marmot. They're tucked far away.

My partner, his dad, and I reach the High Divide Trail on a warm late August afternoon, and I can see nearly everything I had wondered about. Just in front of us looking south, we admire the Blue Glacier wrapped around Mount Olympus like a scarf. We peer down into the Hoh Rainforest, where moss and big trees live in the wide, U-shaped river valley molded by the glacial ice that once covered the mountains almost up to their summits. We can see the entire route that the Hoh River's silty baby-blue water takes from the glaciers that are still there—though much smaller than they used to be, even just thirty years ago.

The river curves around the southern end of the imposing Olympus, which is more like a massive complex of peaks joined by wide ice sheets. The river originates from these nearly eight-thousand-foot peaks and meanders for fifty-six miles until meeting the Pacific Ocean, which we can also see, just barely. To the north, we see the Strait of Juan de Fuca and the Sol Duc Valley, where salmon return around these late summer months to their ancestral waters.

We admire the craggy peaks of Mount Olympus and the Bailey Range that help divide the peninsula into wet and dry sides, similar to how land east of the Cascades is different from the west. It's estimated that more than fifty feet of snow blankets Mount Olympus each year, nourishing glaciers that are only a few dozen miles away from the sea. From land, you'd never know these two worlds exist so close unless you travel up several thousand feet to see it.

The rocks that make up the mountains that marmots tumble around on once held the weight of the Pacific. They were a part of the vast seafloor, far below the water that they now tower over but which still molds their shape and determines the species living on their slopes.

Mount Storm King, Mount Angeles, Mount Constance, the Brothers, Mount Tebo, and Colonel Bob were born from lava spewed underwater some fifty million years ago after the earth's plates started moving and formed a deep marine rift. These ancient basalts were the first of the Olympic Mountains to rise out of the sea. They were forced into a horseshoe shape, which stretches from Victoria in British Columbia south to Coos Bay in Oregon.

Younger sandstone, siltstone, and shale that make up the interior mountains were scraped off the seafloor like frosting off a cake, when the oceanic and continental plates collided again and uplifted the rocks from the water approximately twenty million years ago. The mountains continue to rise, but heavy rain, snow, and ice that have sculpted them for millennia erode the rock and prevent peaks from getting any taller.

Ice and water have separated the Olympic Mountains from the mainland for so long that many animals common in the Cascade Range, like grizzly bears, wolverines, coyotes, pikas, red foxes, lynx, porcupines, and mountain goats never made it to the region naturally. Because of its isolation, at least twenty-seven plants and animals found nowhere else in the world—like Olympic marmots— still live here after surviving the Ice Age in areas of the Olympic alpine that didn't freeze. It's thought that marmots lived on rock islands, called nunataks, where only mountain summits rose above surrounding lowlands hidden underneath glacial ice. The Olympic chipmunk, Olympic torrent salamander, Flett's violet, and Piper's bellflower are also found nowhere else on Earth.

Olympic marmots have one of the smallest ranges of any mammal in North America, living only in meadows above forty-five hundred feet. Before the Ice Age, they likely lived more broadly throughout the Pacific Northwest, and even throughout western North America, perhaps knowing the landscape before the Olympic and Cascade Mountains finished reaching their current heights. Scientists haven't found any marmot fossils from the Ice Age in either the Cascades or Olympics, so it's difficult to know exactly when and where they lived. Some estimate marmots first appeared in North America seven to eleven million years ago.

Researchers for years thought Vancouver Island and Olympic marmots would be more closely related, given their homes are separated only by the Strait of Juan de Fuca. Olympic marmots, though, are a much older species, and branched off from their sisters some 2.6 million years ago, when the Ice Age began. Hoary and Vancouver marmots diverged more recently, by geologic time, between 400,000 to 1.2 million years ago.

Olympic marmots' jaws are peculiarly shaped, which may be a result of millions of years of isolation from other marmots. Some scientists wonder if they may be an ancestor to all living marmots, as other species far away, including one in Russia, have a similar jaw structure.

Although the mountains are isolated, they're not immune to our human presence. Hunters released twelve mountain goats near Lake Crescent in the 1920s, and they quickly populated the high country, damaging unique plants. Warmer weather from our excessive greenhouse gas emissions is inching trees higher into subalpine and alpine meadows, which is expected to encroach on marmots' already limited habitat. Air pollution from Asia is sometimes detected in the park. And extensive logging and hunting of gray wolves brought in a new, non-native predator: coyotes.

COYOTE

Suzanne Cox Griffin assumed Olympic marmot populations were healthy. Given that more than 90 percent of their home is protected within Olympic National Park, the nation's fourth largest national park, she wasn't worried. For her dissertation at the University of Montana in the early 2000s, she initially set out to study how climate change could fragment marmots' alpine habitat and ability to establish new colonies in the future. She soon realized, though, that marmots were already gone from places where they had always been. Many colonies were extinct.

Park biologists first learned about population declines from community members who asked about the marmots. They described to park staff, who also had assumed the marmots were fine, common colonies in the southern reaches of the park that were no longer there. No one knew why.

Initially, Griffin thought lower snowpacks might be the cause, as Barash and other researchers had suggested that marmots need a good insulating snow layer to survive hibernation. Snowpack levels also change plant communities and abundance, so she wondered whether they weren't getting enough to eat. Every marmot that

Griffin studied, though, survived hibernation when the snowpack was much less than it was in the 1960s when Barash observed the animals. Several females even reproduced in consecutive years, perhaps because of earlier access to plants from earlier snowmelt.

Griffin then wondered if habitat loss, increased tourism around Hurricane Ridge, and more hikers and backpackers near remote colonies could affect the marmots. But that also wasn't the cause. No diseases were killing them, and inbreeding wasn't a problem.

During the winter, Griffin knew where marmots slept because she had previously implanted radio transmitters inside some of them to get better data. One year, she noticed coyote tracks in the snow leading from one burrow to another. "They were checking, 'Are the marmots up yet?'" Griffin says.

Once the marmots emerged, adult females were dying before they would normally have babies or begin nursing in June. Females were out in foggy weather and in the evening when other marmots were cozied up inside their burrows. "They were out a lot because they were hungry," Griffin says. "They were acting in a very easy-to-catch way for the coyotes."

Scientists studied nearly one thousand scat samples across the marmots' range. The majority belonged to coyotes. They hunted marmots in most regions of the park, the researchers found, and were marmots' primary predators. Scat also laid around recently extinct colonies, like those near Hurricane Ridge.

Some burrows that used to support marmot families are now empty. Of the 28 colonies observed since the 1950s, 40 percent are gone. At least five colonies went extinct sometime in the early 2000s near Klahhane Ridge.

They're not found at Deer Park anymore. Most are gone from the southern part of the park too, and no one has observed marmots colonizing new meadows in the entire park.

"I wasn't expecting coyotes," says Griffin, who studied the marmots for nearly ten years and helped the park establish a volunteer marmot monitoring program to track their populations. Biologists don't know how many marmots live in the park. Barash estimated in the 1960s that there might be about two thousand, but it's hard to know precise numbers of animals, especially given the remoteness and challenging terrain in the Olympics. The park says there might be less than one thousand marmots now.

Marmots here evolved with relatively few predators. They learned to live with cougars, bobcats, and golden eagles over the course of hundreds of thousands of years. Wolves typically didn't venture above sixteen hundred feet, so they didn't have many encounters with canines. They're relatively naive when it comes to coyotes.

When loggers clear-cut the lowland forests surrounding the park, coyotes came in. They're not forest animals and prefer to move through a habitat that's open, like a freshly logged forest. In the 1800s and early 1900s, newcomers to the area also thought gray wolves—who kept coyote populations in check and perhaps out of the park—posed a threat to their livestock. They killed so many that they went extinct by 1935. People reported the first coyotes in higher elevations in the Olympics soon afterward in the 1940s, which was also when marmots experienced a similar die-off.

Coyotes, it's thought, do well in low-snowpack years. When marmot populations declined in the 1940s, the park saw several unusually low-snow years. Snowpack ebbs and flows over decades as weather patterns change, but overall trends show a sharp decline in the last eighty years, with the lowest recorded snow levels in the 1990s and early 2000s when Griffin researched the marmots. "What we do know about marmot populations is consistent with coyotes being harder on them in low snow years than high snow years," she says.

Snowpack was relatively higher in subsequent years, which is also when the marmot population appeared stable. Surveyors from 2010 to 2015 even noticed marmots in colonies thought to be extinct. The park doesn't have any recent data analyzed to know how the marmots have since fared. Biologists are busy removing goats, reintroducing fishers, and researching martens—an ever-lengthy to-do list that keeps pushing marmots down on the park's priorities. Griffin's work, which is twenty years old, is the most recent in-depth look at the marmots, and the park's wildlife biologist Patti Happe says it's tough to get funding to do more research. So far, recent anecdotal reports of the marmots don't seem good, she says. "People who have repeatedly surveyed have said, 'Boy, I'm just not seeing them like I used to in these areas,'" Happe says.

Researchers and the Washington Department of Fish and Wildlife recommended that the park consider killing coyotes to save the marmots. When just one coyote was killed in the park in the early 2000s after threatening a child near Hurricane Ridge, marmot survival rates in nearby colonies jumped from 60 percent to 80 percent the next summer. Happe says it isn't feasible for the park to control the coyote population, and that reintroducing wolves is a more likely solution.

A wildlife biologist who confirmed wolves were gone from the peninsula in the 1930s also recommended that they be returned to the valleys once the national park was created in 1938. A 1974 management plan and 1981 National Park Service advisory board recommended staff start planning reintroduction programs. Decades have now passed, and wolves still aren't back. A 2018 study even found that the park is one of the best places to reintroduce the apex predator. When wolves returned to Yellowstone National Park in the 1990s, they quickly stabilized the ecosystem and created healthier elk herds. Perhaps more importantly for Olympic marmots, they cut Yellowstone's coyote population in half.

Neighboring Vancouver Island marmots died off to near extinction when logging and road building opened their habitat up to more predators. Just twenty-seven individual marmots were left in the wild two decades ago. Now, more than two hundred marmots live on the island after an intensive and expensive recovery program saved them. Conservationists acted just in time.

Wolves have naturally made their way back to Washington state, though they haven't crossed into areas west of Interstate 5 yet, and it's not guaranteed that they will. Reintroducing them remains on the park's to-do list, but such an endeavor will be slow to navigate through the muck of bureaucracy and politics.

Marmots might not have time to wait.

Moss

Carrie Woods furrows her brows, squints her eyes, leans forward, and looks closer.

"Another NecDou?" she asks her student researchers, referencing a type of moss, *Neckera douglasii*, or "Douglas' Neckera." She's hunched over, peering at what looks like a speck of tangled green thread—a moss in its infancy.

"Looks like a RhyLor," one of the students, Beatrice Bugos, says. "RhyLor" is short for *Rhytidiadelphus loreus*, commonly known as "lanky moss." Woods shines a flashlight on the plant anchored to a branch that's about a foot long and just over an inch wide. For an experiment, the researchers strung up the branch on a thin rope in this sixty-foot-tall bigleaf maple in Olympic National Park's Hoh Rainforest.

"I think I have to loupe it," Woods says. "My eyes."

The University of Puget Sound professor and plant ecologist grabs the small magnifying lens called a loupe that she wears around her neck like a whistle. She brings the branch less than an inch away from her face, peering with her right eye through the glass that makes the minuscule moss fourteen times larger.

"You're right. That is a little RhyLor," she says and laughs. "Jesus."

I observe nearby, as they get so close to the branch, and to each other, to identify these millimeter-sized bits of newly growing mosses that they sometimes bump the helmets they wear in case anything above them in the tree's canopy falls.

"What are these things?" Bugos asks.

"Those little brown things?" Woods replies. "I think it's some type of fungus."

Their eyes continually scan the branch, which to most people would look like nothing is growing on it.

"Ok, so IsoMyo," Woods says of the bits of *Isothecium myosuroides*, or "cattail moss," she spots. "Hold it right there," she says, wondering about another piece and inching closer with her lens as Bugos steadies the flashlight. She pulls the branch to her face, holds her breath, and steadies her gaze. "It's so hard. I cannot see that at all. I need your young eyes."

"It looks like . . ." Bugos trails off as she takes the branch, mumbling some of the scientific nicknames of moss and liverwort species they've come to know well here in the Hoh. She can't figure it out.

"It's unknown," Woods says to another student, Henry Norton, who takes notes on rainproof paper. She guides the branches that they call *tronquitos*—Spanish for "little trunks"—back up into the canopy on a pulley system they created in twelve bigleaf maple trees. The experiment is part of a four-year National Science Foundation-funded project created by ecologist and postdoctoral fellow Michelle Spicer in collaboration with Woods. The two scientists study epiphytes (plants that grow on plants, which includes mosses) in both temperate and tropical rainforests. Spicer created the same *tronquitos* experiment while studying in Panama's rainforests for her PhD. She recently recreated it to study in temperate rainforests too, like the Hoh.

As Woods gently tugs down on the rope, the *tronquitos* move up slowly, back into the high canopy so the researchers can see which mosses colonize the branches first. She starts singing the 1984 Eurythmics song "Here Comes the Rain Again," as water droplets hydrate sword ferns, which grow up to my waist and bounce off golden maple leaves much bigger than the size of my outstretched hand above and around us.

Even though she studies the smallest plants, Woods has a big personality. She yells powerfully, "Hey, bear!" every now and then as we walk through her field sites where black bears are common, just off the main road leading to the Hoh Rainforest Visitor Center on the western side of Olympic National Park. She climbs these trees for her research and insists that the Hoh's famous "Hall of

Mosses" trail be called "Hall of Bryophytes," as that's more scientifically accurate.

We live in one of the mossiest places in the world. Many basic ecological questions, though, remain unanswered about these tiny plants—the mosses, liverworts, and hornworts, known collectively as bryophytes. When trees are young, which species grows first on a branch? Who grows first on the trunk? Who are some of the last to grow? When they do find a home, how did they arrive? Have some mosses evolved to grow only on particular areas of a branch? Do they help each other? Do they compete? Do they make it easier for tree seedlings to grow on nurse logs? How many nutrients do they give to trees?

"When I came here, I thought that I wasn't gonna get anything done because everything's probably already been done," Woods says of one of the last remaining old-growth rainforests in the Northwest. "Well turns out, it was wide open, which is amazing because I can spend the rest of my life studying this system."

We work for eight hours under trees covered in thick green mats from their trunk to the highest branches that I can see. Mosses dangle from anywhere they can, like wispy stalactites. They wrap around every bit of wood becoming thick, poofy sweaters. Somewhere in the distance, we hear elk bugling. We stay relatively dry all day as rain drops rhythmically hit yellow leaves around us as is typical in the fall and winter here, the wettest place in the lower forty-eight. "Thank you mosses," Woods says, looking up at the plants that absorb rain like a sponge.

FIRST ON LAND

Before ferns, grasses, and trees, before any four-legged furry animals existed, and before land masses moved to the Northern Hemisphere, a group of plants made the radical move to live on land when most life was slimy or shelled in the sea. They first acquainted themselves with rocks 470 million years ago, taking what little oxygen the earth had at that time and made do as they spread across the barren land in their new world.

Within a few dozen million years, they carpeted the earth with what I imagine looked like miles of forest floor without anything else, only new, emerald life extending along the contours of the land as far as you can see. Their photosynthesizing powers released oxygen and cut Earth's carbon dioxide levels. They weathered rocks to create the first soil. The planet cooled and glaciers formed. These early, teeny-tiny new land plants created air that ferns, trees, and eventually, humans could breathe.

Ancestors to our modern mosses lived through a world that no one else knew. They somehow transitioned out of water and parted ways with their algae relatives. They survived mass extinctions and climate changes. They learned to adapt, to live with very little, even without water at times, and they kept going. They live nearly everywhere now.

Mosses, liverworts, and hornworts are all similar but differ in complex ways—their endless leaf shapes, textures, and life cycles. Liverworts are typically thicker and shinier, often with flatter leaves or no leaves at all. Hornworts have a flat, green base where green, horn-like spires grow, and to most people all hornworts all look similar and look like moss. Bryophytes are often described for what they don't have, which is a specialized conducting system that sends water and nutrients throughout their bodies. They lack true roots, don't flower, and don't have seeds. They're the simplest plants that get nutrients and water directly from air, rain, and fog. Plants with a vascular system can send nutrients through hardened tissues, which travel longer distances, allowing them to grow large and tall. Plants who lack this system are non-vascular and are, therefore, small.

Despite mosses' inability to grow big, the plants have had endless opportunities over millions of years to evolve unique ways to survive. They don't risk being eaten as they're not palatable to most animals, other than slugs, who may help spread their spores in their feces. Mosses can survive without water and can live underwater. They're found in caves, deserts, and the arctic. They can tumble dozens of feet from a tree branch, latch onto wherever they land, and start life again in a new home. Some types of moss can even photosynthesize while covered in snow—as long as it's not too thick. One moss who was locked away in a drawer with other dried plants for more than one hundred years came back to life with just a little light and water. Scientists also revived a moss estimated to be more than fifteen hundred years old found under Antarctic ice.

Some species have moss in their names, like Spanish moss, but they aren't actually moss. Spanish moss is a flowering plant in the pineapple family. Other moss-like individuals, such as old man's beard and witch's hair, drape elegantly from branches like some mosses, but they're lichens, which are not even plants but pairs of different organisms—a fungus and algae or cyanobacteria—who live together as one. Some of the longest moss-like draperies in the Hoh are *Selaginella oregana*, a vascular plant who grows on other plants. They're a deep green with hardy structures, which is why they become much longer than the mosses, hanging several feet off a branch.

Mosses are also plants that grow on plants, called epiphytes. Since they don't have true roots, they can anchor themselves wherever they want: on rocks, concrete, roofs, cars, or any unoccupied place. They attach tiny, thread-like rhizoids to their new home, which secure them to the surface, and they grow without taking nutrients from their host.

Some 11,000 moss species, 7,000 liverworts, and 220 hornworts are known globally. Just in Olympic National Park, hundreds of bryophyte species live in the park's diverse habitats, though scientists don't know much about those who live in the alpine or on rocks. Some mosses appear so similar to the naked eye, or even under a hand lens, that researchers need to look at them through a microscope to identify them.

Mosses take nutrients from the air and store them in their living and dead tissues, creating a unique, mineral-rich pool, which feeds the forest when a chunk falls off a tree, when an entire branch breaks, or when trees create specialized roots underneath these moss mats to directly absorb their nutrients. Birds, like the Pacific wren, rufous hummingbird, or the endangered marbled murrelet, use moss for their nests, and other birds feed on the small invertebrates who live in them, like the half-a-millimeter tardigrade. Mosses also help hold soil together to prevent erosion, and they might even help trees grow in the first place. Mosses have provided resources for Northwest Coast peoples, too, who used the plants' impressive absorption abilities as diapers and feminine products. Some people lined their shoes with moss for added insulation, and the plants' cushiness proved great for pillows and bedding. Other cultures used some moss species for dyes or spun them with animal hair to weave blankets.

Mosses need water to photosynthesize and reproduce, and they're designed to hold onto it. Some types, like *Sphagnum* moss, can absorb up to seven times their weight in water. Other species have hair-like structures on their leaves that cling to water droplets, while some have specially designed leaves, like long, thin leaf tips, which funnel water. Most mosses grow close together, squeezing tightly into small spaces to maximize water storage. All the moisture they absorb and hold onto keeps things in the forest humid and alive. "They're basically like sponges," says ecologist Michelle Spicer. "You have these giant sponges everywhere, and in the canopy, that can soak up the water and then redistribute the water."

The plants can also shut their system off completely when there's little water. They don't photosynthesize when things are too dry. Although they might look dead in the summer, they're only in a brief dormancy before they quickly green up with the first drop of rain.

Mosses were thought to be "evolutionary dead-ends," Woods says, because ever since they made it onto land, they didn't seem to change much. While other plants developed woody structures that sent them soaring above their petite neighbors to spread their seeds and pollen farther, mosses stayed small. Recent research using DNA-sequencing technology found that they've changed quite dynamically internally, even more so than seed plants, through complex adaptations within their structures that disperse their spores. These variations are too small for us to notice but show mosses' extreme reproductive diversity, a testament to their longevity and endurance since their beginnings on land.

THE RAINFOREST

It's quiet here. No faint refrigerator buzz. No horns or sirens. No cars rumble in the distance. Hardly any planes thunder across the sky. People are generally quiet, too. No headphones or earbuds. Just the sounds of the river, rain, birds, and if you're lucky in the fall, elk bugles. You might even notice how the wind sounds different blowing through Sitka spruce needles compared to bigleaf maple leaves when their subtleties aren't covered by artificial noise. The Hoh Rainforest is considered one of the quietest places in North America.

Trees here have been allowed to grow to their largest potential. Sitka spruces are nearly three-hundred feet tall in the relatively open forest where other plants, like bigleaf maples, also have room to grow big in the understory. Some of the largest known trees nationally and globally, like the biggest spruce, Douglas-fir, subalpine fir, western hemlock, mountain hemlock, yellow-cedar, and western redcedar all live within the peninsula near the Hoh, Queets, Quinault, and Bogachiel River valleys in some of the world's healthiest ecosystems. Mosses have had time to find suitable homes everywhere among hillsides of unlogged forests. So many mosses and other epiphytes live in bigleaf maples in Olympic rainforests that they make up four times the amount of photosynthetic material than the host tree itself.

I thought I knew what old-growth forests looked like living in western Oregon all my life. I didn't realize, though, how much life could exist together, until I visited the Hoh several years ago. Summer sunlight illuminated bigleaf maples that were nearly unrecognizable under the most luxurious moss I've ever seen. We walked through a field where ferns stood as tall as children. We came back the next year to experience the rainforest in October for my 30th birthday. I celebrated with the river, the rain, the mosses, the fungi, the elk, the trees, and the quiet, where age and time follow a different rhythm.

These ancient coastal rainforests once extended from southern Oregon to southeast Alaska, but most have been logged to unrecognizable versions of themselves. Just downstream from the national park, clear-cuts dominate the hillsides for miles.

Other temperate rainforests are found in a few areas in the Southern Hemisphere, like those in Chile, New Zealand, and Australia. Their nearness to ocean rain, fog, plentiful big trees with lots of downed wood, and moderate temperatures, give hundreds of species of epiphytic plants opportunities to grow. During our warm, dry summers, the forest receives less than four inches of rain a month. Nearly all of the Hoh's yearly average of 140 inches of rain falls between November and April.

The Hoh River is one of eleven major rivers in the Olympics that originate from glaciers more than six thousand feet above sea level and complete their journey to the ocean in just several dozen miles. Salmon, elk, deer, redcedars, and abundant plants along the entire watershed made life possible for people here who lived within seven different settlements along the water for thousands of years. So many salmon once lived in the river that one Hoh tribal elder said they could be seen swimming in schools, jumping, and finning. The Hoh earned its name from the Quinault language for the river, Hoxw, though no meaning has been associated with it. If there was an original meaning, it's since been lost. The Hoh people, who speak Quileute and live at the mouth of the river, call the river Chalak'At'sit, meaning the "southern river," as it was the southernmost waterway where Quileute speakers lived. I often read descriptions of these forests as "untouched," as though people have never been here. Families lived along the river. Babies were born here. The forests within the national park just haven't been touched by people seeking profit.

Trees here have grown enough branches, bumps, and nubs on their trunks to support what seems like unlimited moss colonies. Once they topple, their trunks lay on the forest floor for years and become nurseries for future trees and home to even more mosses. Here, Woods has found seventeen different species, compared to only six on the forest floor. When forests are logged, the world's most diverse and productive ecosystems transform into tree plantations. Doug-firs or western hemlocks are planted close together in monocrop tree farms to maximize profits. They'll grow for several decades, then be cut again, leaving no time or room for bigleaf maples and moss colonies to grow.

Warming temperatures are also threatening bigleaf maples here, as they've been declining in western Washington since 2011, especially in urban and suburban areas where they're more exposed. Woods worries that as temperatures increase, fewer wintertime clouds will protect the mosses who are adapted to low-light. "They don't want it to be too sunny," Woods says. "They're happy in the clouds."

ATTENTION

They take time to get to know and appreciate. Once they start growing on our homes, or porches or roofs, we associate them with age or neglect. Even scientists are biased against non-vascular plants, as 92 percent of articles in 2 prominent temperate forest journals from 2000 to 2017 were about trees, while the rest were about herbs, shrubs, and vines.

For their research, Woods and Spicer have a series of three, twenty-by-twenty-centimeter plots within three different heights on bigleaf maple branches and trunks. On one lower plot, the researchers removed the moss mat that had accumulated, a nearly four-inch-thick padding of tiny living and dead plants. Whatever starts growing on the newly exposed trunk will show Woods and Spicer who typically grows first, who follows, how they arrived, and how they interact. Another plot is in its natural state, an explosion of lime, emerald, chartreuse, and yellow all squeezed in together on just this little square, on just one section of the trunk, on just one tree. I gently press my hand against it, and it sinks in, like memory foam. I ask her to identify all the species she can see.

"I remember surveying this last year and was like, 'Oh my god,'" Woods says, as she bends down to look closer. "This one right here is rough moss. This is PorNav, the liverwort."

She carefully inches her fingers across the plot, looking and parting some of the plants to see who else lives here. "There's RhyLor, that's lanky moss. We have SelOre, *Selaginella*, it's the green-green color. And, oh my god, there's Menzies' tree moss. Look at that in there. Goodness."

She continues to scan. "There's MetMen, *Metaneckera menziesii*, it's related to NecDou."

"There's squishy," student researcher Bugos adds, as she touches the vivid lime green liverwort that looks and feels squishy. "What's the scientific name for squishy?" she asks. Woods doesn't know. Her eyes are focused, scanning the plot. "Electrified cattail over here. More tree moss. There's so much going on here. I remember getting to this plot and thinking, 'I'm never gonna finish.'

"And there's curly hypnum. I think that's curly hypnum, or maybe that's ClaCri," she says of a species, *Claopodium crispifolium*, or rough moss. "Crikey."

Within these plots, some fifteen moss and liverwort species can live together, and within the entire tree, more than thirty species coexist. Dozens of species grow next to and on top of each other creating layered moss mats everywhere—on nurse logs, branches, the entire trunk, and forest floor. If you look closely, you can tell different species apart by their tiny rounded or serrated leaves. Some leaves appear more translucent than others. They might grow off of a thin, naked stem or maybe decorate dozens of small, spindly stems, resembling little caterpillars. Under a microscope, some species' leaves reveal teeth along the edges that look like a shark's dorsal fin. Others have rounded edges. Staring at a chunk of moss on the trunk reminds me of *Magic Eye* photos, where everything looks like a blur at first, and then suddenly, I can see a clear picture. I notice who each of them are, their various shades of greens and yellows, where they live on a tree, or forest floor, and all their different personalities, as Woods describes them. I'm not sure what I saw when I looked at moss, or bryophytes, before. Maybe I thought they were all the same. I didn't pay enough attention.

Woods shows me lanky moss, *Rhytidiadelphus loreus*. From a main reddish stem, the plant grows other branched shoots, which are covered in stiff, slightly curved leaves that narrow at the tip and are the color of a green apple. "It's bushy. It's in the same genus as electrified cattail moss," she says of a similar moss that lives up to its name with fluorescent yellowish, greenish leaves that are also nearly translucent when you look close enough. "If you feel them, they feel like pipe cleaners," Woods says. "The end of electrified cattail moss 'whoofs,' though," she says, flicking her fingers out like an explosion. "The end of lanky moss doesn't."

Fan moss, *Rhizomnium glabrescens*, has leaves that look like the cutest little fans. The small, spoon-shaped, shiny leaves surround a naked stem and can grow up to three centimeters tall. We admired them on a nurse log next to dozens of spruce seedlings.

Menzies' tree moss, *Leucolepis acanthoneuron/menziesii*, looks like the teeniest, tiniest palm tree or umbrella. The stem reaches four to eight millimeters tall where it branches out into the shape of a palm, with pointed leaves that are one to two millimeters long. The moss grows only in the Pacific Northwest and is usually found low on the trunk. The Saanich people, of the San Juan Islands and east and north coasts of the Saanich Peninsula, created yellow dye from the plant for baskets.

A similar moss, *Climacium dendroides*, or simply tree moss, looks even more like a miniature tree, growing two to ten centimeters tall on stiff, upright stems. The plants are all connected by underground horizontal stems and together they resemble minuscule forests.

Woods shows me two feathery mosses of the same genus but different species. Initially, as she was learning about them, she thought she'd never figure out who's who. Gradually, she noticed their subtle differences. *Kindbergia oregana*, or Oregon beaked moss, looks like a petite fern and is thicker and more structured compared to its twin, *Kindbergia praelonga*, or slender beaked moss, whose leaves are messier, more haphazard.

Stair-step moss, *Hylocomium splendens*, is all over the forest floor and covers old nurse logs. The moss is tall—up to eight inches—and feathery. They live, on average, for eight years but can live for more than fifteen years. You can tell how old they are by how many "steps" or tiers of leaves they've grown.

Badge moss, *Plagiomnium insigne*, also typically lives on the forest floor. The leaves are large for what we imagine a moss to be, and they grow along the entire stem. Unlike most other mosses, badge moss leaves don't have a water-saving strategy to protect droplets from evaporating because they grow in places that are sufficiently wet year-round.

Cattail moss, *Isothecium myosuroides*, is usually an easy one to identify since it's the most common moss in the Hoh, dominating the understory with thick mats and slate-green wisps dangling from branches. Woods and her students initially thought they were two different species since they can grow in different ways depending on where they live. On top of branches, they grow like a bush. Then, eventually, they can send long bits to hang down. They also grow on the trunk and vine maples. They're everywhere.

Tree-ruffle liverwort, *Porella navicularis*, likes to grow vertically. Liverworts are shinier and flatter compared to mosses. "See, it looks like snakeskin," Woods says.

Then, there's *Selaginella oregana*. Along with licorice fern, they're the only two vascular epiphytes in the Hoh. The plant is waxier, smoother, and thicker because they have advanced nutrient- and water-conducting tissues.

A handful of moss species from the genus *Splachnum* grow only on feces. They specialize in coyote and elk scat, while others prefer owl pellets. They live in coastal bogs west of the Hoh and are rare, as their habitat has been destroyed by logging. Another rare species, *Discelium nudum*, grows on steep, silty, sandy cliffs along stream banks in the Hoh and Bogachiel Rivers. Some colonies have lived in sites for more than fifteen years, which was surprising to researchers given that their homes constantly erode from ever-changing stream and river flows. The moss doesn't have any leaves, just a capsule with structures that bury so deep into the cliff that they're ready to regrow when chunks of the stream banks fall off.

Perhaps most mesmerizing of all, goblin's gold, *Schistostega pennata*, shimmers under the shade of upturned tree roots. Though most identification books will say the plant is rare, they're actually quite common in old-growth forests, if you know where to look. The leaves are tiny, a millimeter or smaller. They have the ability to grow in low light, underneath root wads, or in caves because of lens-shaped cells called protonema that concentrate light. When sunlight hits the cells just right, the plant becomes luminescent with a greenish-gold glow. A beautiful luster.

REPRODUCTION

Moss behavior is complicated. Many moss colonies are either matriarchies or patriarchies, but more commonly they're female dominated. Other species, like *Sphagnum* or peat moss, take on male and female duties and produce both eggs and sperm. Some moss species reproduce both sexually and asexually, while others don't bother with sexual reproduction. They instead reproduce through cloning or fragmentation, when chunks of their colony fall off a branch or are carried by a bird somewhere.

Unlike flowering plants, mosses need water to reproduce, either sexually or asexually because they can't grow without it. Sperm cells are stored within the stem tip or bud-like leaf clusters of male plants, and when a raindrop falls on the plant, males release their sperm, which float up in protective membranes. As raindrops splash around the plants, the droplets containing sperm may fall onto the tip of a female stem. If enough droplets merge to form a water bridge, the sperm can swim across to a female plant, who lures them in by releasing sperm-attracting chemicals.

Once an egg is fertilized, the female plant grows a tall, one-inch stalk that shoots skyward. This skinny new growth contains an oval-shaped capsule at its tip where spores are stored. The structure is sometimes red, brown, green, or yellow depending on the species. I started noticing tall capsules regularly on moss in forests and in my neighborhood after reading Robin Wall Kimmerer's book *Gathering Moss* several years ago. These stalks, though, won't grow to become the next green, leafy moss generation. They're simply an in-between, Kimmerer explains, a facilitator for the next generation as their capsules harbor fertile spores that they'll release from their tower into the wind or a water droplet. If they land in a favorable spot where raindrops, fog, or dew wet the ground, the spores germinate.

The new growth spreads out, sending green threads across their new home until one starts to bud and forms new male and female plants that will repeat the cycle again.

FOCUS

Iwatsukiella leucotricha lives close to the sea. He likes humidity and lots of dew from lingering fog. He prefers views from high up along steep ridges in the upper branches of old fir trees. No one has found a female plant, so he might be the only one of his kind. He likely colonizes new branches by dispersing through the wind, or when birds, small mammals, or invertebrates transport him somewhere new, but no one knows for sure. He resembles a shag carpet with his densely branched stems that fade from orangish-red at the base, to yellow in the middle, and green near the tip. His leaves are sometimes less than a millimeter long and less than half a millimeter wide. No one knows much else about him.

He's confined to forests close to the ocean where rainfall is most intense and where fog perpetually drifts through the trees, keeping his minuscule leaves hydrated. Heavy coastal fog can provide these forests and mosses with more than thirty inches of moisture each year, which is almost the same amount of rainfall that Seattle sees annually. Initially, scientists thought he lived only in southeast Alaska, British Columbia, and two sites in Oregon's Coast Range—Saddle Mountain and Onion Peak—skipping Washington entirely. The gap in his range, though, are coastal forests from the Columbia River to the tip of the Olympic Peninsula, which have been so extensively logged that more than 150 miles of suitable homes he historically occupied are gone.

The US Forest Service in the early 2000s hired bryologist and botanist Martin Hutten to find this moss on the Olympic Peninsula. At first, Hutten didn't think he'd be able to locate the plant without having seen a specimen in person. He needed to get to know the moss's habitat, exactly what they look like when they're wet or dry, and where they grow in the southern part of their range. He read that the moss had been found somewhere on the 3,290-foot Saddle

Mountain, which is home to several rare plant species that don't grow anywhere else. So, Hutten studied what was known about the plant and set out to find them on the coastal mountain, near Seaside and Cannon Beach. "The Germans have a word for what botanists do," Hutten says. "They call it *fingerspitzengefühl*, which is basically the feeling in your fingertips. It describes that level of intuition that you have as a botanist."

He knew the moss prefers more light and typically lives high up in the tree canopy. Quickly, he found them on fallen noble fir branches on an exposed ridge on Saddle Mountain. "You get a feeling for it," he says. "Once you have that you can imagine, 'Well, this place on Saddle Mountain sort of feels like this place on the Olympic Peninsula," he says of a site near the Hoh River outside of the park. "So that's exactly what happened."

Although noble firs don't grow on the Olympic Peninsula, silver firs do, and Hutten knew the perfect spot above the south fork of the Hoh River to look for the moss: high on a sharp ridge where trees get plenty of light and wind that creates lots of fallen branches for Hutten to inspect. Within thirty minutes of arriving at the site, he found the moss—the first time it's been scientifically documented in Washington. "Then you have to pull out your hand lens to look at some fine details to verify that's indeed it," he says. The plant has a long hair point that has a "uniseriate" tip, which is a line of distinct cells. "So, when you know how to look for that, there's nothing you can mistake it with."

Hutten worked for Olympic National Park and spent a lot of time on the peninsula surveying mosses. He co-authored an identification book of common western Oregon and Washington mosses and helped compile the first survey of mosses, liverworts, hornworts, and lichens at sixty-five sites in the Olympics. There he found several rare species, some of which hadn't been seen in the lower forty-eight, including a few lichen species thought to be new to science. Hutten says the survey's scope was limited and didn't include plants in the rocky alpine or mosses that grow on rocks in lower elevations, which he describes as an entirely different and complex suite of species. He now works at Glacier Bay National

Park and Preserve in southeast Alaska, and in his free time he surveys nearby coastal islands for liverworts. He plans to publish an updated liverworts guide.

Hutten grew up in the Netherlands, where sulfurous air pollution killed off most of the country's mosses and lichens. When he moved to Oregon for graduate school, he was astonished. "I thought, 'What is all this stuff? Why is it here, and why don't we have it in the Netherlands?'" He studied lichens for a while, but when he realized how few people study bryophytes, he shifted to mosses, and now specializes in the even lesser-known liverworts. "Most people don't care about bryophytes," he says, "They are small. People relate to things that are more glamorous, or charismatic, and bryophytes aren't really that for most people." He regularly finds new species—dozens new to southeast Alaska—that are easy to miss but also hard to get to in largely roadless, trailless terrain only accessible via boat in choppy, dangerous waters. He often finds the most diversity of non-vascular plants around yellow-cedars in Alaska. "Out here, the bark is perfect for a wide suite for leafy liverworts," he says.

"There's so much more out there than you think," he says of noticing bryophytes. "Habitat is very three dimensional. It's not just looking for mushrooms, which is difficult enough as it is, but they're always on the ground, more or less. But these mosses, they're everywhere. They're up in the trees, they're on the ground, they're in the stream, on the water, it is absolutely overwhelming," he says. "It takes a little while."

ARRIVAL

Some prefer the lower trunk. Others live higher up. Some thrive on the inner branches, while some prefer the bare wood of thin outer branches. Although they can live in nearly any place, once mosses choose their habitat, they become picky. They develop their own preferences within a single bigleaf maple.

Since the late 1800s, researchers, including both Woods and Spicer, have studied epiphytes in tropical rainforests, but the plants in temperate rainforests haven't received as much attention. Pioneering research about Olympic rainforests in the 1980s by forest ecologist Nalini Nadkarni focused mainly on how these moss and epiphyte communities contribute to their ecosystems, or the trees they're growing on, rather than the lives of the plants themselves. "It's a much more complicated community than even I would have thought when I first saw these forests," says Spicer, who started researching the plants with Woods at the University of Puget Sound after earning her doctorate at the University of Pittsburgh in 2019. They're the first to dive deep into patterns of bryophyte diversity and the processes that maintain that diversity within trees here in Northwest rainforests.

The researchers want to learn how and when each species starts to grow on bigleaf maple trees, known in ecology as succession. The small branches they observe hanging in the trees may give them a sense of the plants' primary succession at different heights in the canopy, as the branches were sterilized before being strung up. They also have plots on various heights on the trunk, including some so high up that they have to climb the trees they're studying—a sometimes painstaking and dangerous process that makes me realize why other scientists might have skipped studying plants high above the forest floor. They use an eight-foot-tall slingshot to send a throwline that is then tied to a rope to pull their climbing ropes up and over a sturdy branch. Sometimes, they'll search for hours to simply find a safe tree to climb, let alone execute the perfect shot to start their ascent using a seat harness, leg loops, and climbing ascenders. They send their ropes close to the trunk for more stability, but the branches are covered in so much thick moss and other epiphyte growth that they must use the strength of their entire body to pull the rope through the mats. On her first attempt to climb a tree in the Hoh, Woods says it took her four-and-a-half hours to successfully set up.

Woods' research found that two species, *Neckera douglasii*, or Douglas' Neckera, and *Isothecium myosuroides*, or cattail moss, dominate thin, bare branches in the outer crown in bigleaf maples, vine maples, and other understory Northwest trees. These species start their lives flat against the branch until they eventually become long enough that they drape down like macramé. They choose the outer branches, in part, because they might not be able to grow among the thick mats of *Rhytidiadelphus loreus*, lanky moss, and *Selaginella oregana*, which are commonly found in the inner and mid-branches, though *Selaginella* can also grow on the lower trunk.

I now think of all these unique microhabitats that exist within just one tree. I love knowing that the outer crowns of trees resemble young trees, as Woods taught me. The epiphyte species that grow on the farthest reaches of the branches are those that they think may be among the first to colonize trees. The farther in toward the trunk, the older the tree becomes as you move through their growth, with different moss residents who have different growing preferences. All of these homes within trees, at various heights above ground with various branch sizes, may actually be more important for determining who lives where in these temperate rainforests, rather than the previously assumed availability of moisture.

Some mosses, like *Metaneckera menziesii*, or Menzies' Neckera, don't do well when they grow horizontally on trunks. The stiffer, wavy-leaved moss is usually found vertically on the trunk. They started to brown when Spicer cut a chunk off the trunk and laid them horizontally on a table in the forest to see how they reacted to their new orientation. The moss began creeping down the table, trying to grow upright again.

Bigleaf maple trees host more mosses than any other tree in the rainforest. Though scientists don't know exactly why they attract more bryophytes, one reason could be that maples provide more places for mosses and other epiphytes to grow, Spicer tells me. They're branchy from their trunks to their crowns, giving mosses and liverworts plenty of livable space, while conifers tend to drop their lower branches as they grow. Another reason could be the tree's bark, Spicer explains. It's grooved, doesn't flake off much, and is chemically different from the longer-living conifers who have more defenses and exude chemicals that aren't so great for mosses to grow on.

Bigleaf maples are also one of just a few known trees that grow specialized roots on branches anywhere from six to sixty feet above the forest floor to acquire nutrients from bryophytes. When mosses, liverworts, and other epiphytes grow on branches for a long time, they create their own unique soil, or mats, made up of living and dead plants. The trees send roots, called adventitious roots, up and under the branch mats that become so thick they look like a triple layer, sixteen-inch-tall chocolate cake when cut open. Life on life on life, as acclaimed ecologist Nalini Nadkarni once described it. Nadkarni discovered the roots in the early 1980s and was the first to climb trees to research epiphytes in Olympic rainforests.

TREE LOUNGE

Ellen Bradley fell asleep twenty-five feet up in a bigleaf maple. A huge branch shaped like a chaise lounge supported her, with moss mats several inches thick like a mattress. "It was the best nap I've ever taken," Bradley says. "The whole time I felt the moss was kind of hugging me back, and saying, 'It's ok, you can rest here. You're safe with us.'"

Bradley calls the spot the "tree lounge." After graduating from Gonzaga University, she worked with Spicer and Woods during the summer of 2020 for seven weeks in the rainforest when the coronavirus shut the human world down. Bradley and Spicer worked in trees fifteen to sixty-five feet above ground, spending hours in the canopy, experiencing a new world and gaining new perspectives. "I hadn't spent a lot of time looking at mosses up close and personal like that," Bradley says. "I never appreciated how much moss species diversity we have in the Pacific Northwest, but that becomes super evident when you're twenty meters up in a tree."

From the trees, she could see alders lining the Hoh River, and the mountains rising up beyond the water. She once looked down on a bear walking among the ferns.

Now, on hikes with friends, she stops to observe mosses. She'll notice when the plants have reproductive capsules that they use to spread their spores, and she'll point them out. "I've become the person on every hike or backpack or camping trip, no matter where I am, no matter what environment, if I see mosses, I'll stop and really try to examine them. And people are always like, 'What are you doing?' And I say, 'It's a moss!'

"I'll forever look for moss in all the places I go," she says.

She was able to visit the rainforest again the following summer, to see how the mosses she studied progressed and visit the tree lounge. Bradley, who is an enrolled member of the Tlingit tribe of southeast Alaska, found that days in the trees with the moss helped her process the climate crisis, racial reckoning, and personal trauma during the pandemic. "I realized my connection to the Hoh is that it reminds me of the traditional homelands of my tribe," she says.

The Tlingit's territory stretched from the Tongass area, anywhere between the ocean and the mountains. "Tlingit translated loosely means, 'people of the tide,'" she says, "so I come from a place of rainforests. Of rainforests that are closely connected to the ocean and in temperate areas. The Olympic Peninsula, and the Hoh specifically, really reminds me of home.

"I think being there and being able to experience sitting in one place in a branch for many hours and developing really intimate relationships with some of these species around us allowed me to process a lot of that removal from my home and the whole historical context behind that," she says. "And just being allowed to feel with other people's ancestors because we were visitors on Hoh and Quileute land. So, it felt to me an embracing of those ancestors, that this was also a safe space for me to feel at home to process some of that trauma."

She rested again, up in the canopy, looking out to the river and the mountains, held by the mosses.

UNKNOWN

Woods is endlessly curious and has endless research ideas. The night before we survey their study sites, she explains during dinner the exact chemical process that turns leaves colors in the fall and sums up the evolution of plants in a way that made perfect sense.

"One of the things I'd love to do is extract DNA and select for tardigrades because tardigrades live in liverworts," she says of the microscopic animal, also known as a water bear. "So if we had estimates of biomass and abundance in this whole tree, and if we knew an estimate of tardigrades in PorNav [a liverwort], we could say that one single bigleaf maple in the Hoh Rainforest holds ten billion tardigrades, or some crazy number," she says, excitedly, opening her arms wide and looking up at the trees.

"One of my biggest beefs with bryophyte work is historically people have lumped lichens and bryophytes and called them 'cryptogams,'" she says, and slaps her hands on her hips and looks at me with one eyebrow up, flabbergasted, offended. "They call it the 'cryptogam cover' but they don't differentiate the percentage cover of a bryophyte or a lichen, nor do they differentiate the species of moss or bryophytes. They just say 'moss,'" as she lazily points to some moss as if they're all the same. "The research that we're finding is that each of these has a personality and that plays out in different ways. They're found in different areas of the [tree's] crown, and my research on nurse logs," she interrupts herself, smiling, before she gets into it.

"You're often taught that nurse logs are so beneficial to the forest," she says. "And I'm looking around thinking, 'Not all nurse logs are created equal.' There're differences. What's causing the differences? And I think," she says through a smile, "that the main differences are the moss communities. So if you put this in context—and ahh this is lovely," she says as her smile widens, while grounding her feet evenly on the forest floor. "This means that the giants of the forest, their dynamics, are governed by the tiniest plants. Isn't that fun to think about?"

So, how did each giant spruce grow here in the Hoh? Woods thinks, and other research has suggested, that its seedling landed in the perfect spot at the perfect time, on a young enough nurse log with certain mosses that helped nurture and facilitate its growth. It wasn't inhibited by thick, taller mosses, and the tree made it. "The moss matters," she says.

Some of the first mosses who grow on nurse logs are fan moss, wavy leaf cotton moss, and a liverwort, *Scapania bolanderi*, which was found to facilitate seedling growth in Japan. These tiny plants may help trees mature by providing protection from herbivores and wind, increased moisture and nutrients, and humus for the seedlings to take root. As nurse logs age and decay, the moss communities change, and it's thought that the relationships between the plants and seedlings transition from facilitation to competition.

Stair-step moss may be a final colonizer in forests, as they're found covering the forest floor and nurse logs that are more than thirty years old. The large moss is thought to be too big for any fresh seedlings to survive in it. As we walk around her field sites in the Hoh, I start to look for the moss on nurse logs, and sure enough, when they're covering a decaying log, not as many tree seedlings grow. Some larger seedlings might poke through the moss, but they likely took root and survived before the moss took over.

One of her students dissected moss mats and teased all the different species out. She noticed that one moss, *Orthotrichum lyellii*, and fan moss, were consistently underneath at the very bottom of the mats. Woods wonders if these two mosses kick-start the entire growth of moss communities in the canopy.

"When I walked in that forest, I was like, 'Wow, the story *is* moss.' The story is moss," she says of the Hoh. "And if I'm going to honor the system and really try to understand the system, I have to honor the moss because that's the story. They're the main players here.

"And there are a million unanswered questions."

Clouds

We live with them, with their ever-changing shape and movement, their varying moods and power. They sometimes ride a band of strong winds always blowing high above, raining droplets down on us, made from water that sharks, squids, whales, crabs, and schools of tiny fish once swam through.

We live with them, here, in the sky. They're grounded by their lack of form. The same air and water and wind that passes through our world shapes their world and brings them life, as they shape us and bring us life.

We share the sky with them. We live at the bottom, and they live throughout in their floating world.

"Look at that cloud passing," artist Binky Walker says as we admire the sky from downtown Portland. "Just that subtle shift in color as it's moving. Right in the center, there are very slight clouds underneath. They'll probably just disappear. Very quickly they'll be gone in plain sight. There it goes. It just . . . recedes into whatever."

We watch the clouds together for two hours like old friends reminiscing while looking at photographs. We share a love of their formless form, their acceptance, as she describes it. Their ability to continually transform from gradients of light and dark grays to whites, silvery blues, and morning golds, all mixed in and interacting like a live watercolor. One moment the sky is a slate wall and it's raining, then suddenly the clouds break and reveal hints of blue. Walker points out how they experience light in ways that we can't. As ground creatures, we feel light only from above, but the sun can illuminate clouds entirely—from above, below, and within.

"It always annoys me the signs or sayings that say, 'the clouds will pass,' or 'the sun will reappear.' I want the clouds," she says, smiling. "We're always trying to get to the happy, sunny days. But the weather is here. What is it like to rest in that instead? What is it like to rest inside your own weather, too? We don't need to wish it away."

They make the invisible, visible. They're manifestations of what's present in the air on a given day. They transfer water across the globe and balance Earth's energy. Our human mind isn't even capable of comprehending just how much energy they carry, yet our same mind typically wants them gone. We've even created them ourselves to make rain for warfare and end droughts, but we don't understand all the intricacies or the consequences. We devised long equations to predict their behavior, but they still reserve the ultimate say. We don't know precisely what they'll do, and I find their unpredictability and disregard for us oddly calming. They are complex and mighty, yet soft. They can weigh tens of millions of tons, yet they float. And though we often wish them away, they cool us and keep us warm overnight, tucking us in under their blanket stretched across the sky.

APPRECIATION

My mom and I love dark October mornings when the first frost covers the grass and the neighbors' roofs and fog softens the silhouettes of trees down the block. We would walk extra slowly to school on those mornings, crunching leaves and admiring the arrival of a colder season.

She still sends me a message when it's frosty or foggy out. She tells me to go look at the sunset when the clouds are especially ethereal and sends me a message when the crescent moon is peeking through moody clouds. She still remembers how she'd lay in the grass as a kid, next to an apricot tree in a bright-yellow two-piece outfit and stare up at the sky, watching the clouds form shapes for hours. Her favorite Beatles song growing up was "The Long and Winding Road," and I think that explains her ever-present nostalgia. She taught me to love sad songs and to appreciate what many people don't—the clouds.

Fall is a sentimental season for me: I was born in October and love everything about the season—the colors, pumpkins, sweaters, warm drinks, and welcome change in weather. It's always been my favorite, but I appreciate the clouds and rain even more now, as our summers grow drier and hotter. The first rain is like a deep breath, a rejuvenating sigh of relief.

My partner and I took an online cloud identification class during the pandemic taught by Gavin Pretor-Pinney, the founder of the Cloud Appreciation Society, a United Kingdom-based hub for cloud lovers. It was our first experience in the new Zoom world that we'd live in for a while. We learned about different types of clouds: how they form, and how they appear in paintings, stories, and songs from all over the world. When we think about clouds as not simply getting in the way of the sun, Pretor-Pinney told us, then we can access nature's poetry from anywhere in the world. It's free to all of us.

During the pandemic, I found myself thinking about the world on a larger, longer scale. We were living through things I'd only read about in history books. With all the death, sickness, and loss in our world, the natural world also reminded me of our impermanence, not in an anxiety-inducing way, but in a soft, assuring, comforting way. Like the clouds, we continue to mold and take on new forms.

Without any deadlines, my days felt as open as they were during the summer as a kid. I had time to think, to wonder, and to look up. My partner and I would take long walks with no destination. We'd walk in the middle of the street, since no one was driving anywhere, and look at the sky, our only glimpse into something larger and real, beyond our virtual world. We began calling the clouds by their names: *Cumulus congestus, Nimbostratus, Altocumulus.* We thought we saw a horseshoe vortex cloud that appeared iridescent one sunset. We noticed more color variations, the silvers and mauves, browns and yellows, not just simply gray. When thick *Nimbostratus* rain clouds covered our skies, I imagined the view from space, knowing that clouds over the Pacific Northwest probably stretch for a few dozen miles, maybe hundreds, connecting different towns and people together under one powerful expanse of water droplets and ice crystals. We're under clouds together, and at any point, two-thirds of the earth is covered in them, too.

Every morning, Walker began her day with a meditation, communing with the sky. From her tiny fifth-floor apartment in Paris with windows for walls, she'd sip tea with her new floating friends, taking thousands of photos of them. She'd then choose her preferred photos and draw them with graphite pencils for several hours—an attempt to slow them down, to process their movement, and try to capture their changing form into one moment. She paired three drawings together, with each one representing a photo taken thirty seconds or a minute after the preceding one. In total, she drew six different three-part series. The clouds evolved, subtly. The light shined through in new ways. In one series, layer-like clouds cover nearly half of the frame horizontally, like looking up at them while lying on the ground. Their horizon is jagged, ever-moving wisps. By the third drawing, their edge has morphed, thinned, and feathered into a new form.

"I wanted to know them the way I know a friend," Walker says. "To spend time getting to know them. They're on their own trajectory, and I became very curious. Everything about them is so different from how I move, and I exist. And I really wanted to understand. So, I thought, 'Can I slow that down? Can I just be with them? Can I be with them and just take that ride with them?'

"When I can attend to something, it becomes more beautiful to me."

Walker finished and showed her series in Seattle, calling the work "Ukiyo-e: Pictures of the Floating World." Ukiyo-e is a Japanese art form developed during the seventeenth through nineteenth centuries that depicts moments on detailed woodblock prints, like *Under the Wave off Kanagawa*.

"It's sorrowful beauty—that feeling when we want to hold onto a moment and we can't hold onto it, and then it changes into something else, and they have a word for that," Walker says of Ukiyo-e. "They have an entire art form about exploring that moment you want to grasp onto and that is passing you at the same time."

Often, artists created picture books simply for observation. "The idea was that you would go by yourself, and you would contemplate these different scenes that were just moments. I wanted other people to be able to inhabit that same kind of attention, that quietness that comes just from when you really look at something. And you really decide to be with something."

FORM

Below us, a thick layer of white flooded the valleys and lowlands from Mount St. Helens to Mount Rainier and as far west as I could see. Occasional peaks poked through like islands in the sky. My partner and I watched the sunrise from High Camp, on the northwestern side of Mount Adams, as a layer of falling ice crystals revealed themselves as white brushstrokes that texturized the pastel sky. Even at nearly seven-thousand feet, the wispy clouds still seemed so high up. We were in the middle layer. We even saw the mountain's own shadow, a pyramid stretching along the sea of low clouds.

I had a similar vantage point while climbing Mount St. Helens a few years ago. We had nearly finished scrambling up twenty-five hundred feet, when my fear of heights kicked in, and then calmed when I looked behind me and saw nothing but clouds below us and Mount Adams and Mount Hood in the distance. It was just us, the mountains, and the clouds.

I often think of what our common cloud layer must look like from higher up, how their shape and expanse is much greater than we can see from the ground. I let my mind wander and imagine what the entire western Cascades region's cloud cover looks like on a certain day, how it changes from hour to hour, moment to moment. Maybe the clouds are lingering over us, from Seattle to Eugene, or perhaps they're in patches, with other cloud types layered on top of each other that we can't see, swelling, dissipating, and reforming all at the same time.

Our sky is like an ocean. A sea full of gasses, temperatures, pressures, and winds that change and move and flow and interact with each other like tides and currents. The word for Earth's lowest atmospheric layer that we live in, the troposphere, means change. Here, the air is in constant flux, causing weather and clouds. The troposphere extends five to nine miles up from the ground, depending on where you live, as air is thinner closer to the poles and thicker toward the tropics, extending the height of the sky.

Water from oceans, lakes, rivers, puddles, buildings, or any surface evaporates and transforms from a liquid to an invisible gas: water vapor. Plants also release water vapor into the air through their leaves. Water is always present in our atmosphere, though to form clouds, water molecules need a couple other ingredients: something to latch onto, like a speck of dust, and cooler temperatures. Water molecules are too small to bond together on their own. Once they find a microscopic friend, called a cloud seed, like dust, soil, sea salt, smoke, or airborne bacteria, they join and develop into a cloud. The next step is to find air that is cool enough above ground that will transform molecules into a liquid droplet or ice crystal, and when enough of them gather together—billions and billions—they'll become a visible cloud.

Air, though, needs to be lifted to form clouds, unless the temperature is cold enough at ground level, resulting in fog. Air can rise in a variety of ways, on small, local scales, or large, global scales that create our weather patterns and climate. The earth's surface is unevenly heated, and when a part of the land becomes warm enough, air will move upward in thermals. If there's enough solar energy, thermals can be everywhere. They're the shimmering blur we see on roads or sidewalks. Warm air is less dense, and its buoyancy sends it up until it reaches cool enough temperatures where water molecules condense and a poofy, white cloud appears: *Cumulus*.

A freshly formed *Cumulus* cloud has a flat bottom, the moment where water transforms from a gas to a liquid. *Cumulus*, Latin for heap, are clumpy, detached clouds—what most people imagine when they think of a cloud. They form at low to mid-levels, between two- to three-thousand feet, and they live for just ten minutes until they dissipate and become something else. Even though the average *Cumulus* cloud weighs as much as sixteen gray whales, they stay airborne because as water vapor condenses, the chemical process releases heat and keeps the cloud aloft, like a hot air balloon. The cloud constantly billows and expands all while other droplets evaporate as they encounter new, drier air in the ever-changing movement of the atmosphere.

Cumulus is one of the four main types of clouds that are categorized by their form, altitude, and function. *Stratus*, Latin for flattened or spread out, are clouds that extend for miles, like a gray or white sheet covering the sky, like those filling the lowlands we observed from Mount Adams. They're familiar friends here, mostly featureless, tender, and unpopular, the so-called dreary clouds that linger. They're the lowest clouds, typically staying below sixty-five hundred feet and can even appear at ground level as fog or mist. They can be thick (*Stratus nebulosus*), allowing little sunlight to get through, keeping us cool. Or they can be thin (*Stratus fractus*), giving us glimpses of different textures and possibly the sun beyond them. Different from *Cumulus*, they form not from thermals but when a large mass of air rises at the same time, typically when it encounters a mass of cooler air in a calm, gentle breeze. The warmer air lifts, and as it rises, it cools and forms a smooth, soft *Stratus* cloud.

Cirrus clouds live in the highest reaches of the troposphere and appear wispy or, as their Latin name means, like a curl of hair. Their elegant form is what it looks like when ice crystals fall at 100 or more miles per hour from 16,500 to 45,000 feet above us. They sometimes have feather-like tails or hooks, brush strokes caused by the differing winds, temperatures, and humidity of the air they're descending through until they evaporate. At any point, they cover nearly one-third of the earth and keep us warm by trapping outgoing heat. They form when water vapor latches and freezes onto mineral dust carried across the globe from arid places, like the Sahara and Gobi Deserts. Water molecules can also attach to dust from agriculture, industry, and metallic particles—like lead, copper, and zinc—which are thought to have originated from smelters, small planes, and open-pit electronic burning.

Nimbus, Latin for rain, are thick, dark, precipitating clouds. Though *Stratus* clouds can sometimes drop light drizzles, any significant rain, snow, or ice that makes its way down to us comes from *Nimbostratus*. They can stretch across thousands of square miles, are the thickest clouds, and have the potential to grow taller than Mount Rainier. They form two to eighteen thousand feet up and are most common in mid-latitudes, like the Northwest. If there's hail, lightning, or thunder, it's originating from the mighty *Cumulonimbus*, common in warmer climates. From the humble *Cumulus*, these clouds get taller and taller and taller, fueled by warm, moist air, until they reach the top of a troposphere at forty-five to sixty thousand feet. Reaching this height halts their growth as their tops start icing and flattening, creating what's called an anvil top. Unlike *Nimbostratus* who sticks around for hours, *Cumulonimbus* release their moisture rapidly and dissipate.

Much of the rain that falls on us originates as ice crystals, or snowflakes, in the frigid upper parts of thick *Nimbostratus* clouds. Ice crystals bump into each other, join together, and expand into snowflakes that grow heavy enough to fall through the cloud. As they fall, they journey through a warmer, lower section of the cloud, where they melt and form a rain drop that eventually makes its way to us. Some rain, though, like that from atmospheric rivers, begins in the warmer section of the cloud. When raindrops are large, they were once snowflakes, and when they're small, they were always water droplets.

These basic four cloud forms are included and expanded into ten different types: *Stratus, Stratocumulus, Cumulonimbus, Cumulus, Nimbostratus, Altostratus, Altocumulus, Cirrostratus, Cirrocumulus*, and *Cirrus*. They can take on many variations with their prefixes explaining their form or altitude and added descriptors tagged on to the end, like *Cirrocumulus stratiformis undulatus*, puffy cloudlets rippling high across the sky in waves like fish scales, often called "mackerel sky," which typically hint to a change in weather, for the worse.

Stratocumulus is a familiar friend of ours, a low cloud, never higher than sixty-five hundred feet and often found covering the ocean, like sunscreen reflecting sunlight. It's the most common cloud on Earth, covering about 20 percent of tropical oceans.

Altocumulus are *Cumulus* clouds that are higher up, at sixty-five hundred to eighteen thousand feet, and thus appear smaller to us. They look like cotton balls arranged neatly across the sky, though they can take on different patterns. Portland experienced a sunrise so awe striking in January 2020 when *Altocumulus radiatus* waved across the sky, almost in a corduroy texture. *Radiatus* meaning "with rays," the clouds slightly zig-zagged parallel to each other, seemingly converging toward the horizon and separated by bits of blue above them. Warm, pink light illuminated their bases. Had they not been there, the sky would have been empty. The clouds made it beautiful.

Smooth, silky lens-shaped clouds that appear over or near mountains are another type of *Altocumulus* cloud called *Altocumulus lenticularis*. They form when generally stable air moves over a mountain, condenses, and turns into a stationary cloud, downwind of the crest or spread throughout the area, as waves of air pass through them. They reveal to us an additional way that clouds form—when air is forced over hills or mountains and condenses as it lifts. Other similar clouds, like cap clouds, form as air rises over mountains, though these clouds remain at the summit, giving the mountain a hat. Another type, a banner cloud, forms like a cape along the eastern, less turbulent side of the mountain.

Some unique clouds are considered only a fleeting extension of the ten main types, when, under the right conditions, they reveal themselves, like rare wave clouds, called Kelvin-Helmholtz or *fluctus*. This *Cirrus* formation appears when air is unstable, usually at higher altitudes. My mom, dad, partner, and I saw some as we watched the sunrise last Halloween at Larch Mountain, just northwest of Mount Hood. They were orangish-pink ocean waves one moment, and already fading the next, a blurred wash of light blue blotches. They form when winds blow at different speeds, especially within mountainous areas, where strong gusts blow higher up, creating uniform breaking waves across the cloud layer. Later that day, from Parkdale, we watched some combination of cap and banner clouds hang around Mount Hood. On the western, windy side of the mountain, ever-changing wispier clouds transformed from a crocodile into a frog that became a dragon that turned into a mouse.

The newest recognized cloud type, thanks to Gavin Pretor-Pinney's insistence on its formal recognition, is called *Asperitas*, and it's oddly one of my favorites. They're not especially charismatic and seem to form within a layer of gray. But they give intriguing definition, a new perspective to the sky, making me feel as if I'm either looking at a mountain range or the entire sky flipped upside down. The clouds look like turbulent water from underneath the surface, which is where their Latin name comes from, meaning roughness (to describe choppy water). Scientists aren't yet sure how they form, but they prefer unstable air. I saw some recently near my house, stretching across the entire southern part of the sky, with a Safeway in the foreground, and the rough, powerful sea of clouds passing behind it.

POWER

Storms connote negativity. Merriam-Webster tells me they're "violent," a "tumultuous outburst," a "disturbance." The wind and the earth's temperatures, though, are just doing what they naturally do on this orbiting rock. Is that violent? Violence from my human lens carries an intent to hurt or destroy. We often compare weather to warfare, saying that *Cumulonimbus* clouds pack the same energy as ten atomic bombs. Even the term "polar front" comes from combat when a group of Norwegian meteorologists studied Earth's air movement soon after World War I.

Of course, storms cause damage and take human lives, but that's not their intention. We just happen to be in their path. They're not ready for combat. The storms themselves are simply fulfilling the fundamental task of distributing Earth's temperature and water. Is it accurate to say the atmosphere is being disturbed? Disturbed compared to what? Clear skies and no winds and no water transport? Is the atmosphere violent? If hot and cold air didn't collide to create winds and rains, we wouldn't have our Northwest ecosystems, or the world as we know it. I don't know what else to call storms, but I like to think of them not as tumultuous outbursts, but rather just a natural, enchanting process of living in a dynamic place.

Despite what you might think or what people may tell you, Pacific Northwest cities receive less rain during the year than many East Coast cities, like New York City and Miami, whose regular summer thunderstorms release enormous amounts of rain. Even within the Northwest, rainfall varies drastically depending on where you live. The Cascade and Olympic Mountains suck most of the moisture out of clouds, leaving little for those who live to the east and creating the most dramatic regional precipitation differences in North America.

In the summer, we're one of the driest places in the nation, keeping eastern Oregon and Washington's sagebrush, junipers, and ponderosa pines happy. Even on the wetter western side of the mountains, we see little rainfall in the summer. Klamath Falls, Oregon's "city of sunshine," has three-hundred days of blue skies each year, and most of the southern Oregon town's precipitation falls as snow from November to February. The Cascades protect us western valley dwellers from cold, westward-moving air that chills the interior part of the country and those living east of the mountains.

Though we're not the wettest, our rainfall is more consistent compared to larger gaps in storms on the East Coast. Portland and Seattle see many cloudy days, especially in the fall and winter when we're in the path of a narrow band of high westerly winds, the jet stream, that regularly send enormous amounts of moisture—and clouds—to us. It's a gift from the poles, the equator, the ocean, and ultimately, the sun.

Since Earth isn't heated evenly, warm, moist air from the tropics eventually meets with cold, dry air from the poles in mid-latitudes where we live. When these two air masses meet, they create pressure differences, which creates wind, which creates more temperature changes, and all these things interact together to create weather as the earth tries to reconcile her varying temperatures.

During fall and winter, when the temperature difference is most extreme between the poles and equator, the jet stream blows strongest, sending rain and clouds to us. The winds live in the mid to upper levels of the troposphere about 5 to 8 miles above us, blowing air from west to east at 110 miles per hour, sometimes as strong as 250 miles per hour. In the summer, the jet stream points toward Alaska and British Columbia, and as colder months progress, the winds move south toward Washington and Oregon and, later in winter, toward California. They undulate and move like huge waves flowing north and south, and although they generally blow west to east, they can change unpredictably, sending powerful winds and rains where people aren't expecting them.

"These waves are manifested into large storm systems, a whole system of clouds," says atmospheric scientist and University of Washington professor Lynn McMurdie, who studies storms and is currently working with NASA to understand East Coast snow-storms. "It has its own lifecycle," she says of the storms. "It travels from the ocean, travels to Washington state, changes again, makes a new storm over Montana, and then changes again and makes a new storm over New England. Each storm is unique and has its own distribution of clouds."

These systems, called mid-latitude cyclones, show another way that air is forced up to make clouds, McMurdie explains, but they're much bigger and broader than clouds forming over local thermals or mountain ranges. From space, the cyclones are a stunning spiral of white that sometimes stretch from Canada to California, bringing with them essential water and snow to nourish our landscapes and provide us with drinking water.

There's a quote I love from Maya Angelou where she says that you can learn a lot about someone based on how they handle lost luggage, tangled Christmas tree lights, and rainy days. I think of our rain as connecting us to the tropics, whose heat gives these weather patterns their momentum. The perpetually warm weather around Hawaii and places farther south causes more evaporation over the ocean, and therefore more water vapor that eventually makes its way to us as rain.

ORIGIN

When it rains, where has the water that splashes off my shoulders been? Fifty miles off the Oregon Coast? One-hundred miles? Or, farther, from the warm southern Pacific? What has the water molecule's journey been before this one?

To know, scientists would have to trace a single molecule's path across the Pacific Ocean, and no study has attempted that yet. They do know, though, that the rainfall we get in western Oregon and Washington comes from somewhere in the ocean, always connecting us to the sea.

All the water that's ever been on Earth has continually recycled itself, a basic tenant of the water cycle, but that means that water is extremely old. The oldest glacial ice in Antarctica is thought to be one million years old, an ice crystal that fell eons ago, frozen in time and still here with us.

A significant portion of Earth's water is thought to be even older, perhaps older than the 4.6-billion-year-old sun, according to one theory. Scientists suggest that 30 to 50 percent of our oceans' water could have originated from interstellar ice in the molecular cloud of gas, dust, and ice that birthed the sun. To figure this out, they studied water molecule structure, as some types contain deuterium, a heavier hydrogen with a neutron, or what scientists call heavy water. Researchers don't know exactly where this water came from. It's found throughout our solar system on other planets, comets, maybe even on Jupiter's icy moon Europa. Scientists theorize that it was traveling in space before the sun. Other scientists are even exploring the role galactic cosmic rays play in cloud development, as they've been found to accelerate cloud formation by providing ions for water vapor to latch onto before it can condense.

Clouds can also be made from microscopic plants, called phytoplankton, that help create brighter clouds in the Southern Ocean, which surrounds Antarctica and is the cloudiest region on Earth, a group of University of Washington and Pacific Northwest National Laboratory researchers found. The plants release gas particles that latch onto water molecules to create a floating white mass. Or, bubbly residue on the ocean's surface, especially near big phytoplankton blooms, containing tiny dead plant and animal particles can get launched into the air and create clouds. Researchers say phytoplankton may be present in our Northern Hemisphere clouds, but they're harder to measure, as our air is inundated with pollution and forest particles that water molecules often latch onto to form clouds.

ATMOSPHERIC RIVERS

Although they sound intriguing, special, and seem new in headlines, atmospheric rivers have always been around. They are a critical part of Earth's water cycle. Not until the last few decades, though, were scientists able to understand exactly how Earth's water was transported in these massive rivers in the sky.

At any given time, an atmospheric river is traveling somewhere. Many are weak and simply provide needed rain and snow. But several exceptionally large ones can form as they ride strong, warm mid-latitude cyclones from tropical waters to the West Coast, supplying us with 30 to 50 percent of our annual precipitation. They extend for thousands of miles and are several hundred miles wide, a conveyor belt of water vapor. They're so big that they carry the equivalent of ten to fifteen Mississippi Rivers across the ocean. They bring with them an amount of energy per second that's roughly a factor of ten times greater than the amount of energy that all humans use per second. They're continually evolving on their journey, pulling in and raining out moisture along their path.

It's not until an atmospheric river encounters mountains that the air rises, cools, and rains or snows—a lot. "When you have warm, moist storms slamming into terrain and lifting it," McMurdie says, "you have a way to squeeze out all that water vapor. The amounts are amazing."

McMurdie studies storms over the Olympic Peninsula and observed one atmospheric river dump nearly twelve inches of rain at one location in just one day. "It's really efficient," she says. "You would think it would take a bit of work to go from little, tiny cloud droplets to rain drops, but it just fell out. If you didn't have the mountains, I don't think you'd get a lot of rain out of these atmospheric rivers. They'd just be kind of average."

While writing this in November, an especially powerful atmospheric river struck the region, causing landslides in British Columbia that killed at least four people. Floods killed thousands of farm animals. The storm brought wind gusts of sixty miles per hour, landslides, floods, evacuations, and extensive road closures on the Olympic Peninsula and elsewhere in western Washington. In just twenty-four hours, cities in British Columbia received two to nearly seven inches of rain. Bellingham saw just under five inches.

These storms, although destructive for us, help Earth balance her energy. They make the tropics cooler and the poles warmer than they normally would be, according to Nicholas Siler, an Oregon State University atmospheric science professor. When water changes form, from a liquid to a gas, or gas to a liquid, energy is transferred. "We know that this is why humans sweat," he says. "When water evaporates, it cools your body and the same thing is true in the ocean. Evaporation from the ocean to the atmosphere cools the ocean, and when that water vapor condenses again within the atmosphere, it releases heat into the atmosphere. This process of evaporation and condensation is a really important mechanism by which the earth is transferring energy from the ocean—where most of the sunlight is absorbed—to the atmosphere, and then the atmosphere radiates that energy back into space."

Siler has studied how atmospheric rivers may change in a warming climate. For every degree Celsius increase in warming, which is about two degrees Fahrenheit, the atmosphere can hold about 7 percent more water vapor. Researchers expect that atmospheric rivers will become more intense, carry more water, and potentially cause more flooding. Siler says that as the amount of water these storms carry increases, they become more efficient at transferring energy and moisture, which would lead to fewer moderate storms that supply us with needed rain and snow.

He also studies how climate change might affect snow and rainfall in the Cascades and Sierra Nevada, as models don't accurately account for elevation changes. A higher freezing level might result in more rain than snow in the mountains, and changes in wind patterns could affect when and where moisture falls, potentially causing more precipitation east of mountain ranges.

"We're trying to understand the various mechanisms that can influence this," he says. "It's not something that's well understood, in part because global models aren't able to [compute] mountains at all. So, ranges like the Cascades don't really show up."

COVER

For decades, scientists have provided a range for how much the earth could warm from human-caused emissions. The estimates haven't changed much since the 1970s, though, mostly because of clouds. Clouds are extremely difficult to model in climate studies, as many of their formations happen on local scales that can't be applied globally, and researchers don't know how they'll change in a warmer world. They're the biggest unknown for climate predictions.

Clouds both cool us and keep us warm. At night, the low *Stratus* layer serves as an insulating blanket, and during the day, the same *Stratus* or maybe *Cumulus* clouds, depending on the weather, are bright white, reflecting the sun's energy, sending it back into space, and preventing us from getting too hot. The high, thin *Cirrus* clouds don't reflect as much light and instead mostly trap heat. The heating and cooling effects of different clouds balance each other out and keep our temperatures stable.

Among the most important clouds that scientists are studying are *Stratocumulus* and *Cumulus* that cover large parts of the ocean where most sunlight is absorbed. They don't know whether we'll get more, less, or no change in these clouds as temperatures increase, and whether any change would lead to significant temperature changes globally. One study found that *Stratocumulus*, which shades 20 percent of the oceans, contains less ice than scientists initially thought and could become thinner in a warmer world, reflecting less heat back to space. They might even potentially break up into *Cumulus*, leaving large chunks of the ocean exposed to the sun.

Warmer temperatures result in more evaporation and water vapor, which is a greenhouse gas and traps heat. More water vapor would presumably lead to more clouds to cool us down. However, cloud dynamics are complex, and new climate models show that extra vapor could trap more heat, which would create thinner clouds, which would radiate less heat, and so on, creating a dangerous feedback loop.

Some scientists and states are toying with the controversial idea of creating clouds, called cloud seeding, by injecting particles of silver iodide into the atmosphere for water vapor to latch onto and create rain in drought-stricken areas. Idaho passed legislation for cloud seeding projects and research. One utility company that serves residents in southern Idaho and eastern Oregon is already experimenting with cloud seeding in the upper Snake River basin, as well as Wood River and Boise River basins. Only certain clouds can be created for rain under specific temperatures, though, and it's not guaranteed that enough rain would fall to cut drought conditions.

QUIET

The room softened. People inched closer to the drawings. No one talked.

Afterward, observers told Walker that her cloud art made them feel a sense of missing something. A tenderness, she thinks, that they were looking for in themselves. "We're constantly in-between what we have to do and being able to rest and be held by something," she says.

Clouds are often simply backgrounds: in paintings, drawings, photographs, and our lives, too. The overlooked beautiful part of a landscape and climate, whose presence is fundamental. Walker wants clouds to be the focus, the art. Her latest project explores light within them. She's interested in discovering more of the incidental, the peripheral in nature.

The clouds know who they are, she says to me.

I tell her they ground me. Their movement is like breath.

"Because we are that rhythm, too," she says. "And anything that brings us to where we get to join with their lilt, our whole bodies kind of rest into it. Our whole culture, Western culture, is all about making that less and less."

When we can be with the clouds, quiet, and breathing slowly, she says, it's like medicine.

"I really felt like the clouds chose me," she says. "They wanted to be known. It's different from science. We have to relate. That's what we're doing here. We're relating. Our whole nervous system is sensing all of this, all the time. The cold, the heat, the wind on the skin. It's not that we're thinking about it all the time, but we're relating to the world all the time. We're calibrating, we're sensing.

"What a beautiful gift."

Gray Whale,

Sih-xwah-wiX, Eschrichtius robustus

Open plains of sand and silt and mud stretch below the whales as they travel across the shallow sea. Occasionally, they pass giant boulders once entombed in glacial ice, thousands of years ago, that are now home to corals and sponges on this underwater plateau off the Northwest Coast.

They travel to northern waters every spring, guided by Earth's magnetic fields, while carefully listening, with knowledge passed down to them from their mothers and their mother's mothers. They devour crustaceous critters submerged in seafloor muck on the continental shelf, the last stretch of western North America before the vast, gentle slopes drop steeply into cold darkness.

The whales reach Astoria, where water from all across the Northwest shoots out continuously from the mouth of the Columbia River as a deep underwater canyon cuts through the shelf nearby. They continue along plateaus, which narrow the closer they get to the Olympic Coast. They notice how their thundering, low moans echo differently when they're not too far off the rim of these submarine canyons that sometimes descend five thousand feet. Here, animals who look more like feather dusters cling to vertical muddy cliffs, methane bubbles up, and deep-sea corals live for hundreds of years, tucked away.

As spring and summer winds change, these canyons funnel nutritious deep-ocean water onto the shelf, fertilizing life from the smallest plankton and fish to the largest whales, who time their migrations with these seasonal changes.

The nutrients turn the water a murky bluish-green, blurring the gray whales' world. Although they have eyes the size of baseballs, their vision is poorer than that of a house cat. With their specialized underwater mammalian ears, though, they listen. They hear currents rumble, winds strike the surface, and calls from their fellow gray whale relatives as they all travel north, speaking in low moans, making sure everyone is headed in the right direction. They might hear echolocation clicks of deep-diving beaked whales reverberate off the walls of the fan-shaped Quinault Canyon and know they're getting closer to their preferred Arctic waters. Soon, they're bombarded by the turbulence of the Juan de Fuca Canyon, where water from the Pacific and the Salish Sea mix together at depths of eight hundred feet, in what looks like an underwater river valley. Currents tug and pull water in different directions—around bends and islands and oxbows—as the canyon meanders sixty-two miles across the shelf to the shallower strait near Cape Flattery.

Here, above them, people eagerly await their return. The Makah have lived along this rocky coast forever, in human memory at least. Waves batter cliffs and scattered sea stacks rise from jade waters that mature into a deep navy sea, spread across the horizon. Makah people perfected their seafaring skills over generations to honor and hunt what seemed like an inexhaustible gift of whales, halibut, seals, and salmon, all of which made their famous multi-day feasts and way of life possible.

"Swiftsure is one of the five most dynamic marine ecologies on the planet," Micah McCarty tells me, speaking of a bank along the Juan de Fuca Canyon, about a dozen miles off the coast of Cape Flattery. Plentiful marine life congregates around the deep, cold, nutritious water traveling up from the depths of the canyon. Hundreds of thousands of pounds of fish and whales were sustainably harvested here, continuously, over centuries. "There are ancient teachings and knowledge tied to that place. There are old-growth roots. Those old-growth roots have an umbilical tie to that Swiftsure.

"If you have hereditary rights to one of the most productive marine ecologies, you can develop a wealth of culture and society and continuity of ancient teachings," McCarty says. "Because you're taprooted into the ecosystem. It's the habitat of your culture. It's the symbiosis of cultural diversity and biological diversity at its most ancient core."

McCarty comes from a family of Makah whalers, of chiefs who harpooned the world's largest animals from canoes on north Pacific waters. They were among dozens of other powerful whaling chiefs along the Northwest Coast, from the northwestern tip of the Olympic Peninsula to western Vancouver Island. His family's village of Waʔač, or Waatch, at the southern cusp of the cape, is one of five Makah villages where people whaled for at least thirty-five hundred years, he tells me.

The tribe is the southernmost of the Nuu-chah-nulth peoples of western Vancouver Island. Their name, Qʷidičča?a·tx̌, means "the people who live by the rocks and the seagulls," or more commonly "the people of the cape." To their neighbors, the S'Klallams, they were Makah, meaning "generous with food." McCarty's family name, Hawt'wilth'iayatuk, means "chief who shares his wealth." Makahs danced, sang, and told stories for hours that turned into days during regular ceremonial potlatches, where whaling families affirmed their wealth and shared their bounty with the village.

Every summer, McCarty's great-grandfather brought home to Waatch three or four whales, which sustained the village for a year. His name, Hish-kwee-sah-nahk-sheelth, or Hishka for short, means, "he makes the whales blow on the beach." When he harpooned a whale, according to stories, the animal would tow him home.

Hishka and other Makah chiefs hunted not only gray whales, called *sih-xwah-wiX* in Makah, but also humpbacks who travel farther out to feed on what looks like supernovas of krill in the open water, as well as at Swiftsure. McCarty tells me about a neighboring chief from Ditidaht on Vancouver Island who gifted Hishka a song after marrying his daughter to him. "And that song translates to, 'I can turn my beach black with the backs of whales.' That's not gray whales. That's humpbacks. Humpbacks hit Swiftsure huge every summer."

Whales created Makah society. The hunts brought social structure, power, prestige, wealth, discipline, and spirituality into family life. The Makah traded the animals' rich oil and rope-like sinew with neighboring tribes, north to Nootka Sound and south two hundred miles to the mouth of the Columbia River. Whales today are still considered sacred, supreme beings, McCarty tells me, inspiring art, song, dance, and prayer over centuries. They provided the Makah with nearly all of their food. Babies suckled on their chewy blubber like pacifiers. Their bones became combs, digging sticks, weaving tools, war clubs, retaining walls, and runoff diverters. Oil rendered from their blubber flavored dried halibut and salmon and brightened the dark coast at night.

"The whalers were the light company," McCarty says. "I think about long winter nights in the Pacific Northwest with no electricity. Whale oil is used to keep lights on in a longhouse with fires going, with extended family or single dwellings. Whale oil was not just sacred, it was also very utilitarian. It was a public utility."

McCarty, who grew up in Olympia, visited his dad, John McCarty, every summer at the Makah reservation in Neah Bay on the tribe's ancestral lands and sea. The two would fish together, and his dad would tell him stories about his grandfather, who was a whaler, his great uncle, who was a whaler, and his great-grandfather, who was a whaler.

After graduating high school, McCarty moved to Neah Bay. I ask him if he always knew he wanted to live there. "I knew it all my life," he says. "I remember when there were no car seats and seatbelts, and I was standing on the truck seat looking out of the window. I was probably in diapers, and I could see, and I could remember my homeland. Mountains, ocean, rivers," he says, slowly. "The fog and steam. Yeah, it's always been my home. And the rain.

"I dance in the rain. Well, I love the sun, too. But, you know."

MIGRATION

Their journey is the longest of all mammals—ten to fourteen thousand miles annually along the western coast of North America, venturing nearly half a planet north, then half a planet south, then north, then south, every year, for millennia. Their thirty- to fifty-foot-long, up to ninety-thousand-pound bodies are nourished in the spring and summer as they scoop up mouthfuls of their favorite tiny seafloor-dwelling animals in the northern Bering and Chukchi Seas of the Arctic. A smaller group of gray whales feeds along the Pacific coast, anywhere from Northern California to southeast Alaska. Come November, they head south again, perhaps mating sometime during their travels, until they reach Baja California. There they spend winter in warm lagoons, mating and relaxing. Some mothers will even give birth before traveling back north in spring.

They were the only whales we were likely to see when my parents took my sister and me to headlands along the northern Oregon Coast during whale-watching weeks in spring and winter. We'd catch their occasional spouts far in the distance, and we'd ooh and ahh and cheer, like everyone does whenever they see a whale. From Cape Lookout, my partner and I once saw one breach several times. Her tapered head appeared first, as she defied gravity to thrust most of her body out of the water and wiggled upward for what seemed like several seconds, before dramatically flopping onto her back, returning to her underwater world. We saw several other gray whales from the cape that day, their entire bodies—from head to flukes—visible as we looked down upon one of the most beloved animals, a fellow mammal with a culture and language of their own, with whom we share the same air, yet they choose the sea.

Gray whales, *Eschrichtius robustus*, are a part of the biological order Cetacea, which includes big marine mammals—whales, dolphins, and porpoises. Cetaceans diverged into two groups: toothed whales and non-toothed or baleen whales. Gray whales are among the latter group, called Mysticeti, which translates to "mustached whales" and includes the humpback, fin, and right whales, among others. Baleen whales are the biggest animals on Earth and include the largest animal to ever live, the blue whale. Instead of teeth, these whales grow thin, mustache-like rows of whitish, yellowish keratin, called baleen, that hang from their upper jaws like a stiff curtain. Gray whales dive several dozen feet to the seafloor, roll on their side, scoop up sediment, then push the muck out with their five-foot-long tongue. The baleen filters hundreds to several thousands of pounds of shrimp-like crustaceans for the whales to eat every day.

They're also among the oldest mammals on Earth. Their earliest ancestors were ancient fish who explored life out of water some 375 million years ago. Around fifty million years ago, they still lived on land and kind of looked like small deer, with more of a curved spine. Over the years, they grew curious about the sea again and started hunting in water, becoming muskrat-like. Then, their diets changed from eating only plants to eating meat, and as they started to spend more and more time in the water, they looked and behaved more like alligators. They kept their flexible spine, which was well-suited for running on land. This is why they swim more up-and-down than side-to-side, and why their tail is horizontal and not vertical like that of a shark or fish. Their front legs developed into pectoral fins and contain the same bones we have in our arms and hands. Their back legs basically disappeared, and around thirty million years ago, they began to resemble something closer to the animal we recognize today.

A few million years after that, Earth's oceans began distributing food inconsistently, in patches farther north. Sometime during the Pliocene and Pleistocene, around 11,700 to 5.3 million years ago, strong winds brought nutrient-rich deep water to the surface, giving animals like whales plenty to eat only during spring, summer, and fall. Long-distance migrations are thought to have started around then, some hundreds of thousands of years ago, as food became abundant in specific places at specific times in the year. Whales also evolved bigger and bigger bodies. One study notes that gigantism across the baleen family became the norm, likely to help these animals travel thousands of miles for food while they fast during winter and lose anywhere from 11 to 29 percent of their body weight. Many female baleen whales are larger than males, so that they have enough fat and energy to carry a pregnancy for thirteen months while migrating without eating.

Like the waters they live in, gray whales' entire bodies are a calming shade of bluish gray, almost slate. Their skin starts to molt as they mature, becoming speckled with light gray and white blotches. They also acquire crustaceans and barnacles who attach to their skin, giving the whales an even more spotted appearance and providing each individual with their own unique markings. They don't have a dorsal fin like the humpback, but instead have a dorsal hump followed by six to twelve smaller humps, called knuckles. They can live as long as us, anywhere from twenty-five to eighty years old—long enough for mothers to become grandmothers, then great-grandmothers.

RITUAL

"There's a story about the first whaler," McCarty tells me one evening in December as he's carving a bentwood box with his son in his Neah Bay shop. "He was in a potlatch competition with another rival chief.

"So, they got into this competition. The rivals were throwing potlatches. The biggest feasts of the day were from seals, and so they were hunting seals to have lavish potlatches where they could give away lots of food, and all the guests could go home fat and happy with a bunch of food. It got really unsustainable because they were chasing seals further and further from their home village. It got so bad that one of the chiefs decided, 'This isn't gonna work. I need to pray for a different answer.'

"The chief knew he had to get something big. He said, 'I'm not gonna lose this contest to this chief, and I'm not gonna hunt seals anymore.'

"So, he went to a mountain lake, and he prayed at this rocky ledge that was a nice drop off down to the lake. He sunk in and started praying. When he opened his eyes to come up for a breath, this little baby whale was sitting right in front of him, almost nose-to-nose. When he saw that, he immediately needed his air. He grabbed the whale, went to the surface, and took a deep breath.

"He took that as a sign, and brought that whale to his bedchambers, his part of the lodge. He knew it was something because he was praying for it, and it came in ceremony. He slept with it, laying that little baby whale by his head. That night, the whale came to him in a dream, telling him, 'I know what you're trying to do, and

I can help teach you how to hunt my people and teach you all the rituals you need to do, and how to celebrate the life of the whale,' like when whales mourn for the loss of their own," McCarty explains to me. "Then, the whale said, 'If you keep going to that spot where I came to you and keep praying, I'll keep teaching you these lessons.' And so he started doing that, and the rival chief was like, 'What's this guy doing?' Everybody in the network was trying to find seals and helping the chief in this competition. The gossip was far and wide. And the chief started spying on his rival, thinking, 'Why isn't he out hunting?'

"Then one day, the rival chief found him, watched him go down and dive and sit and pray. The chief who came up for air with the whale's lesson was catching his breath and looking at his rival. He was so aflame with the new, groundbreaking information he was getting that he just started blurting out how special and powerful and amazing the experience was. He said enough that his rival thought he could mimic that medicine, and so his rival killed him and decided he was gonna be the first whaler.

"The son of the slain chief, who had been at all these potlatches, figured something was up, and he started spying on the rival who killed his dad. And, same thing: The day came when the rival came up for air and the son of the slain chief was face-to-face with him. Same as how the slain chief blurted out the medicine, the rival was also so aflame with what he was learning that he also just blurted out what he was doing. The son knew that the rival couldn't take the magic because that magic was born in his house, where his dad took the medicine home. And so he killed that wannabe future whaler. He killed that rival chief, and then he became the first whaler."

Rituals and stories are passed down from father to son. Each family has their own unique ways of channeling the whale spirit, McCarty explains. Once a boy is old enough, he'll begin learning the rivers and lakes where he'll go by himself to cleanse both his body and mind in the cold water.

The success of whale hunts depends not just on the physical talent of the eight-man crew, but how well they spiritually prepare. They spend months centering and bathing themselves to properly take the life of one of the most revered creatures. From a white perspective, as an anthropologist noted, the most important aspects of a whale hunt would be the precise strategies leading up to and the moment hunters harpoon the whale. But for the Makah, proper spiritual ceremonies before and during the hunt are critical and define the crew's success. "That's the thing that a lot of animal rights activists don't get," McCarty says, "is that our hunter-gathering society is so empathetic with taking life and the spirit that's in it. So there was a real attunement to that spiritual awareness with everything, everything is connected," he says, referring to a Nuu-chah-nulth philosophy, *hishuk-ish tsawalk*, meaning everything is one, everything is connected. "It's one of the best remembered words of the Nuu-chah-nulth," he says.

Strict bathing procedures for both whalers and their families, especially the chief's wife, took place from October until the spring whaling season. Similar to how a CEO has a support staff, whalers had that too, which included moon watchers, McCarty tells me. They were trained to observe the moons and count them every year, in every season, using different carving techniques to record each moon phase. "They could predict seasonal forecasts," he says. "They were kind of like living almanacs, kind of like shamans in some ways, too."

Each whaling family had their own moon preference for hunting, while some from other tribal villages would go out when they saw the first new moon in May. Moon watchers didn't just help chiefs get ready to go whaling, but they also assisted with what McCarty likens to an edification process, providing proper timing for prayers and other spiritual practices. Different families have different techniques, rituals, songs, and prayers that are sacred and secret intellectual property, as McCarty describes it. Each of the nine chiefs in his family village had their own moon watchers and whaling traditions, distinguished by their art or the slightly different shape of their canoe bows.

Men also prepare and pray differently depending on their position in the eight-man canoe. The harpooner, the chief of his longhouse, led the way in the front of the canoe using his own whaling equipment. Behind him, to his right, was the line tender, who made sure the lines connected to the harpoon launched correctly. Next to him was the diver, a man tasked with jumping into the icy Pacific once the whale died to tie the mouth shut with rope. This prevented water from seeping in and sinking the whale, while also trapping gasses, which then caused the whale to float. Behind them sat a signaler, who gave directions for which way the canoe should be quickly moved once a harpoon was thrown. Next to and behind the signaler sat strong paddlers, and at the end, the steerer.

"Even the hats differed," McCarty says of their conical cedar or spruce root hats, tightly woven to deflect water. "There are three strata of design work of the whaler's hat. The bottom design around the brim where it's widest is like a whaling scene," he says, "and it describes whose hat it is and what part of the whaling crew he's on. The design above that, where it gets closer to the top of the head, is your Indian medicine for what you do in the canoe as a whaler. And then the knob on the top," which he describes as shaped like an onion, "is a design that ties your Indian medicine to the Great Spirit.

"The whaler's hat today is more like a status symbol for some people because they were so revered. It's like a crown."

McCarty's grandfather and great-grandfather were harpoon men, while his grandmother came from a family trained as divers to sew up the whale's mouth. One of the divers, McCarty's great uncle, used to walk underwater in the middle of a nearby river carrying a big boulder for three hundred yards in one breath. "And when he was an old man my dad remembers him jumping off one of the bridges, and he literally swam downstream underwater the whole time," McCarty says. "He said he was way down and around the bend, and when he came up, he took a big breath and started laughing. My dad said he had a huge lung capacity and was really loud.

"So, somebody training as a long-winded diver might have different prayers than the harpooner," McCarty says, bursting into a laugh. "You know what I mean."

For the first time in seventy years, in the late 1990s, eight Makah men started training, including McCarty. They practiced paddling and swimming in the Pacific and followed traditional bathing procedures and rituals. They acquainted themselves with the skills of relatives who came before them, who preserved in the tribe's treaty with the United States their ancestral right to hunt whales in these waters as they always had. Makah men learned, again, how exactly to launch a giant harpoon into a giant animal from a canoe.

EXPLOITATION

Only two groups of gray whales exist now: a small, critically endangered population that lives in the western Pacific Ocean along the Russian coast, and our eastern Pacific whales. They used to live on both sides of the north Atlantic, but commercial whalers hunted them to extinction by the 1700s.

Colonists relied on whale oil to light their homes. Women used baleen to stiffen corsets and structure hoop skirts, umbrellas, collars, and hat brims. When whale populations on the East Coast were decimated in the late eighteenth century, whalers then headed to the Pacific. They'd target one species, like right whales, hunt them to near extinction, then move on to another type. They went after any whale they could find, harpooning juveniles and lactating females. Whalers built entire colonial towns in the Northwest, like Whaletown on Cortes Island in British Columbia, for processing whale products. They hired Native whalers, taking cultural techniques and expertise and incorporating it into the multi-million-dollar global industry.

Gray whales here on our coasts, like most of the world's whales, were nearly killed off in less than a century. Before commercial whaling in the mid-1800s, it's thought that gray whales numbered anywhere from fifteen to forty thousand. When American whaler Charles Scammon found their birthing lagoons in Baja California, he shot them there, in the teal waters, with a harpoon gun and butchered them on his boat. Just two thousand gray whales were left by the 1880s.

The almost complete loss of the animals and other baleen whales left their ecosystems depleted. Oceans lacked the whales' iron-rich excrement to fertilize the water and create nutrients for tiny plants that feed tiny animals, in turn feeding whales who feed people, sustaining the entire food chain.

As fewer whales made it up to Cape Flattery, the Makah voluntarily suspended their hunts in the 1920s. Commercial whaling wasn't regulated until 1946, when the International Whaling Commission was formed and subsequently banned killing gray whales. However, the commission included an aboriginal subsistence exemption. The United States later passed the Endangered Species Act and the Marine Mammal Protection Act in the early 1970s to save endangered whales, seals, sea lions, and others, all decimated by commercial industries. Alaska Natives, who didn't sign treaties with the United States, also have an exemption to hunt marine mammals for subsistence. Previous legal understandings of treaty rights meant that Makahs were exempt from these conservation laws, too. International commercial whaling of other species continued until 1986, and some countries, like Norway, Iceland, and Japan continue whaling today.

Gray whales quickly rebounded. Their population now numbers anywhere from twenty thousand to twenty-seven thousand in recent years. Some scientists suggest this could be the animal's carrying capacity, as unexplained die-offs over the decades have left hundreds of whales dead on beaches. Scientists aren't sure if it's a result of overpopulation or a scarcity of food in their Arctic waters, possibly from climate change.

In 1994, they were taken off the endangered species list. The next year, the Makah told the government that they intended to resume their hunts.

BEHAVIOR

Solé is a homebody. She's a predictable whale. She's not one for traveling a few extra thousand miles to feed like most of her gray whale relatives. She's content in waters off the Oregon Coast and loves Newport, her home for half the year. She's usually in her spot, feeding on the plentiful mysid shrimp that other whales like herself have decided is enough for them to build up fat for winter.

Once gray whales migrate north, Solé is usually spotted off Newport's coast, from about late March to December. For three or four weeks, though, no one knows where she goes, says Lisa Hildebrand, a doctoral researcher at Oregon State University's Marine Mammal Institute based in Newport.

Researchers collect fecal samples and drone footage for their studies to understand whale behavior and ecology, and some days they might not have any luck finding a whale. "Then we'll say, 'OK, let's go to Solé's spot,'" Hildebrand says. "And she'll be there.

"It's always quite calming to see her again," she says. "Things out in the ocean can be very unpredictable with rain, wind, engine issues, seasickness—all of those things that can be up in the air—and then you have this one whale that you find at the end of the day in the spot where you thought you were going to find her. And you're like, 'Huh, there is some constancy in my life.'"

Although Solé's location is predictable, the researchers don't know how she feeds or what she's doing underwater because she likes to dive deeper than other gray whales they study. As she dives, she rolls off to her side slightly, with her distinctive high tail arc, and ventures far down beyond the point where the researchers' drone can capture her.

Hildebrand works with other researchers to study these gray whales, who cut their northern migration short. They stop about halfway to feed in spring, summer, and fall off of the Oregon Coast, as well as up and down the Pacific coast—anywhere from Northern California to southeast Alaska. Researchers aren't sure exactly why this small group of about two hundred whales don't go to Arctic seas to feed, as they've only recently been studied closely, after the Makah took steps to resume their hunts. These whales are not genetically different from other gray whales. They all migrate around the same time from their feeding to birthing grounds, and they likely mate together. It's possible that these Pacific feeding grounds have become a cultural tradition among the whales, where knowledge of the areas is passed down to calves from their mom, who learned from their mom.

This knowledge transfer may have continued over centuries, although researchers don't know how long they've fed off the Pacific coast.

Their lab within the Marine Mammal Institute found that some whales move around quite a bit, with one roaming nearly eighty-five hundred square miles. Others, like Solé, might be homebodies and stay near the shores of their favorite spots all summer and fall. They typically feed within three miles from shore in water that's less than 120 feet deep. Most whales tagged by researchers seemed to prefer the southern Washington and central Oregon coasts, while an area off Point St. George in Northern California was found to be the most heavily used by them.

Another theory for their behavior might be that they adapted to different feeding grounds when food was scarce in the Arctic, Hildebrand tells me. Algae grows under sea ice, and when there's less ice, less algae falls to the ocean floor to feed small, seafloor-living animals called amphipods that gray whales consume.

To eat food off the Oregon coast, though, the whales have learned unique and surprising techniques. "I would describe them as acrobats," Hildebrand says, "and extremely flexible in terms of how they're able to move their body. It's fascinating how a whale that's so big is able to forage and survive in such shallow environments."

Typically, gray whales feeding on amphipods will dive down and scoop up mud, which they filter for food through their baleen. Off of Newport and Port Orford, however, the whales find food that's not in seafloor sediment but is instead swarming close to rocky reefs. Here, whales have been seen feasting, head down, flukes up, in a whale headstand. Sometimes they aren't in deep enough water to be perfectly upright, so their bodies are bent over slightly while they're in a headstand. Hildebrand says she's seen whales feeding where waves break near the shore, a risky strategy that could leave them stranded. They don't seem bothered if waves crash over them, or if their bodies smash against rocks in a kelp forest, she tells me.

Researchers analyzed drone footage of behaviors from fifty-three whales. They observed whales poking their heads above the surface, baleen exposed, smiling. Others barrel rolled. Some swam upside down or on their sides. They blew out air, likely through their mouth, in what researchers call a "bubble blast." They don't know what it means, but perhaps the whales are chasing prey out of a crevice or out of the kelp. They've also seen whales "sharking" in shallow waters, where they turn on their side, propelled by their tail and pectoral fins, to catch mouthfuls of food. Researchers observed some males racing each other later in the season, around August and October, perhaps to prove dominance to a potential mate.

The researchers hope to better understand behaviors of these whales to help inform the growing fishing and whale-watching industries, both of which threaten these animals with underwater noise from their boats and with fishing gear, particularly crab pots, which whales are increasingly getting tangled in every year.

THE HUNT

From different mountain lookouts on shore, Makahs could see when the whales arrived. They preferred hunting during the whales' northbound migration from March to May when ocean waters were calmer, but if they needed to, they'd hunt in winter.

Gray whales stay closer to shore. They're predictable and don't require elaborate or dangerous hunts and are easier to tow back to home villages, McCarty tells me. Which is all relatively speaking, as catching a forty-ton animal is no easy feat. Whalers could get up before dawn to hunt in the calm morning sea. They knew the animals' feeding grounds both near shore and farther offshore, where other whales, like humpbacks, gathered. McCarty shares with me his great-grandfather's perspective, from when he went out on longer hunts for humpback whales.

They head into the sunset on a summer evening around eight, using yew wood paddles charred jet-black. The men travel silently, stealthily. From a teardrop shape, the paddles come to a point as sharp, skinny, and strong as a blade. The men never lift the paddles out of the water, and instead simply turn the paddle, which turns the blade and pulls water without a sound. Assured by wind, currents, landforms, their training, and ancestral knowledge, the eight men keep going, stroke by stroke, through the night, surrounded by nothing but darkness, stars, the moon, and ocean. They paddle until the landforms retreat, until sunrise the next day, fifteen to twenty miles into the horizon in their twenty-eight-foot cedar canoe, transformed from a single tree into the highest quality seafaring vehicle of its time.

Then, they wait.

As a whale surfaces, they observe the breathing patterns. The paddlers angle the canoe; the chief readies himself. He stands, harpoon in hand, looking out upon the early morning water. He grips the braided cedar bark, wrapped tightly around the thirteen- to sixteen-foot harpoon shaft, so his hands don't slip. At its tip is the harpoon blade, traditionally made from mussel shell, but later of copper or steel. Cut perfectly, the blade is sharp as obsidian and placed in between two elk antler or bone barbs meticulously wrapped together using whale sinew and cherry bark. Before heading out, they kneaded and spread spruce gum over the harpoon head to secure the shell in place and create a smooth, waterproof weapon made to deeply penetrate the whale.

The animal's dark form comes close to the surface. He aims.

Humpbacks are more dangerous and unpredictable than gray whales, as they can dive deeper to try to break off the harpoon. Since gray whales are hunted in shallow water, they can't dive as far down.

He's worked for this moment. His knowledge—passed down to him from his father, and his father's father, and all the whales who have given themselves to his people over centuries—guides him.

Back on shore, the crew's wives stay still. Attempting to channel the movements of the whale, they don't make any sudden movements, hoping that the sea giant will do the same. They skip combing their hair on the day of the hunt because if a strand breaks, then the whaling line might break. They turn their back to the ocean, so that the whale will swim toward the shore and won't tow their husbands out to sea.

The whale comes up for air, blows, and slowly dives again.

The chief grounds his feet and leans back. He powerfully launches the harpoon, sinking it behind the pectoral fin to penetrate the heart that might weigh two times that of his own body.

Keeping his balance, he quickly moves out of the way of the lines attached to the harpoon, as many men before him have gotten tangled and pulled into the water. The injured whale's flukes whip, creating waves. The crew paddles backward, moving the canoe as far away from the whale as possible to avoid the powerful thrashing tail. They might strike again using additional harpoons, waiting possibly for hours until the whale loses strength. Once the animal tires out and is close enough to the canoe, the chief will use a bone-pointed lance to finally kill the animal.

"How would they pull them on shore?" McCarty's son asks.

"That's what the sealskin buoys were for," he says of the large floats the size of beach balls, as depicted in one historic photo of Makah whaler Wilson Parker, carrying two while walking on a beach in 1915. "The sealskin floats were to help slow it down when it was running away and also keep it from getting away if it dove. There'd be four or five sealskin floats. That's why a whaling canoe would be really big to hold those blown-up float bags."

And then there was the plug. One crew member jumps on the dead whale to hammer a chunk of yew wood deep into the blowhole. The diver sews the mouth shut, and once secured, they tow the whale home headfirst, honoring the hydrodynamics of the body.

"My son is having a good time listening," McCarty says. "He's heard some of this before, but it's kind of like refreshing it again."

Being this far out, the men observe the seabirds and waves, how the winds blow westerly as the day progresses, how the current changes every six hours—north to south, then south to west, then west to north, then north to east, as one elder once described. Whalers trust generations of Makah seafaring expertise to carry them and their catch safely home. Photographs from the early 1900s show entire villages awaiting the whale, helping to pull the mammoth mammal on shore, yanking as a group on a long rope, like a tug-of-war.

Stories, songs, knowledge, and rituals continued to be passed down during the seven decades when gray whale populations were too low for Makahs to hunt. Children grew into adults and became elders who passed without ever having a chance to taste whale meat or blubber or oil. Beyond stories, art, and ceremonies, whaling remained a black and white memory depicted in old photos.

The tribe received a quota in 1998 from the National Oceanic and Atmospheric Administration, allowing them to hunt twenty gray whales over a four-year period—five a year, one for each Makah village—after the agency determined their hunts wouldn't threaten the now-healthy gray whale population.

The crew of young men practiced for months, with a few unsuccessful hunts as they learned. Unlike anything their ancestors experienced, though, anti-whaling protesters, led by Paul Watson of Sea Shepherd Conservation Society and co-founder of Greenpeace, aggressively followed close by. They blasted sirens and killer whale sounds from their boats and sprayed fire extinguishers at the crew. Protesters even lowered a submarine painted like an orca that blared orca sounds into waters near Neah Bay to scare off migrating gray whales. Congressmen Jack Metcalf and Slade Gorton, both Republicans from Washington, also criticized the hunt, arguing that killing whales was uncivilized and that tribes should abide by the same laws as other Americans. The conservative politicians formed an unusual alliance with liberal animal rights activists, like Sea Shepherd, in the fight against tribal sovereignty and culture.

News reporters from all over the world traveled to the small and remote Neah Bay. The US Coast Guard was called to protect the tribe as they were exercising a right preserved for them in exchange for ceding their land to the US government.

On May 17, 1999, the crew got up early. They paddled fast in their black canoe, called the Hummingbird, its wide interior painted red. No protesters were around on this particular morning. They targeted a whale off of Cape Alava, paddling one stroke per second in the calm sea to catch up to the animal. As a TV helicopter hovered overhead, tribal members back in Neah Bay watched the hunt live. Once they approached the whale, the harpooner stood up, steadied himself, looked back to make sure everyone was ready, leaned back, and struck the animal. The winds picked up as the whale's tail slapped the water and the animal dove, towing the canoe. The crew continued paddling, and the harpooner threw out rubber floats and helped tend to the lines. A support boat moved in, and a tribal member shot the animal with a large caliber rifle to minimize suffering, though a TV crew initially got in their way. The crew placed their paddles on their knees and prayed.

Just eight minutes after the first harpoon strike, at 6:54 a.m., the female gray whale died. The Makah, once again, brought a whale home.

They went out as a crew of seven, leaving the eighth spot open for McCarty, who was initially part of the crew and started training and making his whaling gear. As anti-whaling activists and racist narratives dominated media coverage and conversations about Makah whaling, McCarty chose to publicly defend Makah rights, traditions, and sovereignty. Suddenly thrust into national and international politics, he traveled to Washington DC, Monaco, and Russia. He helped form the Makah's Whaling Commission and was elected tribal chairman in the early 2000s and served for ten years. "I knew I didn't need to be in the canoe," he says. "I knew certain teachings where the right time will be the right time."

He also assumed this whale wouldn't be the tribe's last for another generation.

COMMUNICATION

They're considered the quiet whale. Their calls aren't as well-known or revered like the songs of their relatives, particularly humpback whales, whose ambient, otherworldly, melodic yet haunting vocalizations are striking and among the most complex communication systems of any animal. Gray whales, though, have nuanced vocalizations, too.

A whale's world is vast, murky, and echoey. They hear a constant low rumble as waves crash and currents pull around them. Creatures' calls, clicks, and songs—some of which seem more natural to a synthesizer than a living animal—can carry for miles, as sound travels four times faster in water than in air.

Baleen whales have the lowest vocal range of all whales and are blessed with the widest vocal range of any mammal. Gray whales can hit notes below the lowest on the piano, sometimes reaching frequencies that humans can't even hear. They can then sweep seven octaves up, all the way to the second highest C on the piano and nail notes more within the range of a marmot.

Their deep, booming moans evolved to resonate as low as possible to travel as far as possible, yet still be heard over noisy water turbulence, which also produces low frequency noise. Their calls can be heard anywhere from five to twenty-eight miles away, while the two largest whale species, blue and fin whales, have been heard hundreds, even thousands, of miles away.

Researchers started noticing and studying gray whale calls about thirty years ago, in their birthing and breeding lagoons. As sound recording and listening technologies improved, scientists like Rianna Burnham can now observe and analyze their vocalizations in more detail off the west coast of Vancouver Island. Burnham, an acoustic ecologist for Canada's Department of Fisheries and Oceans and an adjunct assistant professor at the University of Victoria, says that when she started out some people approached her, asserting that they've never heard gray whales make any sound in their twenty or thirty years of recording them. "And they'd ask, 'Are you saying that I need to go back and look again?' And I say, 'Well,'" as she shrugs her shoulders and nods her head, "Yeah."

They chirp, grunt, rumble, croak, moan, and click. Calves speak to their mothers in special tones, perhaps an attempt to mimic the much larger whale's repertoire.

Burnham says gray whales have about four main calls. They produce what's described as a knocking call, or bongo or conga call, which sounds as the name suggests—a quick, percussive, and sometimes resonant pulse, like a palm striking a drumhead. They can change a lot, she says, as they're short and sharp. They also have a sweeping call, or what she describes as a *whomp, whomp* sound, that most commonly ends with an upward cadence, like a question, but can also produce a down sweep. Another one, the zipper call, sounds like they're zipping up a jacket in their throat, a sort of rumble. Whales may communicate with these higher frequency calls when they're closer together, socializing, or during courtship.

Then, there are the moans. The whales emit these sounds most commonly at night, while they're traveling, to communicate over longer distances through a low boom that thunders across the continental shelf for several miles. "It's almost like checking in. I'm asking you in Oregon, 'How's the food down there?'" Burnham says. Although the calls may not reach that far, other whales can relay the message, like in telephone. "It's that kind of idea," she says, adding that the function of the calls is still speculation.

They might moan for navigation, to hear how their sound carries across the shelf, or echo down a nearby submarine canyon. They also may be teaching their calves and young whales the migration route. Or, they might just be chatty.

Some researchers think there must be a meaning, a biological reason related to survival, as to why the whales would call while they're traveling, without food all winter, and are assumedly trying to save as much energy as possible. "But it could also just be keeping everyone company," Burnham says. "We all sing when we're going on a long car journey. And that has a function, too. It's a more socially inherent function, where they might just be saying, 'Let's keep it moving. Follow me, follow me, follow me.'

"Culture and learning, those are places that I like to live in," she says, "but not many marine mammal people think that way. They think it couldn't be that they're just having a chat to pass the time. You wouldn't take a multi-week journey and not speak to your companion," she says. "It just seems ridiculous. We wouldn't do that, so why would whales do that?"

Their calls originate from their throat, where they have a larynx like ours, but theirs is rotated differently—and it's huge. If our larynx was proportionally as big as theirs, we wouldn't be able to fit it in our throat because it'd be the size of our lungs. Air doesn't cut across their vocal cords like a human larynx. Instead, as whales vocalize, their vocal folds expand and contract like an accordion. The vocalization is then thought to resonate in an acoustic sac attached to the larynx, amplifying their tones, like a choir singing in a church. Air moves through their enormous lungs and several air chambers, where it's then recycled back into their lungs, Burnham tells me. Since they aren't able to take in more air while diving underwater, calls and songs are made through cycling and reshaping air flow. So they don't have to exhale, or breathe, to sing. Exactly how they do this is one of the big unknowns in whale biology, she says. They don't open their mouths, and the sound booms from their throat. "What they don't want to do is take a gulp of air, dive, and need to signal something, but use air to do that, because they're holding their breath," she says. "They're on a limited capacity of air."

To hear underwater, they've evolved unique ear placement, where their internal ears are outside of their skull. When we swim underwater, we can't tell which direction sounds are coming from because our skull and our inner ear bones in both ears are vibrating at the same time. But because whales' ears sit outside their skull and apart from each other, they're able to tell when sound arrives in each ear, allowing them to locate sound accurately. The sound wave is first received by the jawbone, which serves as a huge soundboard, then travels up the jaw through a pocket of fat, and back to the bone of their inner ear, located like a dangly earring behind their jaw. Burnham likens it to if big bat ears were rotated inward and lined the jaw. Marine mammals, especially whales, evolved ears suited for underwater listening since they rely on sound for survival, to navigate, find food, and communicate.

What's become increasingly part of a whale's life is human-caused noise. Giant commercial vessels carry more than ninety-eight percent of the world's goods back and forth across the ocean. Gray whales travel near busy ports throughout their annual migrations, and though whale-watching operations occur in their lagoons in Baja California, they're relatively well regulated and protected there. As they travel north, though, global shipping noises and whale-watching boats are a constant hum or buzz in the background, like white noise. "Acoustically, they're gonna get bombarded the whole time," Burnham says of their several-thousand-mile journey. "These sounds travel quite a long way. Even ports that they wouldn't necessarily go straight by or into, like San Francisco's, which is tucked in a little, they're still gonna get that noise effect."

Noise from boat engines is part of the problem, but most of it comes from large ship propellers, which produce a train-like sound as they spin and also create bubbles. When the bubbles burst, they produce a low frequency sound that is within gray whales' hearing and communication range. "It's almost like the water is boiling because all these bubbles are created," Burnham says, describing the sound as like a consistent hiss.

Gray whales, blue whales, and fin whales hear among the lowest of frequencies, which overlaps with the low frequency noise from commercial ships. Their world is now noisier than it ever has been. Ships are larger and louder, unless quieter propellers are installed, which researchers like Burnham are pushing for. Ocean noise could be the most significant impact humans have on whales, she tells me, and she's urging whale-watching companies to limit their time on the water, to give the whales a break.

In noisier water, some researchers have noticed that blue whale calls are modulating up a bit in pitch to project over the low frequency noise from ships. Gray whales may be doing that as well, Burnham says, though it's hard to know because researchers don't have evidence over time or comparable studies.

In general, the noisier the water, the louder the whales' call. But for gray whale mothers with calves, their calling stops, Burnham says. She studied whales off western Vancouver Island, where they're known to nurse and wean their young. She observed how their calling changed when noise increased from whale-watching boats and float planes. "When they hear something they don't like," Burnham says, "they'll just be quiet." Sometimes, the mother will move so close to the calf that the two might touch. "It's like trying to teach a baby to talk and just playing heavy metal the whole time," she says. "They're not gonna come out as well adapted as other babies."

In addition to commercial ships and whale-watching boats, the National Oceanic and Atmospheric Administration approves requests to "take," meaning harass and sometimes kill, marine mammals with noise under the Marine Mammal Protection Act. Permits are given to oil and gas industries, where drilling creates constant booming. In the Puget Sound, Olympic Coast National Marine Sanctuary, and coastal waters from Northern California to Washington, US Navy sonar training and testing also emits intense and dangerous underwater noise that could harm thousands of marine mammals. The noises are so loud that they can cause temporary hearing loss for humpbacks and gray whales, and permanent hearing loss for harbor porpoises. Sonar has killed beaked whales, and it could affect breathing, feeding, migrating, mating, and nursing behaviors of several dozen species, including the southern resident killer whales and gray whales.

NOAA, meanwhile, still hasn't approved a request from the Makah to resume their hunts.

ART

Thunderbird lives among the glaciers of the Olympic Mountains. He's the overarching protector, the supervisor of the Makah. "There's another story about how a chief was praying for salvation for his people who were starving," McCarty tells me. "He went to a mountain and prayed, and when his prayer was answered he was given a magical cape, a shawl, a cloak, and when he put it on, he turned into a huge Thunderbird. He was given the vision of what to do and how to go get a whale off the ocean and bring it home to his people. So then he swooped off the mountain top and flew out over the ocean wearing his magic cape, and he pulled a whale out of the water and brought it to his home village and dropped it off on the beach."

Using tall ship rigging from vessels that transported timber in the late 1800s, McCarty's great-grandfather, Hishka, designed an elaborate Thunderbird and whale puppet displayed during a dance ceremony on his village's beach. As colonial power began overwhelming tribes decimated from disease, Hishka felt something monumental happening. "He really had an amazing new toolbox with a new insight on how to preserve a memory of a culture that's about to face a forever change," McCarty says, "a tidal wave of change. He knew things were going to be different."

Hishka is remembered as one of the last hereditary whaling chiefs of McCarty's home village. He carved a lot. So did his son. And so does his great-grandson, McCarty, who is now teaching his own son, Khephren McCarty.

McCarty creates masks, wolf headdresses, paddles, wall panels, drums, and wood sculptures of Thunderbirds, eagles, and whales, made mostly of redcedar but also yellow. He often paints with a traditional red, black, and white color palette, as well as navy and royal blue. Some pieces are inlaid with the sparkling iridescence of abalone, and many pieces include elements of Thunderbirds and whales. He recently taught and mentored members of the Pacheedaht First Nation, across the Strait of Juan de Fuca on Vancouver Island, guiding them as they carved their first canoe in more than fifty years. He's carved with both humpback and gray whale bone, making combs and clubs.

I ask McCarty about one of his pieces that depicts a whaling scene etched onto a mirror the size of a door. Thunderbird's wings extend geometrically across the sky. Underneath the water, the whale is visible and much larger than the crew's canoe. From one of the embedded harpoons, blood flows into the shape of a baby whale.

"I call that *The Third Strike*," McCarty says. His brother, Alex McCarty, who is also an artist, created a similar whaling scene that illustrates the first harpoon strike based on a design created by his mother. She used their dad as a model for each of the men sitting in the canoe. "My dad was standing in the living room with a foot up on the chair like he was holding a harpoon and he was the study," McCarty says, "and she was drawing him."

"I loved the design and was always inspired by it, but I didn't want to replicate it," he says. "So that was my tribute."

We talk about a striking historic Makah cedar carving of a humpback's dorsal fin, or saddle, as McCarty calls it, the most prized part of the whale. The piece is hundreds of years old and about two and a half feet tall and wide, painted black and red. It's inlaid with seven hundred otter teeth in precise rows like rhinestones, some outlined in the shape of a Thunderbird. Most teeth are molars, while some along the top and back curve of the fin are sharp canines, creating a jagged edge.

"The hump of the humpback whale is cut off in ceremony to usher the spirit of the whale into the next world," he says. During some rituals, the whaler's daughter swings on the saddle placed over a ceremonial fire to collect the oil. "And the oil from that ceremony would be used in different ceremonies."

The art piece was among thousands of artifacts archeologists found at the famous Ozette whaling village, sixteen miles south of Neah Bay, and the largest of the Makah's five villages. Families lived in Ozette for at least several thousand years until the 1920s, when the federal government forced their children to attend school in Neah Bay. In the 1970s, scientists excavated cedar longhouses that were perfectly preserved under a 450-year-old mudflow. Ozette whaling life was frozen in time, revealing carvings, sculptures, tools, baskets, boxes, harpoons, lances, and paddles, all intricately designed and found as they had originally been left in the longhouses, before Europeans arrived on the Northwest Coast. Some canoe paddles and tool handles were still oily from the hands who last held them and some bowls were coated with whale and seal oil. Scientists found thousands of whale bones, mostly from gray whales and humpbacks, but also from finback and right whales, and one blue whale. The site affirmed that Makahs have been whaling for a very long time, proving to scientists and the public what Makah people have always known.

Makah art, known for its symmetry and precision, also welcomes individual expression. Many of McCarty's cousins, siblings, and several of his five children are also artists, each with their own style. His daughter, who was teething on the 1999 whale, wants to recreate the first whaler story in an animated movie from the perspective of the whaler's wife.

"Everything that's inspired me the most has always been embedded in whaling," he says. "That's who I am, and where I come from. That's what I was raised to understand.

"Right, son-son?" he asks Khephren.

Khephren, who is eighteen, wants to learn more of the Makah language and art. He tells me how his grandmother, who is one of the village's few fluent speakers, taught Makah at the high school. "For a lot of our words, they have us build up a lot of spit in our mouth," he says, "to get some interesting noises that we have."

"Like you got fish bones stuck in your throat," McCarty interjects.

Khephren plans to continue the family business and experiment with new techniques. "I'll try to evolve the art and maybe try blacksmithing and integrating metal with wood," he says.

"We can cut some harpoon heads and spears and lances," McCarty says to him.

"We could make some clubs," Khephren says.

"Make some steel versions of the whaling war clubs, maybe," McCarty adds.

When the Makah hosted the 2010 Tribal Canoe Journeys, McCarty tells me that he and his dad spent five weeks designing their own black, red, and white whale puppet, inspired by his great-grandfather's creation. Hundreds of people from neighboring tribes joined together for a big celebration. During the performance, dancers, singers, and drummers welcomed a group of Makah men as they walked and paddled to the beat with the thirty-foot whale puppet in tow. McCarty's cousin said a prayer and sang a song he wrote, while a whaler wearing a conical hat sprinkled eagle down on the puppet, which soon became alive. Smoke exploded out of the blowhole, the eyes opened, the flippers started moving, and the jaw dropped as four wolf dancers emerged, including McCarty and his dad.

After he was first elected to tribal council, McCarty stood up during a previous Tribal Canoe Journeys and announced that at the next celebration hosted by the Makah: "We will have whale!"

"Well, I didn't say you couldn't eat it," McCarty says now, laughing.

CHANGE

When British fur trader John Meares sailed into Makah waters in the late 1700s in search of the sought-after Northwest Passage, a Makah chief known as Tatoosh prevented Meares from entering and taking claim to the Strait of Juan de Fuca and Puget Sound. As more and more European Americans passed through their waters in the coming decades, though, Makahs supplied them with furs and whale oil. They traded other whale and seal products, as they had with neighboring tribes for centuries, but now they received cash instead of goods, and many Makah families became wealthy in the new economy. Their fishing and hunting skills, as one historian notes, helped fuel the cornerstones of Northwest industries and helped white newcomers acclimate to the north Pacific. Whale oil became a major export of the Hudson's Bay Company, one of the first extractive companies in the Northwest.

From colonization's beginnings, Makah people resisted and adapted their seafaring skills to earn wealth within a new colonial system, while maintaining their culture and subsistence by hunting and fishing. The white people they traded and worked with brought with them deadly diseases and a desire to control the coveted, rich waters of Makah families, like those of Swiftsure, the ancestral bank that McCarty tells me about, full of halibut, salmon, and whales.

Makah treaty signers focused almost exclusively on protecting their ocean resources and preserving the right to whale and fish in their usual, ancestral areas in exchange for ceding three-hundred thousand acres of their land. The 1855 Treaty of Neah Bay is the only treaty between the US government and a tribe with the explicit right to hunt whales, though courts have ruled that fishing rights reserved in other treaties, including those of the Quinault and Quileute tribes, also includes sealing and whaling.

As part of the treaty, officials agreed to provide education, health care, and tools for Makah people to help them transfer their traditional whaling, sealing, and fishing skills into the new economy. Instead, the government sent missionaries, pitchforks, and hoes, in an attempt to turn Makah people into Christian farmers, dependent not on whales and fish they caught themselves, but on agriculture, foreign crops, and ways of the new American culture. The US government also forced this new life on other tribes across the Northwest, like the Kalapuyans of the Willamette Valley, to take power away from chiefs and families. When the Makah received these farming tools, they converted them into fishing hooks, blubber knives, and arrowheads.

The government banned potlatches, ceremonies, and the Makah language. Officials repeatedly ignored the Makah's request for a larger whaling vessel and allocated almost nothing to aid them in their maritime efforts. The rocky, poor soils and densely wooded Olympic Coast made farming unrealistic. Makah families resisted land allotments that would have divided the reservation into individual farms.

Fishing banks and hunting grounds once owned by Makah families were soon open to anyone in an unregulated industry. Historic photographs show non-Native boats packed into Neah Bay. Like whale populations, salmon and halibut numbers were depleted by the end of the nineteenth and early twentieth centuries. White fishermen caught six hundred thousand pounds of the fish in just a few months at fishing banks off Cape Flattery, like Swiftsure, and in the Puget Sound for people in Chicago and New York City to enjoy. Makahs found themselves increasingly pushed out of the industry and caught between new, complex fishing laws and jurisdictions that attempted to conserve declining fish populations but favored white commercial fishermen over Natives. State rules banned Native fishing gear, like nets and weirs. The Makah requested a small fishing season of their own to honor the treaty, but an international commission denied their request. By the early 1900s, one Makah fisherman said all the fish were gone at Swiftsure, which is now within Canadian waters.

Whales were mostly gone, too, and the Makah stopped hunting them.

To try and save salmon and halibut, yet still allow industry to continue, Washington required commercial fishing licenses available only to US citizens, a right denied to Native people until 1924—nearly two decades later. By the early 1960s, Natives caught just 2 to 5 percent of the state's annual salmon and steelhead harvest, but as the state enforced conservation efforts to limit fishing, they targeted Native fishers, arresting them for fishing off-reservation. "Conservation," as a historian notes, became a buzzword and an excuse to regulate Natives out of their own waters, which they weren't responsible for depleting.

The Makah formed their own tribal council in the 1930s to regain their marine space and assert their treaty rights. McCarty's grandfather was the first chairman. In the 1960s and 1970s, the tribe joined other tribal nations in the courts. Together, they won rights to 50 percent of fish harvested in their waters in a landmark treaty case, known as the *Boldt* decision, which led to public outcries fueled by racism.

When gray whale populations recovered and were taken off the endangered species list in 1994, the Makah revived their treaty-protected right and obtained a waiver from the International Whaling Commission and the National Oceanic and Atmospheric Administration to hunt the animals. Non-Native people across the political spectrum suddenly had an opinion on Makah whaling or advice for the tribe on human morality, conservation, and ethics in a modern, advanced, "civilized" society. Whale hunts don't belong, they said, echoing arguments made by colonists to justify the genocide of Indigenous peoples and cultures. Protesters came to Neah Bay. They shouted that Indians shouldn't have special rights. *The Seattle Times* received hundreds of letters to the editor and phone calls expressing outrage and sadness for the whale's death, in addition to racism and hate toward the tribe and Native American people in general. The Makah received death threats. Protesters came up with a slogan: "Save a whale, harpoon a Makah." Letter writers suggested that perhaps white people too, should revive the actions of their ancestors who settled the West, with one saying: "I am anxious to know where I may apply for a license to kill Indians."

Anti-whaling activists called the Makah people "evil." They continue to use language like "barbaric" to describe the hunts in recent news reports. They criticize the crew for not hunting in the "traditional" way—for using a gun to shoot the harpooned whale.

After the hunt, the Makah whaling captain tried to eat at restaurants in Victoria and Seattle, but they wouldn't serve him. Even his mother's chiropractor refused to see her because her son helped kill a whale.

DIET

Many Makah tribal members traveled home to Neah Bay in 1999 to welcome their first whale since the 1920s. More than one thousand people stood in the rain, singing, drumming, and celebrating. They sprinkled the thirty-foot whale with eagle down, prayed, and performed ceremonies. Many people ate raw whale blubber for the first time, including McCarty's infant daughter.

They used the meat, sinew, blubber, baleen, brain, heart, and bones. People made whale stew, steaks, burgers, and sausage. They smoked the meat, stir fried it, and barbecued it. Some made oil from the blubber, others pickled it, and most ate it raw.

A few days after the hunt, the Makah hosted—as they had centuries before—a big feast to give thanks and celebrate the whale, their guest of honor, as they called the animal. They gave out copies of their 1855 treaty, tied with a bow, to people from neighboring coastal tribes, and all over the world, to places like Fiji and Africa, to celebrate Indigenous rights. They sang, danced, and fed the people who filled the high school gym to capacity, three separate times. High school students later reassembled the whale's skeleton, which hangs in the Makah Museum, displayed alongside ancient artifacts from Ozette.

The vast majority of Makah households want whale meat and oil on a regular basis, surveys by anthropologists have found. Many Makahs had never tasted the animal who defined their culture. Over the decades, the tribe couldn't even harvest drift whales that washed ashore on their beaches, as federal officials dynamited them, buried them, or placed armed guards around the whale's body.

Fatty acids from marine mammal oil protect against inflammation, heart disease, hypertension, type 2 diabetes, and rheumatoid arthritis, among other chronic diseases. Western foods like beef, poultry, pork, and dairy, as well as processed foods high in fat and sugar were forced into Northwest Natives' diets. Though Makah people haven't regularly eaten whale since the early twentieth century, their bodies are still built for it. Studies suggest that Native people evolved unique genetics suited to their environment.

Indigenous people have the highest rates of food-related diseases in the United States and Canada. Coastal people have been found to have the highest rates of digestive issues among Native Americans, as their diets never included dairy, or many plants before colonization.

"There are special enzymes in coastal people who have been living with marine mammals for generations," McCarty says. "Our bodies are genetically designed to metabolize whale. It's just been a few generations that we couldn't. It's the high-octane fuel for our bodies, and we're not healthy without it."

REVIVAL

Soon after the 1999 hunt, the community experienced a "cultural renaissance," McCarty says, not seen since the Ozette archeological digs. Other families, including McCarty and his dad, made plans for their own hunt. The rigors of whaling inspired young people. They wrote new songs. Elders told more stories. The protests and racism were like a "lightning rod for solidarity for the people," McCarty explains. "It made us feel even more empowered toward our treaty rights, toward our ancestors, toward the sacredness of keeping the living breath of our ancestors alive," he says. "That has been a conduit of all the teaching behind what it means to be a whaler and what it means to usher the spirit of a whale into the next world.

"Those teachings, I'm saying them in English, but my ancestors knew it, and they lived it."

His second-born daughter, as McCarty proudly tells me several times, was born two years and two hours after the 1999 whale's time of death. "She's my whale baby," he says.

Congressman Jack Metcalf along with animal rights activists secured a court ruling soon after the hunt that has prevented the Makah from whaling for more than twenty years. The tribe has continually received quotas from the International Whaling Commission since 1997 for subsistence hunts, but they also need a domestic waiver under the Marine Mammal Protection Act approved by NOAA. They applied for one in 2005, but after nearly a generation of convoluted legal processes and extensive scientific reviews, NOAA still hasn't made a decision. "We have learned in this waiver process that delays of days tend to turn into weeks, weeks become months, and months become years," Makah Tribe Vice Chairman Patrick DePoe wrote in a court statement in 2019.

The current proposal would allow the tribe to take three whales in even years and one in odd years, over a ten-year waiver period, with some hunts restricted largely to winter months in rough waters. Their proposal has been whittled down to reduce the chance of accidentally killing a whale from the group that feeds on the Pacific coast, like those in Oregon, or the low chance they might target a whale from the endangered western Pacific population. An administrative law judge in 2021 found that the hunts would have no impact on the healthy gray whale population and recommended NOAA grant the Makah a waiver. The judge, though, suggested even further restrictions that could limit the tribe to land only five whales over a decade.

Tribal members, like McCarty and the captain of the 1999 whaling crew, Wayne Johnson, feel the government has been slow walking the process. To protest, five Makah men, including Johnson, killed a gray whale in 2007 without a waiver. Johnson served time in prison, and the fiasco further delayed and derailed the tribe's efforts.

Even if the waiver is approved, animal rights activists will likely challenge it. "You're only sovereign if you have the capacity to exercise it," McCarty says. "We're still building capacity."

He and his father thought they'd be able to whale together. His dad has since passed. "And we haven't gotten our whale that we wanted," he says.

Many of my conversations with McCarty frame Makah whaling in broad, contextual perspectives. He critiques the consumption, materialism, and constant market growth that a few generations of colonists created during the past two hundred years, robbing new generations, Native and non-Native, of a chance to form deep, meaningful connections to their landscapes, to Swiftsure, to Willamette Valley prairies, or to huckleberry fields, where people can create art, song, dance, spirituality—an entire culture—connected to place. Many of us live far from our ancestral homes and lack ancient family teachings rooted to specific waters, to trees like yellow-cedars, and mountains like Marys Peak.

Activists and the government can legislate people out of their environments, as Makahs have experienced, and they can ban traditional burning in huckleberry fields, like Yakamas experienced. Natural systems are off-balance when people exploit and when people are taken out of ecosystems. Laws and regulations pushed by conservationists that attempt to heal capitalistic exploitation can also lack holistic, long-term ecological views, McCarty says, which further separates people from place—especially Indigenous people. He explains how decades of protecting seals and sea lions has led to their populations exploding without enough fish to eat, and they're now depleting critically endangered salmon.

"They want to come in from far away and impose values into a living ecosystem that people are part of," he says of non-Native environmentalists and conservationists. "When you get too extreme on either side, it's bad. And the Indian reality has always been ground center. Ground-truth reality.

"Some of the hardest opponents to Makah whaling were also suffering from an orphanage from their own cultural heritage," he says. "Other cultures suffer and lose that internal flame that is knowing who you are and where you come from.

"I know people who don't have that ground truth to fall back on that's deeply rooted," he says. "And if I ever feel down and out, I know my roots.

"That's the essence of the lesson."

Gratitude

When I had my last interview for this project in December 2021, it felt like the final day of a favorite college class: I was filled with new knowledge yet already nostalgic. All the people I met and talked with, listed below, gave me a greater awareness of the natural world. They helped me make sense of scientific jargon and the complexities of animal and plant biology and evolution. They shared their own research, resources, experiences, and knowledge, and several met with me in-person, or in the field. They provided invaluable historical context for each species, helping me to connect the past to the present. Many of our talks also broadened my understanding of where people fit into ecosystems and helped me in my journey to decolonize my way of thinking. Without their expertise, these essays wouldn't have been possible. Each person was so generous with their time, and I am deeply grateful. The work they do inspires me and gives me hope.

Thank you Edward Alverson, David Harrelson, Lindsay McClary, Tom Kaye, Bart Johnson, Paul B. Reed, Gary Ivey, Teresa Wicks, James B. Pearson, Carter G. Crouch, Paul Hennon, Nancy J. Turner, Ariane Xay Kuyaas, Richard Cronn, David D'Amore, William Downing, Joseph Rausch, Don Hann, Nan MacDonald, Lincoln Best, Andony Melathopoulos, Jeff Everett, Jamie Strange, Liam Whiteman, Ashley Rohde, Rich Hatfield, Mark Leppin, Deanna Olson, Doug Heiken, Suzanne Cox Griffin, David P. Barash, Dave Conca, Patti Happe, Maia Murphy-Williams, Bill Baccus, Elaine Harvey, Emily Washines, Cheryl Mack, Bernadine Strik, Jessica Hudec, Jamie Tolfree, Amit Dhingra, Carrie Woods, Michelle Spicer, Ellen Bradley, Beatrice Bugos, Henry Norton, Martin Hutten, Binky Walker, Lynn McMurdie, Nicholas Siler,

Micah McCarty, Rianna Burnham, Lisa Hildebrand, Jenny Waddell, and extra special thank you to David G. Lewis.

I am also so grateful to Ooligan Press for the opportunity to share my writing with others. Thank you for the support and guidance. Thank you, Ramon Shiloh, for lending your talents, time, and inspiration.

Thank you...

Ms. Hunter—for letting me read the first stories I wrote to my fellow second-grade classmates.

Michelle Ma at the University of Washington and Sean Nealon at Oregon State University—for connecting me with several of the researchers listed above.

Blue Cliff Zen Center—for the tools to keep me centered, calm, and focused.

Professor Kyu Ho Youm—for setting the bar high, teaching me how to write accurately and concisely, and making me even more passionate about journalism.

Professor Tom Wheeler—for inviting me into your home and introducing me to good stories while listening to good music.

Former Register-Guard colleagues—for showing me how to write, report, and care about a local community with a healthy dose of skepticism.

Liz Rusch—for the guidance, connections, and confidence.

My Literary Arts book proposal classmates—for reading crappy drafts and helping me shape my ideas, especially Amie Riley.

Christine Sherk—for your keen eye, suggestions, and friendship in nature.

Clouds, neighborhood birds, and trees—for helping me flesh out ideas and grounding me.

Friends—for assuring me, checking in, and understanding why I was trapped inside in front of my computer for seven months.

Gladys—for the purrs, moral support, and always being on or near me while I was researching and writing.

Ken—for our backcountry conversations that help me see things differently.

Mary—for your encouragement, support, and delicious nourishments.

My sister, Babe—for teaching me, pushing me, inspiring me, hunting bumble bees with me, and always reminding me of the power of words.

Mom and Dad—for your selflessness, attention, and the opportunities you've provided to me. For the home-cooked meals, oil changes, car washes, sweet stress-relieving animal videos, binoculars, and love.

Adam—for listening to me talk about these species in detail for months, reading and rereading drafts, feeding me, doing the dishes, joining me on trips, pointing out wildflowers, noticing birds, taking me places that I would have never gone without you, and helping me deepen my relationship to nature.

Bibliography

Camas

Aikens, C. Melvin, Thomas J. Connolly, and Dennis L. Jenkins. "The Willamette Valley." Chap. 5 in *Oregon Archaeology*, 284–327. Corvallis: Oregon State University Press, 2011.

Altman, Bob, Sara Evans-Peters, Elspeth Hilton Kim, Nicole Maness, Jaime Stephens, and Bruce Taylor. *Prairie, Oaks, and People: A Conservation business plan to revitalize the prairie-oak habitats of the Pacific Northwest.* Cascadia Prairie-Oak Partnership, 2017. https://pacificbirds.org/wp-content/uploads/2017/10/Oak_Plan2017_v100517.pdf.

Altman, Bob. "Historical and Current Distribution and Populations of Bird Species in Prairie-Oak Habitats in the Pacific Northwest." *Northwest Science* 85, no. 2 (2011): 194–222. http://dx.doi.org/10.3955/046.085.0210.

Archuleta, Greg. "Greg Archuleta: Tribes Have Been Rebuilding Since Termination." *Living Culture: Interview Collection,* June 28, 2019. Video, 1:58. https://www.confluenceproject.org/library-post/greg-archuleta-treaties/.

Barlow, Jim. "UO graduate students get a taste of Native camas cooking." University of Oregon Communications, Department of Anthropology. July 11, 2017.https://anthropology.uoregon.edu/2017/07/11/uo-graduate-students-get-a-taste-of-native-camas-cooking/.

Bart Johnson (professor and head of University of Oregon's department of landscape architecture) in discussion with the author, April 5, 2021.

Boyd, Robert. "Indian Use of Fire in Early Oregon." *Oregon Encyclopedia*. Last updated January 15, 2019. https://www.oregonencyclopedia.org/articles/anthropogenic_fire/#.YSFx-pNKhjs.

Christy, John A. and Edward R. Alverson. "Historical Vegetation of the Willamette Valley, Oregon, circa 1850." *Northwest Science* 85, no. 2 (2011). https://doi.org/10.3955/046.085.0202.

David G. Lewis (anthropologist, Oregon State University assistant professor) in discussion with the author, June 25, 2021.

David Harrelson (Confederated Tribes of Grand Ronde cultural resources manager) in discussion with the author, April 13, 2021.

Dennehy, Casey, Edward R. Alverson, Hannah E. Anderson, David R. Clements, Rod Gilbert, Thomas N. Kaye. "Management Strategies for Invasive Plants in Pacific Northwest Prairies, Savannas, and Oak Woodlands." *Northwest Science* 85, no. 2 (2011): 329–351. https://doi.org/10.3955/046.085.0219.

Douglas, David. *Journal kept by David Douglas during his travels in North America 1823-1827*. London: W. Westley & Son, 1914.

Dunwiddie, Peter W., and Edward R. Alverson. "Prairies, Savannas, and Oak Woodlands of the Pacific Northwest." In *Encyclopedia of the World's Biomes* (2020): 489–504. https://doi.org/10.1016/B978-0-12-409548-9.11953-0.

Dunwiddie, Peter W., and Jonathan D. Bakker. "The Future of Restoration and Management of Prairie-Oak Ecosystems in the Pacific Northwest." *Northwest Science* 85, no. 2 (2011): 83–92. https://doi.org/10.3955/046.085.0201.

Edward Alverson (botanist, Lane County Parks natural areas coordinator) in discussion with the author, April 20, 23, 2021 November 15, 2021.

"Endangered and Threatened Wildlife and Plants; Removing Bradshaw's Lomatium (*Lomatium bradshawii*) From the Federal List of Endangered and Threatened Plants." *Federal Register: The Daily Journal of the United States Government*, March 8, 2021. https://www.federalregister.gov/documents/2021/03/08/2021-04693/endangered-and-th reatened-wildlife-and-plants-removing-bradshaws-lomatium-lomatium-bradshawii-from.

"Golden paintbrush: Range" Oregon Fish and Wildlife Office. https://www.fws.gov/oregonfwo/articles.cfm?id=149489433.

Hamman, Sarah T., Peter W. Dunwiddie, Jason L. Nuckols, Mason McKinley. "Fire as a Restoration Tool in Pacific Northwest Prairies and Oak Woodlands: Challenges, Successes, and Future Directions." *Northwest Science* 85, no. 2 (2011): 317–328. https://doi.org/10.3955/046.085.0218

Harrelson, David. "The Kalapuya and Marys Peak," US Forest Service. January 4, 2021. YouTube video, 2:42. https://www.youtube.com/watch?v=K0ea80BVzyE.

Jacobs, Melville. *Kalapuya texts*. Seattle: University of Washington, 1945. https://digitalcollections.lib.washington.edu/digital/collection/lctext/id/9509.

Lewis, David G. "Kalapuyan Eyewitnesses to the Megaflood in the Willamette Valley." *Quartux: Journal of Critical Indigenous Anthropology*, April 8, 2017. https://ndnhistoryresearch.com/2017/04/08/kalapuyan-eyewitnesses-to-the-megaflood-in-the-willamette-valley/.

Lewis, David G. "Kalapuyans: Seasonal Lifeways, TEK, Anthropocene." *Quartux: Journal of Critical Indigenous Anthropology*, November 8, 2016. https://ndnhistoryresearch.com/2016/11/08/kalapuyans-seasonal-lifeways-tek-anthropolocene/.

Lewis, David G. "The Red Road to Self-Extermination." *Quartux: Journal of Critical Indigenous Anthropology*, June 12, 2016. https://ndnhistoryresearch.com/2016/06/12/the-red-road-to-self-extermination/.

Lewis, David G. "Tribal Forced Removal 'Trail of Tears.'" *Quartux: Journal of Critical Indigenous Anthropology*. https://ndnhistoryresearch.com/tribal-history-themes/tribal-forced-removal-trails-of-tears/.

Lewis, David G. "Two Schools at Grand Ronde Indian Reservation, 1863." *Quartux: Journal of Critical Indigenous Anthropology*, September 10, 2019. https://ndnhistoryresearch.com/2019/09/10/two-schools-at-grand-ronde-indian-reservation-1863/.

Lewis, David Gene. "Termination of the Confederated Tribes of the Grand Ronde Community of Oregon: Politics, Community, Identity." PhD diss., University of Oregon, 2009. https://scholarsbank.uoregon.edu/xmlui/bitstream/handle/1794/10067/Lewis_Daivd_Gene_phd2009wi.pdf.

Lindsay McClary (Confederated Tribes of Grand Ronde restoration ecologist, and fish & wildlife policy analyst) in discussion with the author, April 20, 2021.

Macnaughtan, Don. "Kalapuya: Native Americans of the Willamette Valley, Oregon." LCC Library. https://libraryguides.lanecc.edu/kalapuya.

Marin, Ian P. "Geologic Map of the Oregon City 7.5' Quadrangle, Clackamas County, Oregon." In *Geologic Map Series GMS-119*, 4. Portland: Oregon Department of Geology and Mineral Industries, 2009. https://maps.orcity.org/galleries/dynamicContent/DOGAMI%20-%20Geologic%20Map/GMS-11 9-text_onscreen.pdf.

McClary, Lindsay. "Sips 'n' Science: Tribal Lands Management with Lindsay McClary." Luckiamute Watershed Council. March 31, 2021. Video, 1:12:56. https://www.luckiamutelwc.org/tribal-lands-mgmt.html.

Medley, Erica. "Ancient Cataclysmic Floods in the Pacific Northwest: Ancestors to the Missoula Floods." Master's thesis, Portland State University, 2012. https://pdxscholar.library.pdx.edu/cgi/viewcontent. cgi?article=1580&context=open_access_etds.

Merrill, Brent, and Yvonne Hajda. "The Confederated Tribes of the Grand Ronde Community of Oregon." In *The First Oregonians*, edited by Laura Berg, 123– 127. Portland: Oregon Council for the Humanities, 2007.

Nuckols, Jason L., Nathan T. Rudd, Edward R. Alverson, and Gilbert A. Voss. "Comparison of Burning and Mowing Treatments in a Remnant Willamette Valley Wet Prairie, Oregon, 2001-2007." *Northwest Science* 85, no. 2 (2011): 303–316.https://doi.org/10.3955/046.085.0217.

"Our Story." Confederated Tribes of Grand Ronde. https://www.grandronde. org/history-culture/history/our-story/.

Paul B. Reed (University of Oregon Institute of Ecology and Evolution postdoctoral scholar) in discussion with the author, March 31, 2021.

Reed, Paul B., Megan L. Peterson, Laurel E. Pfeifer-Meister, William F. Morris, Daniel F. Doak, Bitty A. Roy, Bart Johnson, Graham T. Bailes, Aaron A. Nelson, and Scott D. Bridgham. "Climate manipulations differentially affect plant population dynamics within versus beyond northern range limits." *Journal of Ecology* 109, no. 2 (2020): 665–673. https://doi.org/10.1111/1365-2745.13494.

Rich Hatfield (Xerces Society for Invertebrate Conservation senior endangered species conservation biologist) in discussion with the author, July 7, 2021.

"Rooted in Culture: Oregon's Wild Camas." *Travel Oregon*. June 4, 2021. YouTube video, 2:34. https://m.youtube.com/watch?v=kl-mc70jm98.

Schultz, Cheryl B., Erica Henry, Alexa Carleton, Tyler Hicks, Rhiannon Thomas, Ann Potter, Michele Collins, Mary Linders, Cheryl Fimbel, Scott Black, Hannah E. Anderson, Grace Diehl, Sarah Hamman, Rod Gilbert, Jeff Foster, Dave Hays, David Wilderman, Roberta Davenport, Emily Steel, Nick Page, Patrick L. Lilley, Jennifer Heron, Nicole Kroeker, Conan Webb, and Brian Reader."Conservation of Prairie-Oak Butterflies in Oregon, Washington, and British Columbia," *Northwest Science* 85, no. 2 (2011). https://doi.org/10.3955/046.085.0221.

Stanley, Amanda G., Peter W. Dunwiddie, and Thomas N. Kaye. "Restoring Invaded Pacific Northwest Prairies: Management Recommendations from a Region-Wide Experiment." *Northwest Science* 85, no. 2 (2011): 233–246. https://doi.org/10.3955/046.085.0212.

Stevens, Michelle, Dale C. Darris, and Scott M. Lambert. "Plant Guide for Common Camas: Ethnobotany, Culture, Management, and Use." Natural Resources Conservation Service, US Department of Agriculture, 2000. https://www.nrcs.usda.gov/Internet/FSE_DOCUMENTS/nrcs142p2_042942.pdf.

Sultany, Molly L., Susan R. Kephart, H. Peters Eilers. "Blue Flower of Tribal Legend: 'Skye blue petals resemble lakes of fine clear water.'" *Kalmiopsis* 14 (2007): 29–32. https://www.semanticscholar.org/paper/Blue-Flower-of-Tribal-Legend%3A-%22Skye-blue-petals-of-Sultany-Kephart/eadf3f2b983168115bae6567a528e6e902b15f8c.

The Nature Conservancy of Washington, "Integrated Prairie-Oak Conservation Report for Oregon and Washington." 2010. https://cascadiaprairieoak.org/documents/integrated-prairie-oak-conservation-report-for-oregon-and-washington.

Thomas Kaye (ecologist at the Institute for Applied Ecology) in discussion with the author, April 14, 2021.

Thompson, Sara. "Our Connection to the Falls." Confederated Tribes of Grand Ronde. June 10, 2019. https://www.grandronde.org/press-media/tribal-announcements/our-connection-to-the-falls/#:~:text=1%20The%20historical%20and%20cultural,by%20the%20United%20States%20Government.

Tomimatsu, Hiroshi, Susan R. Kephart, and Mark Vellend. "Phylogeography of *Camassia* quamash in western North America: postglacial colonization and transport by indigenous peoples." *Molecular Ecology* 18, no. 18 (2009): 3918–3928. https://doi.org/10.1111/j.1365-294X.2009.04341.x.

Wilkes, Charles. *Narrative of the United States Exploring Expedition*, Vol. 5. Philadelphia: Lea and Blanchard, 1844. https://www.sil.si.edu/DigitalCollections/usexex/navigation/NarrativePages/USExEx19_05b.cfm?start=270.

"Willamette Valley Grass Seed Production." Willamette Valley Field Crops, Oregon State University. https://valleyfieldcrops.oregonstate.edu/grass-seed.

"Willamette Valley," Oregon Conservation Strategy, Department of Fish and Wildlife, 2016. https://www.oregonconservationstrategy.org/ecoregion/willamette-valley/.

Sandhill Crane

Aikens, C. Melvin, Thomas J. Connolly, and Dennis L. Jenkins, "Northern Great Basin." Chap. 5 in *Oregon Archaeology*, 31–148. Corvallis: Oregon State University Press, 2011.

Ackerman, Jennifer. *The Genius of Birds*. New York: Penguin Books, 2016.

Altman, Bob. "Historical and Current Distribution and Populations of Bird Species in Prairie-Oak Habitats in the Pacific Northwest," *Northwest Science* 85, no. 2 (2011): 194–222 https://doi.org/10.3955/046.085.0210.

Carter G. Crouch (Burns Paiute Tribe wildlife program manager) in discussion with the author, May 17, 2021.

Contreras, Alan L., ed. *Edge of Awe: Experiences of the Malheur-Steens Country*. Corvallis: Oregon State University Press, 2019.

Engels, Mike. "Migration Routes and Winter Areas of Lesser Sandhill Cranes from Homer, Alaska." International Crane Foundation, 2010.

"Fur Trappers, Wagon Trains and Military Expeditions." Malheur National Wildlife Refuge, US Fish and Wildlife. Last updated November 19, 2014. https://fws.gov/refuge/malheur/about/trappers.html.

Gabrielson, Ira N. "Malheur Then and Now." In *Edge of Awe: Experiences of the Malheur-Steens Country*, 34. Corvallis: Oregon State University Press, 2019.

Gary Ivey (International Crane Foundation researcher) in discussion with the author, May 25, 2021.

Gaunt, Abbot S., Sandra L. L. Gaunt, Henry D. Prange, and Jeremy S. Wasser. "The effects of tracheal coiling on the vocalizations of cranes (Aves; Gruidae)." *Journal of Comparative Physiology A* 161 (1987): 43–58. https://doi.org/10.1007/BF00609454.

"Geology and Geomorphology," Malheur National Wildlife Refuge, US Fish and Wildlife. Last updated November 20, 2014. https://fws.gov/refuge/malheur/about/geology.html.

Happ, George and Christy Yuncker-Happ. *Sandhill Crane Display Dictionary: What Cranes Say with Their Body Language*. Tampa, FL: Waterford Press, 2011.

"Important Bird Areas: Malheur National Wildlife Refuge." National Audubon Society. https://www.audubon.org/important-bird-areas/malheur-national-wildlife-refuge.

Ivey, Gary L. "Travels and Traditions of Sandhill Cranes." International Crane Foundation. 2020. Video, 57:38. https://www.youtube.com/watch?v=rb5d4W8681U.

Ivey, Gary L., and Bruce Dugger. "Factors Influencing Nest Success of Greater Sandhill Cranes at Malheur National Wildlife Refuge, Oregon." *Waterbirds* 31, no. 1 (2007): 52–61. https://doi.org/10.1675/1524-4695(2008)31[52:FINSOG]2.0.CO;2.

Ivey, Gary L., Caroline P. Herziger, and Thomas J. Hoffmann. "Annual Movements of Pacific Coast Sandhill Cranes." *Proceedings of the North American Crane Workshop* (2005): 25–35. http://digitalcommons.unl.edu/nacwgproc/13.

Ivey, Gary L., Caroline P. Herziger, David A. Hardt, and Gregory H. Golet. "Historic and Recent Winter Sandhill Crane Distribution in California." *Proceedings of the North American Crane Workshop* (2016): 54–66. https://digitalcommons.unl.edu/cgi/viewcontent.cgi?article=1340&context=nacwgproc.

Ivey, Gary. "Sandhill crane: One of the oldest known bird species." *Herald and News* (Klamath Falls, OR), January 25, 2019. https://www.heraldandnews.com/news/local_news/sandhill-crane-one-of-the-oldest-known-bird species/article_c31d04af-e287-5be2-b56b-4ec37bc00a19.html.

James B. Pearson (former fish biologist at Malheur National Wildlife Refuge) in discussion with the author, May 27, 2021.

Johnsgard, Paul A. "Individualistic and Social Behavior." In *Cranes of the World*, 11–24. Bloomington: Indiana University Press, 1983. https://digitalcommons.unl.edu/bioscicranes/1/.

Johnsgard, Paul A. "Vocalizations." In *Cranes of the World*, 25–34. Bloomington: Indiana University Press, 1983. https://digitalcommons.unl.edu/bioscicranes/1/.

Jones, M. R. and C. C.Witt. "Migrate small, sound big: functional constraints on body size promote tracheal elongation in cranes." *Journal of Evolutionary Biology* 27, no. 6 (2014): 1256-1264. https://doi.org/10.1111/jeb.12397.

Krapu, Gary L., Gary L. Ivey, and Jeb A. Barzen. "Species Review: Sandhill Crane (*Grus canadensis*)." Crane Conservation Strategy. International Crane Foundation. https://savingcranes.org/wp-content/uploads/2021/12/crane_conservation_strategy_sandhill_crane.pdf.

Leopold, Aldo. "Marshland Elegy." In *A Sand County Almanac*, 95-101. New York: Oxford University Press, 1949.

Littlefield, Carroll D., and Gary L. Ivey. "Washington State Recovery Plan for the Sandhill Crane." Washington Department of Fish and Wildlife, 2002 https://wdfw.wa.gov/sites/default/files/publications/00396/wdfw00396.pdf.

Meine, Curt D., George W. Archibald, eds. *The Cranes: Status Survey and Conservation Action Plan.* Gland, Switzerland: IUCN, 1996. https://www.researchgate.net/publication/307436974_The_Cranes_Status_Survey_and_Conserva tion_Action_Plan.

Miller, Marli B. "Basin and Range." In *Roadside Geology of Oregon*, 346. Missoula, MT: Mountain Press Publishing Company, 2014.

Sallinger, Bob. "Malheur National Wildlife Refuge: Past, Present and Future." Audubon Society of Portland. 2016. Video, 1:08:27. https://www.youtube.com/watch?v=vGD2H1mRG4I.

"Sandhill Crane." All About Birds, The Cornell Lab. 2019. https://www.allaboutbirds.org/guide/Sandhill_Crane/overview#.

"Sandhill Crane." Species Field Guide. International Crane Foundation. 2021. https://savingcranes.org/species-field-guide/sandhill-crane/.

"Sandhill Cranes." US Fish and Wildlife. https://www.fws.gov/uploadedFiles/Region_1/NWRS/Zone_2/Mid-Columbia_River_Complex/Columbia/Documents/sandhill-crane-facts.pdf.

"Settling the Land: Ranching in the Blitzen Valley," Malheur National Wildlife Refuge, US Fish and Wildlife Service. Last updated November 19, 2014. https://fws.gov/refuge/malheur/about/settling.html.

Schwartz, Devan. "Turning Around Malheur Wildlife Refuge One Carp Carcass At A Time." *Oregon Public Broadcasting*, June 9, 2014. https://www.opb.org/news/article/turning-around-malheur-refuge-one-carp-carcass-at-/.

Sibley, David Allen. *What It's Like to Be A Bird.* New York: Alfred A. Knopf, 2020.

Soucie, Minerva T. "Burns Paiute Tribe." In *The First Oregonians*, edited by Laura Berg, 44–59. Portland: Oregon Council for the Humanities, 2007.

Stinson, Derek W. *Periodic Status Review for the Sandhill Crane.* Olympia: Washington Department of Fish and Wildlife, 2017. https://wdfw.wa.gov/sites/default/files/publications/01854/wdfw01854.pdf.

Teresa Wicks (Audubon Society of Portland's Eastern Oregon field coordinator) in discussion with the author, May 13, 2021.

Yellow-Cedar

Ariane Xay Kuyaas (Haida weaver) in discussion with the author, July 8, 2021.

Arno, Stephen F. and Ramona P. Hammerly. "Conifers: What Is a 'Cedar'?" In *Northwest Trees: Identifying and Understanding the Region's Native Trees*, 118. Seattle: Mountaineers Books, 2020.

Beier, Colin M., Scott E. Sink, Paul E. Hennon, David V. D'Amore, and Glenn P. Juday. "Twentieth-century warming and the dendroclimatology of declining yellow-cedar forests in southeastern Alaska." *Canadian Journal of Forest Research* 38 (2008): 1319–1334. https://www.fs.usda.gov/Internet/FSE_DOCUMENTS/fsbdev2_038022.pdf.

Christodoulides, Christy. "Unpacking a Phrase: The Chilkat Blanket." Burke Museum, February 29, 2012. https://www.burkemuseum.org/news/unpacking-phrase-chilkat-blanket.

Comeau, Vanessa M., Lori D. Daniels, and Stefan Zeglen. "Climate-Induced Yellow-Cedar Decline on the Island Archipelago of Haida Gwaii." *Ecosphere* 12, no. 3 (2021). https://doi.org/10.1002/ecs2.3427.

D'Amore, David V., Paul E. Hennon, Paul G. Schaberg, and Gary J. Hawley. "Adaptation to Exploit Nitrate in Surface Soils Predisposes Yellow-Cedar to Climate-Induced Decline While Enhancing the Survival of Western Redcedar: A New Hypothesis." *Forest Ecology and Management* 258, no. 10 (2009): 2261–2266. https://doi.org/10.1016/j.foreco.2009.03.006.

David D'Amore (US Forest Service soil scientist) in discussion with the author, June 28, 2021.

Donald Hann (retired US Forest Service archeologist) in discussion with the author, June 17, 2021.

Downing, William M., James D. Johnston, Meg A. Krawchuk, Andrew G. Merschel, and Joseph H. Rausch. "Disjunct and Decoupled? The Persistence of a Fire-Sensitive Conifer Species in a Historically Frequent-Fire Landscape." *Journal for Nature Conservation* 55 (2020). https://doi.org/10.1016/j.jnc.2020.125828.

Goldberg, Jamie, and Jayati Ramakrishnan. "Portland Records All-Time High Temperature of 116, Setting New Record for Third Day in a Row." *The Oregonian/OregonLive*, June 28, 2021. https://www.oregonlive.com/weather/2021/06/portland-records-all-time-high-temperature-of-113-setting-new-record-for-third-day-in-a-row.html.

Hennon, Paul E., Carol M. McKenzie, David D'Amore, Dustin T. Wittwer, Robin L. Mulvey, Melinda S. Lamb, Frances E. Biles, and Rich C. Cronn. "A Climate Adaptation Strategy for Conservation and Management of Yellow-Cedar in Alaska," General Technical Report. US Department of Agriculture, Forest Service, Pacific Northwest Research Station. 2016. https://doi.org/10.2737/pnw-gtr-917.

Hennon, Paul E., David V. D'Amore, Dustin T. Wittwer, and John P. Caouette. "Yellow-Cedar Decline: Conserving a Climate-Sensitive Tree Species as Alaska Warms," Proceedings of the 2007 National Silviculture Workshop, 2007. https://www.fs.usda.gov/Internet/FSE_DOCUMENTS/fsbdev2_038120.pdf.

Jensen, Edward C. "Common and Scientific Names of Trees." In *Trees to Know in Oregon and Washington*. Corvallis: Oregon State University Press, 2021.

Joling, Dan. "Yellow Cedar Rejected for Threatened Species Listing." *The Spokesman-Review*, October 4, 2019. https://www.spokesman.com/stories/2019/oct/04/yellow-cedar-rejected-for-threatened-species-lis ti/.

Joseph Rausch (US Forest Service botanist, vegetation management staff officer) in discussion with the author, May 20, 2021.

Karchesy, Joseph J., Rick G. Kelsey, and M. P. González-Hernández. "*Yellow-Cedar, Callitropsis (Chamaecyparis) Nootkatensis*, Secondary Metabolites, Biological Activities, and Chemical Ecology." *Journal of Chemical Ecology* 44, no. 5 (2018): 510–24. https://doi.org/10.1007/s10886-018-0956-y.

Krapek, John, Paul E. Hennon, David V. D'Amore, and Brian Buma. "Despite Available Habitat at Range Edge, Yellow-Cedar Migration Is Punctuated with a Past Pulse Tied to Colder Conditions." *Diversity and Distributions* 23, no. 12 (2017): 1388–90. https://doi.org/10.1111/ddi.12630.

Mobley, Charles M. and Morley Eldridge. "Culturally Modified Trees in the Pacific Northwest." *Arctic Anthropology* 29, no. 2 (1992): 91–110. http://www.jstor.org/stable/40316316.

Murray, Marshall D. "Ancient Yellow-Cedar Groves in the Olympic Mountains." In *A Tale of Two Cedars PNW-GTR-828*. *Portland*, OR: US Forest Service, 2010. https://www.fs.fed.us/pnw/olympia/silv/publications/opt/612_Murray2010b.pdf.

Nan MacDonald (traditional weaver) in discussion with the author, February 18, 2022.

Nancy J. Turner (ethnobotanist) in discussion with the author, June 24, 2021.

Oakes, Lauren E. "What Mass Die-off of an Iconic Tree Says about Changing Climate." *National Geographic*, November 27, 2018. https://www.nationalgeographic.com/environment/article/mass-death-yellow-cedar-climate-chan ge-canary-tree-book.

Oliver, Marie. "Forests in Decline: Yellow-Cedar Research Yields Prototype for Climate Change Adaptation Planning." *Science Findings*, no. 150 (February 2013): 1–5. https://www.fs.fed.us/pnw/sciencef/scifi150.pdf.

Parfitt, Ben. "The Battle for Haida Gwaii's Cedars." *The Narwhal*, August 14, 2019. https://thenarwhal.ca/battle-haida-gwaiis-cedars/.

Paul Hennon (retired US Forest Service plant pathologist) in discussion with the author, July 1, 2021 and October 12, 2021.

"Petition to List Yellow-Cedar, *Callitropsis nootkatensis*, Under the Endangered Species Act." Center For Biological Diversity, The Boat Company, Greater Southeast Alaska Conservation Community, and Greenpeace, June 24, 2014. https://www.biologicaldiversity.org/species/plants/pdfs/Yellow_Cedar_CenterBiologicalDiversit y_6-24-14.pdf.

Pojar, Jim and Andy MacKinnon. *Plants of the Pacific Northwest Coast*. The B.C. Ministry of Forests and Lone Pine Publishing, 1994. Revised edition, 2014.

Popovich, Nadja. "How Severe Is the Western Drought? See For Yourself." *New York Times*, June 11, 2021. https://www.nytimes.com/interactive/2021/06/11/climate/california-western-drought-map.html.

Pringle, Heather. "In the Land of Lost Gardens." *Hakai Magazine*, June 6, 2017. https://hakaimagazine.com/features/land-lost-gardens/.

Pynn, Larry. "Lyell Island: 25 Years Later." *Vancouver Sun*, November 17, 2010. https://www.wildernesscommittee.org/news/lyell-island-25-years-later.

Rich Cronn (US Forest Service geneticist) in discussion with the author, June 11, 2021.

"Shake Table fire is a hot topic." *Blue Mountain Eagle*, November 21, 2006. https://www.bluemountaineagle.com/news/shake-table-fire-is-a-hot-topic/article_6b18d57b-5268 -58a8-8c05-7c9c01bb213a.html.

Stewart, Hilary. *Cedar: Tree of Life to Northwest Coast Indians*. Seattle: University of Washington Press, 1984.

Turner, Nancy J. *The Earth's Blanket: Traditional Teachings for Sustainable Living*. Seattle: University of Washington Press, 2005.

Turner, Nancy J., Douglas Deur, and Dana Lepofsky. "Plant Management Systems of British Columbia First Peoples." *BC Studies*, no. 179 (2013): 107–133. https://ojs.library.ubc.ca/index.php/bcstudies/article/view/184112.

Turner, Nancy J., Marianne Boelscher Ignace, and Ronald Ignace. "Traditional Ecological Knowledge and Wisdom of Aboriginal Peoples in British Columbia." *Ecological Applications* 10, no. 5 (2000): 1275–1287. http://www.ask-force.org/web/TraditionalKnowledge/Turner-TK-British-Columbia-2000.pdf.

Turner, Nancy. "'Passing on the News': Women's Work, Traditional Knowledge and Plant Resource Management in Indigenous Societies of North-western North America." In *Women & Plants: Gender Relations in Biodiversity Management & Conservation*, edited by Patricia L. Howard, 133–145. London: Zed Books Ltd., 2003.

William Downing (Oregon State University faculty research assistant) in discussion with the author, June 9, 2021.

"Yellow-Cedar: The Tree. What's in a Name?" US Forest Service. https://www.fs.usda.gov/detail/r10/communityforests/?cid=fsbdev2_038767.

Zoledziowski, Anya. "Residential School Survivors Tell Us What Intergenerational Trauma Really Is." *Vice*, July 26, 2021. https://www.vice.com/en/article/k78xyx/intergenerational-trauma-residential-school-survivors-in digenous.

Western Bumble Bee

Andony Melathopoulos (Oregon State University assistant professor, Oregon's pollinator health extension specialist) in discussion with the author, June 11, 2021.

Ashley Rohde (US Geological Survey ecologist and Utah State University PhD candidate) in discussion with the author, June 29, 2021.

Cameron, Sydney A., Haw Chuan Lim, Jeffrey D. Lozier, Michelle A. Duennes, and Robbin Thorp. "Test of the Invasive Pathogen Hypothesis of Bumble Bee Decline in North America." *Proceedings of the National Academy of Sciences* 113, no. 16 (2016): 4386–91. https://doi.org/10.1073/pnas.1525266113.

Center for Biological Diversity. "Petition to List Suckley's Cuckoo Bumble Bee (*Bombus suckleyi*) Under the Endangered Species Act and Concurrently Designate Critical Habitat." 2010. https://www.biologicaldiversity.org/species/invertebrates/pdfs/Suckleys-cuckoo-bumble-bee-peti tion.pdf.

Cordes, Nils, Wei-Fone Huang, James P. Strange, Sydney A. Cameron, Terry L. Griswold, Jeffrey D. Lozier, and Leellen F. Solter. "Interspecific Geographic Distribution and Variation of the Pathogens *Nosema Bombi* and Crithidia Species in United States Bumble Bee Populations." *Journal of Invertebrate Pathology* 109, no. 2 (2012): 209–16. https://doi.org/10.1016/j.jip.2011.11.005.

Dodgson, Lindsay. "This Myth People Keep Quoting about How Bees Shouldn't Be Able to Fly Is Scientifically Incorrect—Here's Why." *Business Insider*, December 27, 2017. https://www.businessinsider.com/bees-cant-fly-scientifically-incorrect-2017-12.

Goulson, Dave. "The Beguiling History of Bees [Excerpt]." *Scientific American*, April 25, 2014. https://www.scientificamerican.com/article/the-beguiling-history-of-bees-excerpt/.

Graves, Tabitha A., William M. Janousek, Sarah M. Gaulke, Amy C. Nicholas, Douglas A. Keinath, Christine M. Bell, Syd Cannings, Richard G. Hatfield, Jennifer M. Heron, Jonathan B. Koch, Helen L. Loffland, Leif L. Richardson, Ashley T. Rohde, Jessica Rykken, James P. Strange, Lusha M. Tronstad, and Cory S. Sheffield. "Western Bumble Bee: Declines in the Continental United States and Range-Wide Information Gaps." *Ecosphere* 11, no. 6 (2020): 5. https://doi.org/10.1002/ecs2.3141.

Greshko, Michael. "First US Bumblebee Officially Listed as Endangered." *National Geographic*, March 22, 2017. https://www.nationalgeographic.com/science/article/bumblebees-endangered-extinction-united-st ates#:~:text=The%20 rusty%20patched%20bumblebee%20.

Hanson, Thor. "Empty Nests." In *Buzz: The Nature and Necessity of Bees*, 177–78. New York: Basic Books, Hachette Book Group, 2018.

Hatfield, R., S. Jepsen, R. Thorp, L. Richardson, S. Colla, and S. Foltz Jordan. "*Bombus occidentalis*." The IUCN Red List of Threatened Species, 2015. http://dx.doi.org/10.2305/IUCN.UK.2015-2.RLTS.T44937492A46440201.en.

Hatfield, Rich, Sarina Jepsen, Eric Mader, Scott Hoffman Black, and Matthew Shepherd. "Conserving Bumble Bees. Guidelines for Creating and Managing Habitat for America's Declining Pollinators." Portland, OR: The Xerces Society for Invertebrate Conservation, 2012. https://www.xerces.org/sites/default/files/2018-05/12-028_01_XercesSoc_Conserving-Bumble-B ees-Guidelines_web.pdf.

Hatfield, Richard G., James P. Strange, Jonathan B. Koch, Sarina Jepsen, and Isaak Stapleton. "Neonicotinoid Pesticides Cause Mass Fatalities of Native Bumble Bees: A Case Study From Wilsonville, Oregon, United States." *Environmental Entomology* 50, no 5. (2021): 1095-1104. https://doi.org/10.1093/ee/nvab059.

Heinrich, Bernd. *Bumblebee Economics*. Cambridge, MA: Harvard University Press, 1979, 2004.

Hines, Heather M. "Historical Biogeography, Divergence Times, and Diversification Patterns of Bumble Bees (Hymenoptera: Apidae: Bombus)." *Systematic Biology* 57, no. 1 (2008): 58–75. https://doi.org/10.1080/10635150801898912.

"How Bees Fly." Smithsonian National Air and Space Museum. 2020. Video, 1:16. https://www.youtube.com/watch?v=6cMB_YeUh1o.

"Identifying Bumble Bees in the Pacific Northwest." Pacific Northwest Bumble Bee Atlas, 2021. https://www.pnwbumblebeeatlas.org/species-illustrations.html.

James Strange (Ohio State University professor, chairman of department of entomology) in discussion with the author, July 20, 2021.

Jeff Everett (US Fish and Wildlife biologist) in discussion with the author, July 13, 2021.

Koch, Jonathan, James Strange, and Paul Williams. "Bumble bees of the western United States." US Forest Service, 2012. https://www.fs.fed.us/wildflowers/pollinators/documents/BumbleBeeGuideWestern2012.pdf.

Leonard, Anne. "Buzz Pollination." Leonard Lab. University of Nevada, Reno. http://www.anneleonard.com/buzz-pollination/.

Liam Whiteman (Ohio State University entomology graduate student) in discussion with the author, July 20, 2021.

Lincoln Best (Oregon State University native bee taxonomist) in discussion with the author, June 7, 2021.

"Petition before the United States Department of Agriculture, Animal and Plant Health Inspection Service." Xerces Society for Invertebrate Conservation, January 12, 2010. https://www.xerces.org/sites/default/files/publications/17-063.pdf.

Rich Hatfield (Xerces Society for Invertebrate Conservation senior endangered species conservation biologist) in discussion with the author, July 7, 2021.

Strange, Jamie. "Melittology 101: An Introduction to Bee Science." The Bee Short Course for Community Scientists webinar. 2021. Video, 1:08:00. https://m.youtube.com/watch?v=eCEj1G0awcY&t=831s.

"This Vibrating Bumblebee Unlocks a Flower's Hidden Treasure." *KQED Deep Look.* PBS Digital Studios. 2016. Video, 3:48. https://www.youtube.com/watch?v=SZrTndD1H10.

Thorp, Robbin, Sarina Jepsen, Sarah Foltz Jordan, Elaine Evans, and Scott Hoffman Black. "Petition to List Franklin's Bumble Bee, *Bombus Franklini* (Frison), 1921 as an Endangered Species Under the US Endangered Species Act," The Xerces Society for Invertebrates Conservation, 2010. https://www.xerces.org/sites/default/files/2019-10/bombus-franklini-petition.pdf.

Walther-Hellwig, Kerstin, Gerriet Fokul, Robert Frankl, Ralph Büchler, Klemens Ekschmitt, and Volkmar Wolters. "Increased Density of Honeybee Colonies Affects Foraging Bumblebees." *Apidologie* 38, no. 1 (2007): 124–24. https://doi.org/10.1051/apido:200701.

"Western Bumble Bee: A Conservation Tale." The Xerces Society for Invertebrate Conservation, June 30, 2020. https://storymaps.arcgis.com/stories/c5e591a19eb24d28af483ede7b174434.

Woodard, S. Hollis, Jeffrey D. Lozier, David Goulson, Paul H. Williams, James P. Strange, and Shalene Jha. "Molecular Tools and Bumble Bees: Revealing Hidden Details of Ecology and Evolution in a Model System." *Molecular Ecology* 24, no. 12 (2015): 2916–2936. https://doi.org/10.1111/mec.13198.

"Yellow Banded Bumble Bee." The Xerces Society for Invertebrate Conservation. https://xerces.org/endangered-species/species-profiles/at-risk-bumble-bees/yellow-banded-bumbl e-bee.

Coastal Tailed Frog

Alexander Pyron, R., and John J. Wiens. "A Large-Scale Phylogeny of Amphibia Including over 2800 Species, and a Revised Classification of Extant Frogs, Salamanders, and Caecilians." *Molecular Phylogenetics and Evolution* 61, no. 2 (2011): 543–83. https://doi.org/10.1016/j.ympev.2011.06.012.

"Amphibian Species by the Numbers." University of California, Berkeley, CA. AmphibiaWeb. https://amphibiaweb.org/amphibian/speciesnums.html.

Arno, Stephen A. and Carl E. Fiedler. "The Tree That Built an Empire." In *Douglas-Fir: The Story of the West's Most Remarkable Tree,* 71–91. Seattle: Mountaineers Books, 2020.

Bolsinger, Charles L., and Karen L. Waddell. "Area of old-growth forests in California, Oregon, and Washington." Forest Service, United States Department of Agriculture, 1993. https://www.fs.fed.us/pnw/pubs/pnw_rb197.pdf.

Bury, R. Bruce. "Low Thermal Tolerances of Stream Amphibians in the Pacific Northwest: Implications for Riparian and Forest Management." *Applied Herpetology* 5, no. 1 (2008): 63–74. https://doi.org/10.1163/157075408783489211.

"Coastal Tailed Frog - *Ascaphus Truei*." A Guide to the Amphibians and Reptiles of California. http://www.californiaherps.com/frogs/pages/a.truei.html.

"Coastal Tailed Frog" The Oregon Conservation Strategy. Oregon Department of Fish and Wildlife. https://www.oregonconservationstrategy.org/strategy-species/coastal-tailed-frog/.

Corn, Paul Stephen, and R. Bruce Bury. "Logging in Western Oregon: Responses of Headwater Habitats and Stream Amphibians." *Forest Ecology and Management* 29, no. 1–2 (1989): 39–57. https://doi.org/10.1016/0378-1127(89)90055-8.

Davis, Rob. "Polluted by Money: How Corporate Cash Corrupted One of the Greenest States in America." *The Oregonian/OregonLive*. February 22, 2019. https://projects.oregonlive.com/polluted-by-money/part-1.

Davis, Rob and Tony Schick. "What Happened When a Public Institute Became a De Facto Lobbying Arm of the Timber Industry." *ProPublica*, August 4, 2020. https://www.propublica.org/article/what-happened-when-a-public-institute-became-a-de-facto-lobbying-arm-of-the-timber-industry.

Deanna Olson (US Forest Service research ecologist) in discussion with the author, July 9, 2021.

Doug Heiken (Oregon Wild conservation and restoration coordinator) in discussion with the author, August 3, 2021.

Dupuis, Linda. "Wildlife in British Columbia at Risk: tailed frog" Ministry of Environment, Lands and Parks, British Columbia, 1998. https://www2.gov.bc.ca/assets/gov/environment/plants-animals-and-ecosystems/species-ecosyste ms-at-risk/brochures/tailed_frog.pdf.

Durbin, Kathie. *Tree Huggers: Victory, Defeat & Renewal in the Northwest Ancient Forest Campaign*. Seattle: The Mountaineers, 1996.

Elderkin, Susan. "What a Difference a Year Makes." *High Country News*, September 2, 1996. https://www.hcn.org/issues/89/2748.

Essner, Richard L., Daniel J. Suffian, Phillip J. Bishop, and Stephen M. Reilly. "Landing in Basal Frogs: Evidence of Saltational Patterns in the Evolution of Anuran Locomotion." *Naturwissenschaften* 97, no. 10 (2010): 935–39. https://doi.org/10.1007/s00114-010-0697-4.

Graves, Mark. "Public and Private Lands in Oregon." *The Oregonian/OregonLive*. https://projects.oregonlive.com/maps/land-ownership/index.php.

Hall, Bennett. "Marys Peak: Island in the Sky." *Corvallis Gazette-Times*, April 11, 2017. https://www.gazettetimes.com/philomathexpress/local/marys-peak-island-in-the-sky/article_77b5 b4ab-9f1e-5543-99fe-f645c3252add.html.

Hayes, Marc P., and Timothy Quinn, eds. "Review and Synthesis of the Literature on Tailed Frogs (genus *Ascaphus*) with Special Reference to Managed Landscapes." *Cooperative Monitoring Evaluation and Research Report* CMER 01-107. Washington State Forest Practices Adaptive Management Program. Washington Department of Natural Resources. 2015. https://www.dnr.wa.gov/publications/fp_cmer_01_107.pdf.

Hays, Phillip R., Robert E. Frenkel, and Esther H. G. McEvoy. "Marys Peak Scenic Botanical Area." *Kalmiopsis* 19 (2012): 21–35. https://www.npsoregon.org/kalmiopsis/kalmiopsis19/4maryspeak.pdf.

Jade Keehn (Oregon Department of Fish and Wildlife conservation biologist) email correspondence with author, July 8, 2021, August 17, 2021, and August 18, 2021.

Larmer, Paul. "Cut to the Past: Logging Wars Resume." *High Country News*, October 16, 1995. http://www/hcn/org/issues/45/1378.

Law, Beverly E., Tara W. Hudiburg, Logan T. Berner, Jeffrey J. Kent, Polly C. Buotte, and Mark E. Harmon. "Land Use Strategies to Mitigate Climate Change in Carbon Dense Temperate Forests." *Proceedings of the National Academy of Sciences 115*, no. 14 (2018): 3663–68. https://doi.org/10.1073/pnas.1720064115.

Lorensen, Ted, Chip Andrus, and John Runyon. "The Oregon Forest Protection Act Water Protection Rules." Forest Practices Policy Unit, Oregon Department of Forestry, 1994. https://www.oregon.gov/odf/Documents/workingforests/waterprotectionrulessciencepolicy1994. pdf.

Mallory, Agi, and L. Dupuis. "Coastal Tailed Frog." *Accounts and Measures for Managing Identified Wildlife*, 2004, 1–8. https://www.env.gov.bc.ca/wld/frpa/iwms/documents/Amphibians/a_coastaltailedfrog.pdf.

Mark Leppin (Oregon State University graduate student) in discussion with the author, July 10, 2021.

Mason, Robert T., Matthew J. Asay, Polly G. Harowicz, and Lixing Su. "Chemically Mediated Mate Recognition in the Tailed Frog (Ascaphus Truei)." In *Chemical Signals in Vertebrates* 10, edited by Robert T. Mason, Michael P. LeMaster, and Dietland Müller-Schwarze. New York: Springer, 2005.

Morin, Ricardo. "Logging in Oregon." Oregon Wild. Online Map. 2019. https://logging.oregonhowl.org/.

Nielson, Marilyn, Kirk Lohman, and Jack Sullivan. "Phylogeography of the Tailed Frog (Ascaphus truei): Implications for the Biogeography of the Pacific Northwest." *Evolution* 55, no. 1 (2001): 147–60. https://doi.org/10.1554/0014-3820(2001)055[0147:pottfa]2.0.co;2.

Olson, Deanna H. and Kelly M. Burnett. "Geometry of forest landscape connectivity: pathways for persistence." In *Density Management in the 21st Century: West Side Story*, 220–238. General Technical Report. Portland, OR: US Department of Agriculture, Forest Service, Pacific Northwest Research Station, 2013. https://www.fs.usda.gov/treesearch/pubs/44786.

Olson, Deanna H., and Julia I. Burton. "Climate Associations with Headwater Streamflow in Managed Forests over 16 Years and Projections of Future Dry Headwater Stream Channels." *Forests* 10, no. 11 (2019): 1–28. https://doi.org/10.3390/f10110968.

Olson, Deanna H., and Kelly M. Burnett. "Design and Management of Linkage Areas across Headwater Drainages to Conserve Biodiversity in Forest Ecosystems." *Forest Ecology and Management* 258S (2009): S117–S126. https://doi.org/10.1016/j.foreco.2009.04.018.

Olson, Deanna H., and Matthew R. Kluber. "Plethodontid Salamander Distributions in Managed Forest Headwaters in Western Oregon, USA." *Herpetological Conservation and Biology* 9, no. 1 (2014): 76–96. https://www.fs.fed.us/pnw/pubs/journals/pnw_2014_olson005.pdf.

Olson, Deanna H., Paul D. Anderson, Christopher A. Frissell, Hartwell H. Welsh Jr., and David F. Bradford. "Biodiversity management approaches for stream-riparian areas: Perspectives for Pacific Northwest headwater forests, microclimates, and amphibians." *Forest Ecology and Management*, 246 (2007): 81–107. https://www.fs.usda.gov/treesearch/pubs/29704.

Oregon Department of Fish and Wildlife Priority Strategy Species List. 2017. https://oregonconservationstrategy.org/media/ODFW-Wildlife-Priority-Strategy-Species-by-Ecoregion_3.2018.pdf.

Pough, F. Harvey, Robin M. Andrews, Martha L. Crump, Alan H. Savitzky, Kentwood D. Wells, and Matthew C. Brandley. "Anura: Frogs and Toads." In *Herpetology*, Fourth Ed., 60–61. Sunderland, MA: Sinauer Associates, Inc., 2016.

"Rocky Mountain Tailed Frog - *Ascaphus Montanus*." Montana Field Guide. http://fieldguide.mt.gov/speciesDetail.aspx?elcode=AAABA01020.

Samayoa, Monica, and David Steves. "More National Forest Logging Expected from Last-Minute Environmental Rule Change." *Oregon Public Broadcasting*, November 19, 2020. https://www.opb.org/article/2020/11/19/us-forest-service-rule-change-national-environmental-policy-act/.

Scott, Aaron. *Timber Wars*. Produced by Oregon Public Broadcasting. 2020. Podcast. https://www.opb.org/show/timberwars/.

Scully-Engelmeyer, Kaegan, Elise F. Granek, Max Nielsen-Pincus, Andy Lanier, Steven S. Rumrill, Patrick Moran, Elena Nilsen, Michelle L. Hladik, and Lori Pillsbury. "Exploring Biophysical Linkages between Coastal Forestry Management Practices and Aquatic Bivalve Contaminant Exposure." *Toxics* 9 (March 2, 2021): 1–25. https://doi.org/10.3390/toxics9030046.

Sickinger, Ted. "Failing Forestry: Oregon's forestry department is on an unsustainable path." *The Oregonian/OregonLive*. October 20, 2019. https://www.oregonlive.com/environment/2019/10/failing-forestry-oregons-forestry-department-is-on-an-unsustainable-path.html.

Spies, Thomas A., Jonathan W. Long, Susan Charnley, Paul F. Hessburg, Bruce G. Marcot, Gordon H. Reeves, Damon B. Lesmeister, Matthew J. Reilly, Lee K. Cerveny, Peter A. Stine, and Martin G. Raphael. "Twenty-Five Years of the Northwest Forest Plan: What Have We Learned?" *Frontiers in Ecology and the Environment* 17, no. 9 (2019): 511–20. https://doi.org/10.1002/fee.2101.

Huckleberry

Amit Dhingra (Professor, plant genomics researcher at Washington State University, Texas A&M University) in discussion with the author, August 18, 2021.

Anzinger, Dawn L. "Big huckleberry (*Vaccinium membranaceum* Dougl.) Ecology and Forest Succession, Mt. Hood National Forest and Warm Springs Indian Reservation, Oregon." Master's thesis, Oregon State University, 2002. https://ir.library.oregonstate.edu/concern/graduate_thesis_or_dissertations/cc08hh65r?locale=en.

Ayer, Tammy "Yakama elder, leader and cultural champion dies at 86." *Yakima Herald-Republic*, April 25, 2020. https://www.yakimaherald.com/news/local/yakama-elder-leader-and-cultural-champion-dies-at-a ge-86/article_fad-cbb83-7de9-509a-a02e-14b57f8e8a15.html.

Bernadine Strik (Oregon State University berry crops specialist) in discussion with the author, August 24, 2021.

Carson, Rob. "Boldt Decision on tribal fishing still resonates after 40 years." *The Olympian*, February 9, 2014. https://www.courts.wa.gov/content/PublicUpload/eclips/2014%2002%2010%20Boldt%20Decisi on%20on%20tribal%20fishing%20still%20resonates%20after%2040%20years.pdf.

Charnley, Susan, A. Paige Fischer, and Eric T. Jones. "Integrating traditional and local ecological knowledge into forest biodiversity observation in the Pacific Northwest." *Forest Ecology and Management*, 246 (2007): 14–28. https://ecoshare.info/uploads/ccamp/synthesis_paper_tools/huckleberry/Charnley_et_al.__2007._Integrating_TEK_into_biodiversity_conservation.pdf.

Cheryl Mack (retired US Forest Service archeologist) in discussion with the author, August 19, 2021.

Durbin, Kathie. "Huckleberry fields benefit from flames." *The Columbian*, October 4, 2011. https://www.columbian.com/news/2011/oct/05/huckleberry-fields-benefit-from-flames/.

Elaine Harvey (Yakama Nation fish biologist, hydro systems oversight coordinator) in discussion with the author, August 25, 2021.

Emily Washines (native plants, food, and Yakama War scholar) in discussion with the author, September 3, 2021.

Fisher, Andrew H. "The 1932 Handshake Agreement: Yakama Indian Treaty Rights and Forest Service Policy in the Pacific Northwest." *Western Historical Quarterly* 28 (1997): 186–217. https://academic.oup.com/whq/article-abstract/28/2/186/1891954?redirectedFrom=fulltext.

Friesen, Cheryl. "Ecology and Management of Big Huckleberry." US Forest Service Region 6 Ecology Program. 2016. https://drive.google.com/file/d/1sQouSshxPtRjpwOhdt3-xmyWIjaUj-Nn/view?usp=drivesdk.

Goschke, Lauren. "Tribes, Treaties, and the Trust Responsibility: A call for Co-Management of Huckleberries in the Northwest." *Colorado Natural Resources, Energy, and Environmental Law Review* 27 (2016): 315–360. https://www.colorado.edu/law/sites/default/files/CNREELR-V27-I2-Lauren.pdf.

Hudec, Jessica. "Gifford Pinchot National Forest Huckleberry Management Strategy." US Department of Agriculture, US Forest Service. November 2018. https://drive.google.com/file/d/1sQouSshxPtRjpwOhdt3-xmyWIjaUj-Nn/view?usp=drivesdk.

Hunn, Eugene S. with James Selam and Family. *Nch'i-Wána, "The Big River:" Mid-Columbia Indians and Their Land.* Seattle: University of Washington Press, 1990.

Jamie Tolfree (former US Forest Service archeologist, retired Pinchot Partners coordinator) in discussion with the author, August 10, 2021.

Jessica Hudec (US Forest Service ecologist, fire specialist) in discussion with the author, August 10, 2021.

"Lesson Eleven: Overview of American Indian Policies, Treaties, and Reservations in the Northwest." Center for the Study of the Pacific Northwest, University of Washington. https://www.washington.edu/uwired/outreach/cspn/Website/Classroom%20Materials/Pacific%20 Northwest%20History/Lessons/Lesson%2011/11.html.

Ligori, Crystal. "Northwest Huckleberries Could Be Close to Domestication." *Oregon Public Broadcasting,* August 10, 2018. https://www.opb.org/news/article/northwest-huckleberries-backyard-domestication/.

Mack, Cheryl A. "A Burning Issue: American Indian Fire Use on the Mt. Rainier Forest Reserve." *Fire Management Today* 63, no. 2 (2003): 20–24. http://npshistory.com/publications/usfs/fmt-v53n2-2003.pdf

Mack, Cheryl A. and Richard H. McClure. "*Vaccinium* Processing in the Washington Cascades." Heritage Program, Gifford Pinchot National Forest. *Journal of Ethnobiology* 22, no. 1 (2002): 35–60. https://ethnobiology.org/sites/default/files/pdfs/JoE/22-1/MackMcClure2002.pdf.

"Map of Ceded Area and Reservation." Yakama Nation History. Confederated Tribes and Bands of the Yakama Nation. https://www.yakama.com/about/.

Minore, Don. "The wild huckleberries of Oregon and Washington—a dwindling resource." Pacific Northwest Forest and Range Experiment Station, US Department of Agriculture, US Forest Service. 1972. https://www.fs.fed.us/pnw/pubs/pnw_rp143.pdf.

Pojar, Jim and Andy MacKinnon. *Plants of the Pacific Northwest Coast.* The BC Ministry of Forests and Lone Pine Publishing, 1994. Revised edition, 2014. 56–59.

Prevéy, Janet S., Lauren E. Parker, Constance A. Harrington, Clayton T. Lamb, and Michael F. Proctor. "Climate change shifts in habitat suitability and phenology of huckleberry (*Vaccinium membranaceum*)" *Agricultural and Forest Meteorology* 280 (2020): 1-12. https://www.fs.fed.us/pnw/pubs/journals/pnw_2020_prevey001.pdf.

Richards, Rebecca T. and Susan J. Alexander. "A Social History of Wild Huckleberry Harvesting in the Pacific Northwest." US Department of Agriculture, US Forest Service. February 2006. https://www.fs.fed.us/pnw/pubs/pnw_gtr657.pdf.

Robbyn Bergher (US Forest Service special forest products program coordinator) email correspondence with the author, September 3, 2021.

Senos, René, Frank K. Lake, Nancy Turner, and Dennis Martinez. "Traditional Ecological Knowledge and Restoration Practice." In *Restoring the Pacific Northwest: The Art and Science of Ecological Restoration in Cascadia*, 393–426. Washington, DC: Island Press, 2006. https://www.fs.fed.us/psw/publications/lake/psw_2006_lake001_senos.pdf

Sorts, Danielle J., Andrew G. Fountain, and Matthew J. Hoffman. "Twentieth Century Glacier Change on Mount Adams, Washington, USA." *Northwest Science* 84, no. 4 (2010): 382. http://www.glaciers.pdx.edu/fountain/MyPapers/SittsEtAl2010_GlaciersMt.Adams.pdf.

Tidwell, Tom. "Thinking Like a Mountain, About Fire." Speech given at the Big Burn Centennial Commemoration, Boise, ID, May 22, 2010. https://www.fs.usda.gov/speeches/thinking-mountain-about-fire.

Tove, Danovich. "For the Love of Huckleberries: August Brings Out Hunters of Elusive Fruit." *National Public Radio, Oregon Public Broadcasting*, August 11, 2017. https://www.npr.org/sections/thesalt/2017/08/11/542690164/for-the-love-of-huckleberries-august -brings-out-hunters-of-elusive-fruit.

"Tribal Nations and the United States: An Introduction." National Congress of American Indians. https://www.ncai.org/tribalnations/introduction/Tribal_Nations_and_the_United_States_An_Intr oduction-web-.pdf.

Washines, Emily and Jerry Peltier. "Natural Restoration and Cultural Knowledge of the Yakama Nation." Olympia, WA: Evergreen State College, 2010. http://nativecases.evergreen.edu/sites/nativecases.evergreen.edu/files/case-studies/washinescases tudy.pdf.

Olympic Marmot

"Alaska Marmot Species Profile." Alaska Department of Fish and Game. https://www.adfg.alaska.gov/index.cfm?adfg=alaskamarmot.main.

Armitage, Kenneth B. "Evolution of Sociality in Marmots." *Journal of Mammalogy* 80, no. 1 (1999): 1–10. https://www.researchgate.net/publication/271950278_Evolution_of_Sociality_in_Marmots.

Armitage, Kenneth B. "Hibernation as a major determinant of life-history traits in marmots." *Journal of Mammalogy* 98, no. 2 (2017): 321–331. https://doi.org/10.1093/jmammal/gyw159.

Armitage, Kenneth B. "The evolution, ecology, and systematics of marmots." *Oecologia Montana* 9 (2000): 1–18. https://om.vuvb.uniza.sk/index.php/OM/article/view/116/103.

Armitage, Kenneth B., Daniel T. Blumstein, and Brett C. Woods. "Energetics of hibernating yellow-bellied marmots (*Marmota flaviventris*)" *Comparative Biochemistry and Physiology* Part A 134 (2003): 101–114. https://citeseerx.ist.psu.edu/viewdoc/download?doi=10.1.1.700.7455&rep=rep1&type=pdf.

Barash, David P. *Marmots: Social Behavior and Ecology.* Redwood City, CA: Stanford University Press, 1989.

Blumstein, Daniel T. "Alarm Calling in Three Species of Marmots." *Behaviour* 136, no. 6 (1999): 731–757. https://blumsteinlab.eeb.ucla.edu/wp-content/uploads/sites/104/2017/05/Blumstein1999_Behavi our.pdf.

Blumstein, Daniel T. "The Marmot Burrow." Last modified 2009. http://www.marmotburrow.ucla.edu/.

Cardini, Andrea. "The Geometry of the Marmot (Rodentia: Sciuridae) Mandible: Phylogeny and Patterns of Morphological Evolution." *Systematic Biology* 52, no. 2 (2003): 186–205. https://doi.org/10.1080/10635150390192807.

Cox, Sarah. "Bringing the endangered Vancouver Island marmot back from the brink." *The Narwhal*, August 29, 2020. https://thenarwhal.ca/vancouver-island-marmot/.

"Cute Marmots Waking Up from Hibernation." BBC Studios. February 17, 2009. Video, 2:20. https://www.youtube.com/watch?v=Z9R3jVLXuxI.

Daniel G. Gavin, David M. Fisher, Erin M. Herring, Ariana White, and Linda B. Brubaker. "Paleoenvironmental Change on the Olympic Peninsula, Washington: Forests and Climate from the Last Glaciation to the Present." Final report to Olympic National Park (2013): 1–40. https://depts.washington.edu/pnwcesu/reports/J8W07100028_Final_Report.pdf.

Daniel, Janice C. and Daniel T. Blumstein. "A test of the acoustic adaptation hypothesis in four species of marmots." *Animal Behaviour* 56 (1998): 1517–1528. https://citeseerx.ist.psu.edu/viewdoc/download?doi=10.1.1.486.7137&rep=rep1&type=pdf.

Dave Conca (Olympic National Park cultural resource program manager) in discussion with the author, August 5, 2021 and August 30, 2021.

David P. Barash (University of Washington professor emeritus) in discussion with the author, September 29, 2021.

del Moral, Roger. "The Impact of the Olympic Marmot on Subalpine Vegetation Structure." *American Journal of Botany* 71, no. 9 (1984): 1228–1236. https://doi.org/10.2307/2443647.

Dryden, Carley. "Marmots wear out welcome." *The Spokesman- Review*, June 28, 2008. https://www.spokesman.com/stories/2008/jun/28/marmots-wear-out-welcome/#:~:text=They've%20become%20an%20unofficial%20city%20mascot.&text=Greenstone%20Homes%2C%20the%20developer%20of,resident%20complaints%20in%20recent%20months.

"Geology of the Olympic Peninsula." Olympic National Park. https://www.nps.gov/olym/planyourvisit/upload/geology_printer-friendly.pdf.

Griffin, Suzanne Cox. "Demography and Ecology of a Declining Endemic: The Olympic Marmot." PhD, diss., University of Montana. 2007. https://www.proquest.com/openview/0c5117421510b24e09cabc593edaf479/1?pq-origsite=gschol ar&cbl=18750.

Gussman, John. "The Olympic Marmot, Whistleblowers of the Alpine." 2020. Video, 3:36. https://vimeo.com/367369676.

Kerhoulas, Nicholas J., Aren M. Gunderson, and Link E. Olson. "Complex history of isolation and gene flow in hoary, Olympic, and endangered Vancouver Island marmots." *Journal of Mammalogy* 96, no. 4 (2015): 810–826. https://doi.org/10.1093/jmammal/gyv089.

Maia Murphy-Williams (wildlife ecologist) in discussion with the author, August 3, 2021.

McCaffery, Rebecca and Kurt Jenkins, eds. "Natural Resource Condition Assessment." Olympic National Park (2018): 189–211. http://npshistory.com/publications/olym/nrr-2018-1826.pdf

McNulty, Tim. *Olympic National Park: A Natural History*. Seattle: University of Washington Press, 2009.

"Mountain Goat Capture and Translocation." Olympic National Park. https://www.nps.gov/olym/planyourvisit/mountain-goat-capture-and-transloca-tion.htm.

Murphy-Williams, Maia. "Climate Change Impacts in Alpine Meadows: Environmental Factors Correlated with the Decline of the Olympic Marmot (*Marmota olympus*) Population in Olympic National Park, Washington State." Master's Thesis, University of Washington, 2020. https://digital.lib.washing-ton.edu/researchworks/bitstream/handle/1773/45499/MurphyWilliams_washington_0250O_21159.pdf?sequence=1&isAllowed=y.

Nash, Matthew. "Locals spot possibly more non-native, yellow-bellied marmots." *Sequim Gazette*, May 26, 2021. https://www.sequimgazette.com/news/locals-spot-possibly-more-non-native-yellow-bellied-marmots/.

"Olympic marmot (*Marmota olympus*)." Conservation Threats and Actions Needed. Washington Department of Fish and Wildlife. https://wdfw.wa.gov/species-habitats/species/marmota-olympus#desc-range.

"Olympic Marmot," Washington Department of Fish and Wildlife, Annual Report, 2012. https://wdfw.wa.gov/sites/default/files/2019-03/olympic_marmot.pdf.

Polly, P. David, Andrea Cardini, Edward B. Davis, and Scott J. Steppan. "Marmot evolution and global change in the past 10 million years." In *Evolution of the Rodents: Advances in Phylogeny, Palaeontology and Fundamental Morphology*, edited by Philip G. Cox and Lionel Hautier, 246–276. Cambridge: Cambridge University Press, 2015. https://doi.org/10.1017/CBO9781107360150.010.

Patti Happe (Olympic National Park wildlife biologist, branch chief) in discussion with the author, August 9, 2021.

Peterson, Christine. "25 years after returning to Yellowstone, wolves have helped stabilize the ecosystem." *National Geographic*, July 10, 2020. https://www.nationalgeographic.com/animals/article/yellowstone-wolves-reintroduc-tion-help ed-stabilize-ecosystem.

"Secrets of Marmot Hibernation." Nature on PBS. Video, 2:56. Jan. 12, 2021. https://www.youtube.com/watch?v=NJXi3s59sn0

"Squirrels, Chipmunks and Marmots." Oregon Department of Fish and Wildlife. https://myodfw.com/wildlife-viewing/species/squirrels-chipmunks-and-marmots.

Steppan, Scott J., G.J. Kenagy, Christopher Zawadzki, Rafael Robles, Elena A. Lyapunova, and Robert S. Hoffmann. "Molecular data resolve placement of the Olympic marmot and estimate dates of trans-Beringian interchange." *Journal of Mammalogy* 92, no. 5 (2011): 1028–1037. https://doi.org/10.1644/10-MAMM-A-272.1.

Suzanne Cox Griffin (University of Montana doctoral researcher) in discussion/communication with author August 8, 2021 and September 15, 2021.

"The Olympic Marmot: Ecology and Research." National Park Service. https://www.nps.gov/olym/learn/nature/upload/The-Olympic-Marmot-Ecology-Research-2.pdf.

"Weather and Climate." Olympic National Park. Last updated November 9, 2021. https://www.nps.gov/olym/planyourvisit/weather-brochure.htm.

"Wildlife and Other Sightings: Marmot is returned to Yosemite!" National Park Service, August 26, 2012. https://www.nps.gov/yose/blogs/wildlife-and-other-sightings-marmot-is-returned-to-yosemite.htm.

William Baccus (Olympic National Park physical science technician) email communication with the author, October 25, 2021.

Witczuk, Julia, Stanisław Pagacz, and L. Scott Mills. "Disproportionate predation on endemic marmots by invasive coyotes." *Journal of Mammalogy* 94, no. 3 (2013): 702–713. https://doi.org/10.1644/12-MAMM-A-199.1.

Wolf, Christopher and William J. Ripple. "Rewilding the world's large carnivores." *Royal Society Open Science* 5, no. 3 (2018): 1–15. https://doi.org/10.1098/rsos.172235.

Moss

Beatrice Bugos (University of Puget Sound undergraduate student) in discussion with the author, September 26, 2021

Betzen, Jacob J., Amy Ramsey, Daniel Omdal, Gregory J. Ettl and Patrick C. Tobin. "Bigleaf maple, *Acer macrophyllum* Pursh, decline in western Washington, USA." *Forest Ecology and Management* 501 (2021): 1–11. https://doi.org/10.1016/j.foreco.2021.119681.

Carrie Woods (University of Puget Sound professor, ecologist) in discussion with the author, September 26, 2021 and November 5, 2021.

Crooks, Vanessa. "Bryophytes: Tiny plants in a big changing world." *Smithsonian Tropical Research Institute*, February 22, 2021. https://stri.si.edu/story/bryophytes.

"Draft Management Recommendations for Goblin's gold *Schistostega pennata* (Hedw.) Web & Mohr." Version 1.1 (1996). https://www.blm.gov/or/plans/surveyandmanage/MR/Bryophytes/scpe.pdf.

Ellen Bradley (scientist who conducted research with Carrie Woods and Michelle Spicer) in discussion with the author, September 15, 2021.

Fretwell, Kelly and Brian Starzomski. "Badge moss, coastal leafy moss, plagiomnium moss." Biodiversity of the Central Coast. 2013. https://www.centralcoastbiodiversity.org/badge-moss-bull-plagiomnium-insigne.html.

Glime, Janice M. *Bryophyte Ecology*. Houghton, MI: Michigan Technological University, 2021. https://digitalcommons.mtu.edu/cgi/viewcontent.cgi?article=1001&context=bryophyte-ecology1.

Haig, David. "Living together and living apart: the sexual lives of bryophytes." *Philosophical Transactions of the Royal Society B* 371, no. 1706 (2016): 1–9. https://doi.org/10.1098/rstb.2015.0535.

Harpel, Judy A. and John Davis. "Conservation Assessment for *Iwatsukiella leucotricha*." US Department of Agriculture, US Forest Service, Region 6 and US Department of Interior Bureau of Land Management, Oregon and Washington. 2009. https://www.blm.gov/or/plans/surveyandmanage/files/ca-br-iwatsukiella-leucotricha-2009-12.pdf.

Henry Norton (University of Puget Sound undergraduate student) in discussion with the author, September 26, 2021.

Hutten, Martin and Andrea Woodward. "Bryophytes and Lichens: Small but Indispensable Forest Dwellers." US Department of the Interior, US Geological Survey. December 2002. https://www.fws.gov/pacific/Climatechange/pdf/boise/DeCrappeo/Recommended%20Reading/Bryophytes%20and%20Lichens.pdf.

Hutten, Martin, Andrea Woodward, and Karen Hutten. "Inventory of the Mosses, Liverworts, Hornworts, and Lichens of Olympic National Park, Washington: Species List." US Geological.

Survey, Scientific Investigations Report 2005–5240. 2005. https://pubs.usgs.gov/sir/2005/5240/sir20055240.pdf.

Jensen, Larry. "Reproductive Cycle of Mosses." In *The Amazing Lives of Plants*. McGraw-Hill Companies, Inc. April 1, 2005. Video, 10:15, June 10, 2013. https://www.youtube.com/watch?v=_MFnZjpTFT8.

Johnson, Matthew G. and A. Jonathan Shaw. "Genetic diversity, sexual condition, and microhabitat preference determine mating patterns in *Sphagnum* (Sphagnaceae) peat-mosses." *Biological Journal of the Linnean Society* 115, no. 1 (2015): 96–113. https://doi.org/10.1111/bij.12497.

Kimmerer, Robin Wall. "The Role of Slugs in Dispersal of the Asexual Propagules of *Dicranum flagellare*." *The Bryologist* 98, no. 1 (1995): 149–153. https://doi.org/10.2307/3243652.

Kimmerer, Robin Wall. *Gathering Moss: A Natural and Cultural History of Mosses.* Corvallis: Oregon State University Press, 2003.

Kirk, Ruth. *Ozette: Excavating a Makah Whaling Village.* Seattle: University of Washington Press, 2015.

Lenton, Timothy M., Tais W. Dahl, Stuart J. Daines, Benjamin J. W. Mills, Kazumi Ozaki, Matthew R. Saltzman, and Philipp Porada. "Earliest land plants created modern levels of atmospheric oxygen." *Proceedings of the National Academy of Sciences of the United States of America* 113, no. 35 (2016): 9704–9709. https://doi.org/10.1073/pnas.1604787113.

Liu, Yang, Matthew G. Johnson, Cymon J. Cox, Rafael Medina, Nicolas Devos, Alain Vanderpoorten, Lars Hedenas, Neil E. Bell, James R. Shevock, Blanka Aguero, Dietmar Quandt, Norman J. Wickett, A. Jonathan Shaw, and Bernard Goffinet. "Resolution of the ordinal phylogeny of mosses using targeted exons from organellar and nuclear genomes." *Nature Communications* 10 (2019): 1–11. https://doi.org/10.1038/s41467-019-09454-w.

Loften, Adam and Emmanuel Vaughan-Lee. "Sanctuaries of Silence." *New York Times*, March 27, 2018. https://www.nytimes.com/2018/03/27/opinion/silence-forests.html.

Marshall, Michael. "Timeline: The evolution of life." *New Scientist*, July 14, 2009. https://www.newscientist.com/article/dn17453-timeline-the-evolution-of-life/.

Martin Hutten (bryologist and botanist) in discussion with the author, September 30, 2021.

McCune, Bruce and Martin Hutten. *Common Mosses of Western Oregon and Washington.* Corvallis, OR: Wild Blueberry Media, 2018.

McGrath, Matt. "Frozen Antarctic moss brought back to life after 1,500 years." *BBC News*, March 17, 2014. https://www.bbc.com/news/science-environment-26614092.

Michelle Spicer (Yale School of the Environment postdoctoral fellow and ecologist) in discussion with the author, September 14, 2021.

Nadkarni, Nalini M. "Biomass and mineral capital of epiphytes in an *Acer macrophyllum* community of a temperate moist coniferous forest, Olympic Peninsula, Washington State." *Canadian Journal of Botany* 62, no. 11 (1984): 2223–2228. https://nalininadkarni.com/wp-content/uploads/2019/01/Biomass-and-mineral-capital-of-epiphytes-in-an-Acer-macrophyllum-community-of-a-temperate-moist-coniferous-forest-Olympic-Peninsula-Washington-State.pdf.

Nadkarni, Nalini M. "Canopy Roots: Convergent Evolution in Rainforest Nutrient Cycles." Science. New Series 214, no. 4524 (1981): 1023–1024. https://nalininadkarni.com/wp-content/uploads/2019/01/Canopy-roots-convergent-evolution-in-rainforest-nutrient-cycles.pdf.

Nadkarni, Nalini. *The stuff I'm here to study: Life on life on life.* Produced by Meditative Story, 2021. Podcast. https://meditativestory.com/nalini-nadkarni/.

Nadkarni. Nalini M. "The Moss Shall Set Them Free." *Orion Magazine.* https://orionmagazine.org/article/the-moss-shall-set-them-free/.

Olympic Peninsula Intertribal Cultural Advisory Committee. *Native Peoples of the Olympic Peninsula.* Edited by Jacilee Wray. Norman: University of Oklahoma Press, 2015.

Pojar, Jim and Andy MacKinnon. *Plants of the Pacific Northwest Coast.* The BC Ministry of Forests and Lone Pine Publishing, 1994. Revised edition, 2014.

Powell, Jay. "Cultural Resources. Hoh Tribe". https://hohtribe-nsn.org/culture/cultural-resources/.

Radford, Tim. "All hail the humble moss, bringer of oxygen and life to Earth." *The Guardian,* August 15, 2016. https://www.theguardian.com/science/2016/aug/15/all-hail-the-humble-moss-bringer-of-oxygen-and-life-to-earth.

"Record Trees: Forests of Giants." Olympic National Park. https://www.nps.gov/olym/planyourvisit/upload/record-trees-printer-friendly.pdf.

Spicer, Michelle Elise, Hannah Mellor, and Walter P. Carson. "Seeing beyond the trees: a comparison of tropical and temperate plant growth forms and their vertical distribution." *Ecology* 101, no. 4 (2020): 1–9. https://doi.org/10.1002/ecy.2974.

Tejo, Camila F., Darlene Zabowski, and Nalini M. Nadkarni. "Total and epiphytic litter under the canopy of *Acer macrophyllum* in an old-growth temperate rainforest, Washington State, USA." *Canadian Journal of Forest Research* (2015). https://doi.org/10.1139/cjfr-2014-0492.

"Temperate Rain Forests." National Park Service. https://www.nps.gov/olym/learn/nature/temperate-rain-forests.htm.

Woods, Carrie L. "Primary ecological succession in vascular epiphytes: The species accumulation model." *BIOTROPICA* 49, no. 4 (2017): 452–460. https://doi.org/10.1111/btp.12443.

Woods, Carrie L., Katy Maleta, and Kimmy Ortmann. "Plant-plant interactions change during succession on nurse logs in a northern temperate rainforest." *Ecology and Evolution* 11, no. 14 (2021): 9631–9641. https://doi.org/10.1002/ece3.7786.

Woods, Carrie L., Laura M. Nevins, and Emma J. Didier. "Structural heterogeneity of trees influences epiphyte distributions in a northern temperate rainforest." *Journal of Vegetation Science* 30, no. 6 (2019): 1134–1142. https://doi.org/10.1111/jvs.12797.

Clouds

Ali, Shirin. "Controversial practice of seeding clouds to create rainfall becoming popular in the American West." *The Hill*, November 22, 2021. https://thehill.com/changing-america/resilience/smart-cities/582689-controversial-practice-of-seeding-clouds-to-create.

"An Introduction to Clouds." National Weather Service. https://www.weather.gov/jetstream/clouds_intro.

"Asperitas clouds." Met Office. https://www.metoffice.gov.uk/weather/learn-about/weather/types-of-weather/clouds/other-clouds /asperitas.

Barnes, Hannah C., Joseph P. Zagrondnik, Lynn A. McMurdie, Angela K. Rowe, and Robert A. Houze Jr. "Kelvin-Helmholtz Waves in Precipitating Midlatitude Cyclones." *Journal of the Atmospheric Sciences* 75, no. 8 (2018): 2763–2785. https://doi.org/10.1175/JAS-D-17-0365.1.

Baumann, Lisa. "'Atmospheric river' causes floods, evacuations in Northwest." *Associated Press*, November 15, 2021. https://www.seattletimes.com/seattle-news/weather/major-flooding-expected-on-skagit-river-tow n-of-hamilton-evacuated/.

Binky Walker (artist) in discussion with the author, November 6, 2021.

Chu, Jennifer. "Dust in the clouds." *MIT News*, May 9, 2013. https://news.mit.edu/2013/cirrus-clouds-mineral-dust-0509.

Cleeves, L. Ilsedore, Edwin A. Bergin, Conel M. O'D. Alexander, Fujun Du, Dawn Graninger, Karin I. Oberg, and Tim J. Harries. "The Ancient Heritage of Water Ice in the Solar System." *Science* 345, no. 6204 (2014):1590–1593. http://dx.doi.org/10.1126/science.1258055.

"Clouds and Climate." Physical Sciences Laboratory. National Oceanic Atmospheric Administration. https://psl.noaa.gov/outreach/education/science/clouds_and_climate.html#:~:text=Clouds%20pla y%20a%20vital%20role,warmer%20our%20climate%20will%20grow.

"Clouds." Met Office. https://www.metoffice.gov.uk/weather/learn-about/weather/types-of-weather/clouds.

"Cloudy Earth." NASA Earth Observatory. https://earthobservatory.nasa.gov/images/85843/cloudy-earth.

Dello, Kathie and Cally Whitman. "Water and Climate in the Pacific Northwest." A report prepared for the Institute for Water and Watersheds, Oregon State University (2012): 1–11. https://water.oregonstate.edu/sites/water.oregonstate.edu/files/water_and_climate_in_the_pacific_northwest_v3.pdf.

Dettinger, Michael D. and B. Lynn Ingram. "The Coming Megafloods." Scientific American, January 2013. http://www.hydrology.bee.cornell.edu/BEE3710Handouts/DettingerSCIAM2013_Megafloods.pdf.

Ennis, Chris. "The origins of cirrus: Earth's highest clouds have dusty core." NOAA Research News, May 9, 2013. https://research.noaa.gov/article/ArtMID/587/ArticleID/1503/The-origins-of-cirrus-Earth%E2%8 0%99s-highest-clouds-have-dusty-core.

Gillies, James. "CLOUD shows pre-industrial skies cloudier than we thought." CERN, May 25, 2016. https://home.cern/news/news/experiments/cloud-shows-pre-industrial-skies-cloudier-we-thought.

Hansen, Kathryn. "Water Vapor Confirmed as Major Player in Climate Change." NASA's Goddard Space Flight Center. https://www.nasa.gov/topics/earth/features/vapor_warming.html.

Hausfather, Zeke. "Explainer: How scientists estimate 'climate sensitivity'" CarbonBrief, June 19, 2018. https://www.carbonbrief.org/explainer-how-scientists-estimate-climate-sensitivity.

Hersh, Seymour M. "Rainmaking Is Used As Weapon by U.S." New York Times, July 3, 1972. https://www.nytimes.com/1972/07/03/archives/rainmaking-is-used-as-weapon-by-us-cloudseedin g-in-indochina-is.html.

Hickey, Hannah. "Marine plankton brighten clouds over Southern Ocean." University of Washington News, July 17, 2015. https://www.washington.edu/news/2015/07/17/marine-plankton-brighten-clouds-over-southern-ocean/

"How old is glacier ice?" US Geological Survey. https://www.usgs.gov/faqs/how-old-glacier-ice?qt-news_science_products=0#qt-news_science_products.

Lynn McMurdie (University of Washington professor and atmospheric scientist) in discussion with the author, October 21, 2021.

Mangione, Kendra. "Another 'atmospheric river' expected to hit B.C. as province deals with flooding from 1st." *CTV News Vancouver*, November 21, 2021. https://bc.ctvnews.ca/another-atmospheric-river-expected-to-hit-b-c-as-province-deals-with-flood ing-from-1st-1.5675183.

Mass, Cliff. *The Weather of the Pacific Northwest*. Seattle: University of Washington Press, 2021.

McCoy, Daniel T., Susannah M. Burrows, Robert Wood, Daniel P. Grosvenor, Scott M. Elliot, Po-Lun Ma, Phillip J. Rasch, and Dennis L. Hartmann. "Natural aerosols explain seasonal and spatial patterns of Southern Oregon cloud albedo." *Science Advances* 1, no. 6 (2015): 1–12. https://doi.org/10.1126/sciadv.1500157.

Milman, Oliver. "Make it rain: US states embrace 'cloud seeding' to try to conquer drought." *The Guardian*, March 23, 2021. https://www.theguardian.com/environment/2021/mar/23/us-stated-cloud-seeding-weather-modifi cation.

"NASA: Why does the sun matter for earth's energy budget?" NASA Goddard. November 29, 2017. Video, 1:39. https://www.youtube.com/watch?v=82jE-yvB8xU.

Nicholas Siler (Oregon State University professor and atmospheric scientist) in discussion with the author, September 16, 2021.

Pearce, Fred. "Why Clouds Are the Key to New Troubling Projections on Warming." *Yale Environment 360*, February 5, 2020. https://e360.yale.edu/features/why-clouds-are-the-key-to-new-troubling-projections-on-warming.

Pretor-Pinney, Gavin. "Cloudspotting for Beginners," The Eye Towards the Sky lecture series, The American Meteorological Society. Boston Public Library. October 30, 2019. Video, 1:15:22. https://www.youtube.com/watch?v=dDXtGuGNfuc.

Pretor-Pinney, Gavin. "Nature Speaks Cloudspotting for Beginners with Gavin Pretor-Pinney." Prospect Heights Public Library District. April 1, 2021. Video, 1:03:22. https://www.youtube.com/watch?v=4JheqmRCZ7s.

Pretor-Pinney, Gavin. *The Cloudspotter's Guide: The Science, History, and Culture of Clouds*. New York: TarcherPerigee, 2007.

Ruth, Maria Mudd. *A Sideways Look at Clouds*. Seattle: Mountaineers Books, 2017.

Schmunk, Rhianna. "Thousands of animals have died on flooded B.C. farms in 'agriculture disaster.'" *CBC News*, November 17, 2021. https://www.cbc.ca/news/canada/british-columbia/bc-flooding-2021-livestock-deaths-abbots-ford 1.6252774.

Schneider, Tapio. Earnest C. Watson Lecture by Professor Tapio Schneider, "Clouds and the Climate Tipping Point." Caltech. April 24, 2019. Video, 46:44. https://www.youtube.com/watch?v=eGshzvKAM3w&t=88s.

"Severe flooding in the Pacific Northwest." NASA Earth Observatory. November 14, 2021. https://earthobservatory.nasa.gov/images/149100/severe-flooding-in-the-pacific-northwest

Siler, Nicholas and Gerard Roe. "How will orographic precipitation respond to surface warming? An idealized thermodynamic perspective." *Geophysical Research Letters* 41, no. 7 (2014): 2606–2613. https://doi.org/10.1002/2013GL059095.

St. Fleur, Nicholas. "The Water in Your Glass Might Be Older Than the Sun." *New York Times*, April 15, 2016. https://www.nytimes.com/2016/04/16/science/the-water-in-your-glass-might-be-older-than-the-s un.html.

"The science behind atmospheric rivers." National Oceanic Atmospheric Administration. https://psl.noaa.gov/arportal/about/pdf/noaa-atmospheric-rivers-infographic.pdf.

"The Water Cycle." National Science Foundation. July 12, 2013. Video, 6:46. https://www.youtube.com/watch?v=al-do-HGuIk.

Walker, Binky. "Ukiyo-e: pictures of the floating world." https://www.binkywalker.net/drawings/ukiyo-e-pictures-of-the-floating-world/1.

Water Science School. "How Much Does a Cloud Weigh?" US Geological Survey. July 7, 2019. https://www.usgs.gov/special-topic/water-science-school/science/how-much-does-a-cloud-weigh?qt-science_center_objects=0#qt-science_center_objects.

"What are atmospheric rivers?" National Oceanic Atmospheric Administration. https://www.noaa.gov/stories/what-are-atmospheric-rivers.

"What are clouds?" STEMvisions Blog. Smithsonian Science Education Center. https://ssec.si.edu/stemvisions-blog/what-are-clouds.

"What is the Jet Stream?" SciJinks. National Oceanic and Atmospheric Administration. https://scijinks.gov/jet-stream/.

"Why do clouds stay up?" *It's Okay To Be Smart*, PBS Digital Studios. October 6, 2014. Video, 6:28. https://www.youtube.com/watch?v=DjByja9ejTQ.

Zagrodnik, Joseph P., Lynn A. McMurdie, and Robert A. Houze Jr.. "Stratiform Precipitation Processes in Cyclones Passing over a Coastal Mountain Range." *Journal of Atmospheric Sciences* 75 (2018): 983-1004. https://doi.org/10.1175/JAS-D-17-0168.1.

Gray Whale

Alford, Matthew H. and Parker MacCready. "Flow and mixing in Juan de Fuca Canyon, Washington." *Geophysical Research Letters* 41, no. 5 (2014):1608–1615. https://doi.org/10.1002/2013GL058967.

"Amazing Facts About Whales!" *Be Smart.* PBS Digital Studios. Aug. 24, 2015. Video, 7:19. https://www.youtube.com/watch?v=Ozi7lcyatt0.

Andersen, Peggy. "Whale goes down: Makah rejoice; protesters mourn." *Associated Press*, May 16, 1999. https://products.kitsapsun.com/archive/1999/05-16/0042_makah__whale_shakes_off_harpoon.html.

Braby, Caren, Kelly Corbett, Amanda Gladics, and Leigh Torres. "Hatfield Marine Science Center Research Seminar." May 28, 2020. Video, 1:09:27. https://www.youtube.com/watch?v=0FE0aJW4HG0&t=1775s.

Burnham, Rianna and David Duffus. "Gray whale calling response to altered soundscapes driven by whale watching activities in a foraging area." *Journal of Ocean Technology* 14, no. 3 (2019): 85–106. https://www.thejot.net/article-preview/?show_article_preview=1090.

Burnham, Rianna, David Duffus, and Xavier Mouy. "Gray Whale (*Eschrictius robustus*) Call Types Recorded During Migration off the West Coast of Vancouver Island." *Frontiers in Marine Science* 5 (2018): 1–11. https://doi.org/10.3389/fmars.2018.00329.

Burnham, Rianna. "Whale geography: Acoustics, biogeography and whales." *Progress in Physical Geography* 41, no. 5 (2017): 675–685. https://doi.org/10.1177/0309133317734103.

Bush, Evan. "Navy plans extensive training in Pacific Northwest. Here's how many animals could be hurt." *Seattle Times*, May 24, 2019. https://www.seattletimes.com/seattle-news/navy-plans-testing-of-futuristic-technology-sonar-harm-to-mammals-in-pacific-northwest/.

Calambokidis, John, Alie Pérez, and Jeffrey Laake. "Updated analysis of abundance and population structure of seasonal gray whales in the Pacific Northwest, 1996–2017." Cascadia Research Collective. https://www.cascadiaresearch.org/files/publications/Gray_whale_abundance_2017-Rev.pdf.

Collins, Cary C. "Subsistence and Survival: The Makah Indian Reservation, 1855–1933." *Pacific Northwest Quarterly* 87, no. 4 (1996): 180–193. https://digitalcollections.lib.washington.edu/digital/collection/lctext/id/1532.

Coté, Charlotte. "hishuk'ish tsawalk—Everything is one. Revitalizing place-based Indigenous food systems through the enactment of food sovereignty." *Journal of Agriculture, Food Systems, and Community Development* 9, no. A (2019) 37–48. https://doi.org/10.5304/jafscd.2019.09A.003.

Coté, Charlotte. *Spirits of our Whaling Ancestors.* Seattle: University of Washington Press, 2010.

Daugherty, Richard and Janet Friedman. "An Introduction to Ozette Art." In *Indian Art Traditions of the Northwest Coast*, 183–195. Burnaby, BC: SFU Archaeology Press, 1982. http://archpress.lib.sfu.ca/index.php/archpress/catalog/download/46/17/796-1?inline=1.

"Description of the USA Aboriginal Subsistence Hunt: Makah Tribe." International Whaling Commission. https://iwc.int/makah-tribe.

Dennison, Jean, Josh Reid, Lisa Wilson, and Melvinjohn Ashue. "What is at stake for Washington's Native nations today," Seattle Channel. October 8, 2018. Video, 1:29:01. https://www.youtube.com/watch?v=siRN18UsNC4.

DePoe, Patrick. "Declaration of Patrick DePoe in re: Proposed Waiver and Regulation Governing the Taking of Eastern North Pacific Gray Whales by the Makah Indian Tribe." Docket No. 19-NMFS-0001, United States of America Department of Commerce, National Oceanic and Atmospheric Administration, May 15, 2019. https://www.uscg.mil/Portals/0/Headquarters/Administrative%20Law%20Judges/NOAA%20files%202019/24%20-%20Makah%20-%20Declaration%20of%20Patrick%20DePoe.pdf?ver=2019-05-28-151157-063.

Dougherty, Phil. "Boldt Decision: *United States v. State of Washington.*" *HistoryLink.org*, Essay 21084. August 24, 2020. https://www.historylink.org/file/21084.

Duhamel, Frédérik-Xavier. "U.S. renews navy's right to harm marine mammals during testing and training off Pacific Coast." *CBC News*, November 17, 2020. https://www.cbc.ca/news/canada/british-columbia/u-s-renews-navy-s-right-harm-marine-mamma ls-1.5802652.

Eligon, John. "A Native Tribe Wants to Resume Whaling. Whale Defenders Are Divided." *New York Times*, November 14, 2019. https://www.nytimes.com/2019/11/14/us/whale-hunting-native-americans.html.

Feltes, Alex. "Learning About Whales From the Inside Out!" Catalina Island Marine Institute. https://cimioutdoored.org/learning-about-whales-from-the-inside-out/.

Floyd, Mark. "Study finds Oregon's unique 'resident' gray whales actually move around quite a bit." *Oregon State University Newsroom*, February 12, 2019. https://today.oregonstate.edu/news/ study-finds-oregon%E2%80%99s-unique-%E2%80%9Cresident%E2%80%9D-gray-whales-actually-move-around-quite-bit.

"Genetics and Gray Whale Behavior." University of California Television, April 4, 2013. Youube video, 44:00. https://www.youtube.com/watch?v=_F4VdrSGs0w.

"Gray whale facts." The Whale's Tail: Chartered Whale Watching. https://whalestaildepoebay.com/gray-whale-facts/.

Hildebrand, Lisa, Kim S. Bernard and Leigh G. Torres. "Do Gray Whales Count Calories? Comparing Energetic Values of Gray Whale Prey Across Two Different Feeding Grounds in the Eastern North Pacific." *Frontiers in Marine Science* 8 (2021): 1–13. https://doi.org/10.3389/fmars.2021.683634.

Hopper, Frank. "Whale Wars Group vs. Makah: Who Decides If Traditions Are Authentic?" *Indian Country Today*, June 23, 2015. https://indiancountrytoday.com/archive/whale-wars-group-vs-makah-who-decides-if-traditions-a re-authentic.

"Incidental Take Authorizations Under the Marine Mammal Protection Act." Protected Resources Permits & Authorizations. National Oceanic and Atmospheric Administration. https://www.fisheries.noaa.gov/permit/incidental-take-authorizations-under-marine-mammal-prot ection-act.

"International Whaling Commission." National Oceanic and Atmospheric Administration. https://www.fisheries.noaa.gov/international-affairs/ international-whaling-commission.

Jenny Waddell (Olympic Coast National Marine Sanctuary research ecologist) in discussion with the author, December 16, 2021.

Johnson, Gene. "Tribe wins major step toward resuming whaling off Washington's Olympic Peninsula." *Associated Press*, September 27, 2021. https://www.opb.org/article/2021/09/27/tribe-wins-major-step-toward-resuming-whaling-off-was hington/.

Kirk, Ruth. *Ozette: Excavating a Makah Whaling Village*. Seattle: University of Washington Press, 2015.

Kitch, Troy and Leila Hatch. "Listen Up: What You Need to Know About Ocean Noise." Produced by National Oceanic and Atmospheric Administration. *NOAA Ocean Podcast*. https://oceanservice.noaa.gov/podcast/aug18/nop18-ocean-noise.html.

Lagerquist, Barbara A., Daniel M. Palacios, Martha H. Winsor, Ladd M. Irvine, Thomas M. Follett, and Bruce R. Mate. "Feeding home ranges of Pacific Coast Feeding Group gray whales." *The Journal of Wildlife Management* 83, no. 4 (2019): 925–937. https://doi.org/10.1002/jwmg.21642.

Lang, Aimée R., John Calambokidis, Jonathan Scordino, Victoria L. Pease, Amber Klimek, Vladimir N. Burkanov, Pat Gearin, Dennis I. Litovka, Kelly M. Robertson, Bruce R. Mate, Jeff K. Jacobsen, and Barbara L. Taylor. "Assessment of genetic structure among eastern North Pacific gray whales on their feed grounds." *Marine Mammal Science* 30, no. 4 (2014): 1473–1493. https://doi.org/10.1111/mms.12129.

"Large Submarine Canyons of the United States Outer Continental Shelf Atlas." Bureau of Ocean Energy Management (2019). https://espis.boem.gov/final%20reports/BOEM_2019-066.pdf.

Larry D. Taylor, Aaron O'Dea, Timothy J. Bralower, and Seth Finnegan. "Isotopes from fossil coronulid barnacle shells record evidence of migration in multiple Pleistocene whale populations." *PNAS* 116, no. 15. (2019): 7377–7381. https://doi.org/10.1073/pnas.1808759116.

Lewis, David G. "Captain Abel Douglass." *Quartux: Journal of Critical Indigenous Anthropology*, December 22, 2014. https://ndnhistoryresearch.com/2014/12/22/captain-abel-douglass/.

Linthicum, Kate. "Why are so many gray whales dying in the Pacific?" *National Geographic*, April 13, 2021. https://www.nationalgeographic.com/animals/article/why-are-so-many-gray-whales-dying-in-the-pacific.

Lisa Hildebrand (doctoral researcher at Oregon State University's Marine Mammal Institute) in discussion with the author, December 2, 2021.

"Makah Tribal Members Sentenced For Violating Marine Mammal Protection Act." The United States Attorney's Office Western District of Washington. June 30, 2008. https://www.justice.gov/archive/usao/waw/press/2008/jul/whalesentencing.html.

"Makah Tribal Whale Hunt Chronology." National Oceanic and Atmospheric Administration. https://www.fisheries.noaa.gov/west-coast/marine-mammal-protection/makah-tribal-whale-hunt chronology.

"Makah Tribe History and More." https://makah.com/makah-tribal-info/.

Mapes, Lynda V. "Celebrating The Whale––Native Peoples From All Over Share Makah Potlatch." *Seattle Times*, May 23, 1999. https://archive.seattletimes.com/archive/?date=19990523&slug=whal23.

Marrero, Meghan E. and Stuart Thorton. "Big Fish: A Brief History of Whaling." *National Geographic*, November 1, 2011. https://www.nationalgeographic. org/article/big-fish-history-whaling/.

McCarty, Polly and Maria Pascua. "Makah Model Canoe." Smithsonian National Museum of the American Indian. March 13, 2012. Video, 3:33. https://www. youtube.com/watch?v=vaD5p1-mWco.

Melica, Valentina, Shannon Atkinson, John Calambokidis, Aimée Lang, Jonathan Scordino, and Franz Mueter. "Application of endocrine biomarkers to update information on reproductive physiology in gray whale (*Eschrichtius robustus*)" PLoS ONE 16, no. 8 (2021): 1–23. https://doi.org/10.1371/journal. pone.0255368.

Micah McCarty (Makah artist, former chairman of Makah Tribal Council) in discussion with the author, November 4, 9, 19, and 30, 2021, and December 6, 2021.

Olympic Peninsula Intertribal Cultural Advisory Committee. *Native Peoples of the Olympic Peninsula*. Edited by Jacilee Wray. Norman: University of Oklahoma Press, 2015.

Pascua, Maria. "Declaration of Maria Pascua in re: Proposed Waiver and Regulation Governing the Taking of Eastern North Pacific Gray Whales by the Makah Indian Tribe." Docket No. 19-NMFS-0001, United States of America Department of Commerce, National Oceanic and Atmospheric Administration. May 13, 2019. https://www.uscg.mil/Portals/0/ Headquarters/Administrative%20Law%20Judges/NOAA%20files%20 2019/33%20-%20c%20-%20Makah%20-%20Declaration%20%20of%20 Maria%20Pascua. pdf?ver=2019-05-29-111852-007.

Rannankari, Lynn, Rianna E. Burnham, and David A. Duffus. "Diurnal and Seasonal Acoustic Trends in Northward Migrating Eastern Pacific Gray Whales (*Eschrichtius robustus*)" *Aquatic Mammals* 44, no. 1 (2018): 1–6. https://doi.org/10.1578/AM.44.1.2018.1.

"Recommended Decision Issued by George J. Jordan, Administrative Law Judge in re: Proposed Waiver and Regulation Governing the Taking of Eastern North Pacific Grey Whales by the Makah Tribe." Docket No. 19-NMFS-0001. United States of America Department of Commerce, National Oceanographic and Atmospheric Administration. https://media.fisheries.noaa.gov/2021-09/ recommended-decision-19nmfs0001.pdf.

Reid, Joshua L. *The Sea is My Country*. New Haven, CT: Yale University Press, 2015.

Reid, Joshua. "Dr. Joshua L. Reid - From 'Fishing Together' to 'Fish in Common With.'" One Ocean Hub. June 7, 2020. Video, 32:03. https://www.youtube.com/watch?v=QV3NiBdocHE&t=1s.

Reidenberg, Joy. "Why Whales are Weird." Video, 24:21. 2012. https://vimeo.com/45448010.

Renker, Ann M. "Whale Hunting and the Makah Tribe: A Needs Statement." International Whaling Commission. May 2012. https://iwc.int/document_2968.

Rianna Burnham (acoustic ecologist for Canada's department of fisheries and oceans, adjunct professor at the University of Victoria) in discussion with the author, December 9, 2021.

Rugh, David J., Roderick C. Hobbs, James A. Lerczak and Jeffrey M. Breiwick. "Estimates of abundance of the eastern North Pacific stock of gray whales (*Eschrichtius robustus*) 1997–2002." *Journal of Cetacean Research and Management* 7, no. 1 (2005): 11. https://www.researchgate.net/publication/258808884_Rugh_DJ_RC_Hobbs_JA_Lerczak_and_J M_Breiwick_2005_Estimates_of_abundance_of_the_eastern_North_Pacific_stock_of_gray_wha les_Eschrichtius_robustus_1997-2002_Journal_Cetacean_Research_and_Management_711-1.

Sanchez, Rene. "As Tribe Pursues Whales, Protesters Pursue Tribe." *Washington Post*, October 17, 1998. https://www.washingtonpost.com/archive/politics/1998/10/17/as-tribe-pursues-whales-protesters-pursue-tribe/c41e7c86-8168-432a-904c-afbb8e8b410c/.

Sardelis, Stephanie. "Why do whales sing? -Stephanie Sardelis." TED-Ed. November 10, 2016. Video, 5:12. https://www.youtube.com/watch?v=7Xr9BYhlceA.

Sato, Chris and Gary J. Wiles. "Periodic Status Review for the Gray Whale." Washington Department of Fish and Wildlife: Wildlife Program. March 2021. https://wdfw.wa.gov/sites/default/files/publications/02170/wdfw02170.pdf.

Savoca, Matthew S., Max F. Czapanskiy, Shirel R. Kahane-Rapport, William T. Gough, James A. Fahlbusch, K. C. Bierlich, Paolo S. Segre, Jacopo Di Clemente, Gwenith S. Penry, David N. Wiley, John Calambokidis, Douglas P. Nowacek, David W. Johnston, Nicholas D. Pyenson, Ari S. Friedlaender, Elliott L. Hazen and Jeremy A. Goldbogen. "Baleen whale prey consumption based on high-resolution foraging measurements." *Nature* 599 (2021): 85–90. https://doi.org/10.1038/s41586-021-03991-5.

"Species directory: Gray Whale." National Oceanic and Atmospheric Administration. https://www.fisheries.noaa.gov/species/gray-whale.

"Supplemental Environmental Impact Statement/Overseas Environmental Impact Statement." Northwest Training and Testing, US Navy (2019): 181–182. https://nwtteis.com/Portals/nwtteis/files/draft_seis/section/NWTT_Draft_Supplemental_EIS-OEI S_3.4MarineMammals.pdf.

Stewart, Joshua D. and David W. Weller. "Abundance of Eastern Pacific Gray Whales 2019/2020." NOAA Technical Memorandum National Marine Fisheries Service (2021). https://doi.org/10.25923/bmam-pe91.

Sullivan, Robert. A Whale Hunt. New York: Scribner, 2000.

Tizon, Alex. "E-mails, Phone Messages Full Of Threats, Invective." Seattle Times, May 23, 1999. https://archive.seattletimes.com/archive/?date=19990523&slug=race23m.

"The Makah Whaling Tradition." https://makah.com/makah-tribal-info/whaling/.

Torres, Leigh G. "A sense of scale: Foraging cetaceans' use of scale-dependent multimodal sensory systems." Marine Mammal Science 33, no. 4 (2017): 1170–1193. https://doi.org/10.1111/mms.12426.

Torres, Leigh G., Sharon L. Nieukirk, Leila Lemos, and Todd E. Chandler. "Drone Up! Quantifying Whale Behavior From a New Perspective Improves Observational Capacity." Frontiers in Marine Science 5 (2018): 1–14. https://doi.org/10.3389/fmars.2018.00319.

"Upwelling." Oregon Department of Fish and Wildlife Marine Reserves. June 8, 2016. Video, 1:12. https://www.youtube.com/watch?v=60_y6-CiUMA.

Waterman, T.T. The Whaling Equipment of the Makah Indians. Seattle: University of Washington Publications in Anthropology 1, no. 1 (1920). Reprint, Seattle: University of Washington Press, 1955.

Webb, Robert Lloyd. On the Northwest: Commercial Whaling in the Pacific Northwest, 1790–1967. Vancouver: University of British Columbia Press, 1988.

Weiss, Rick. "Whales' Deaths Linked to Navy's Sonar Tests." Washington Post, December 31, 2001. https://www.washingtonpost.com/archive/politics/2001/12/31/whales-deaths-linked-to-navys-sonar-tests/2d2f3124-394d-4d25-a68a-5ec983834efc/.

"Whale Anatomy." National Oceanic and Atmospheric Administration. Ocean Today. Video, 3:36. https://oceantoday.noaa.gov/whaleanatomy/.

"Whale Products." New Bedford Whaling National Historical Park. Last updated August 29, 2018. https://www.nps.gov/nebe/learn/historyculture/whale-products.htm.

About the Author

Josephine Woolington is a writer, musician, and educator. She previously worked at several newspapers in Oregon and is currently a freelance journalist, focusing on stories about the natural world. She lives in Portland.

About the Artist

Ramon Shiloh has volunteered at educationally focused nonprofit organizations for almost three decades. As a writer, artist, and instructor, he curates thoughtful insights, teaches analytic skills and applied knowledge, and distributes tools relative to the creative mediums of art, food sovereignty, writing, and spoken word.

Shiloh focuses many of his efforts on supporting Indigenous children. He uses his knowledge of food, art, and culture to help Native youth develop a connection to good health and their histories, in our ever-changing world. Shiloh resides in Portland.

Ooligan Press

Ooligan Press is a student-run publishing house rooted in the rich literary culture of the Pacific Northwest. Founded in 2001 as part of Portland State University's Department of English, Ooligan is dedicated to the art and craft of publishing. Students pursuing master's degrees in book publishing staff the press in an apprenticeship program under the guidance of a core faculty of publishing professionals.

Project Managers
Rylee Warner
Jackie Krantz

Editorial
Rachel Lantz
Rachel Howe
Kelly Morrison
Sienna Berlinger

Design
Katherine Flitsch
Elaine Schumacher

Digital
Amanda Hines
Anna
  Wehmeier Giol

Marketing
Sarah Moffatt
Sarah Bradley

Publicity
Emma St. John
Tara McCarron

Social Media
Riley Robert
Nell Stamper

Acquisitions
Amanda Fink
Kelly Zatlin
Jennifer Ladwig
Michael Shymanski

Book Production
Jenna Amundson
Megan
  Vader Bongolan
Sienna Berlinger
Anna
  Wehmeier Giol
Alexander Halbrook
Megan Haverman
Jazzminn Morecraft
Alena Rivas
Kali Carryl
Alexandra Burns
Ashley Lockard
Elaine Schumacher
Elliot Bailey

John Huston
Kelly Morrison
Kyndall Tiller
Rebecca Gordon
Tara McCarron
Rachel Adams
Frances
  Fragela Rivera
Brenna Ebner